Building Big

earth

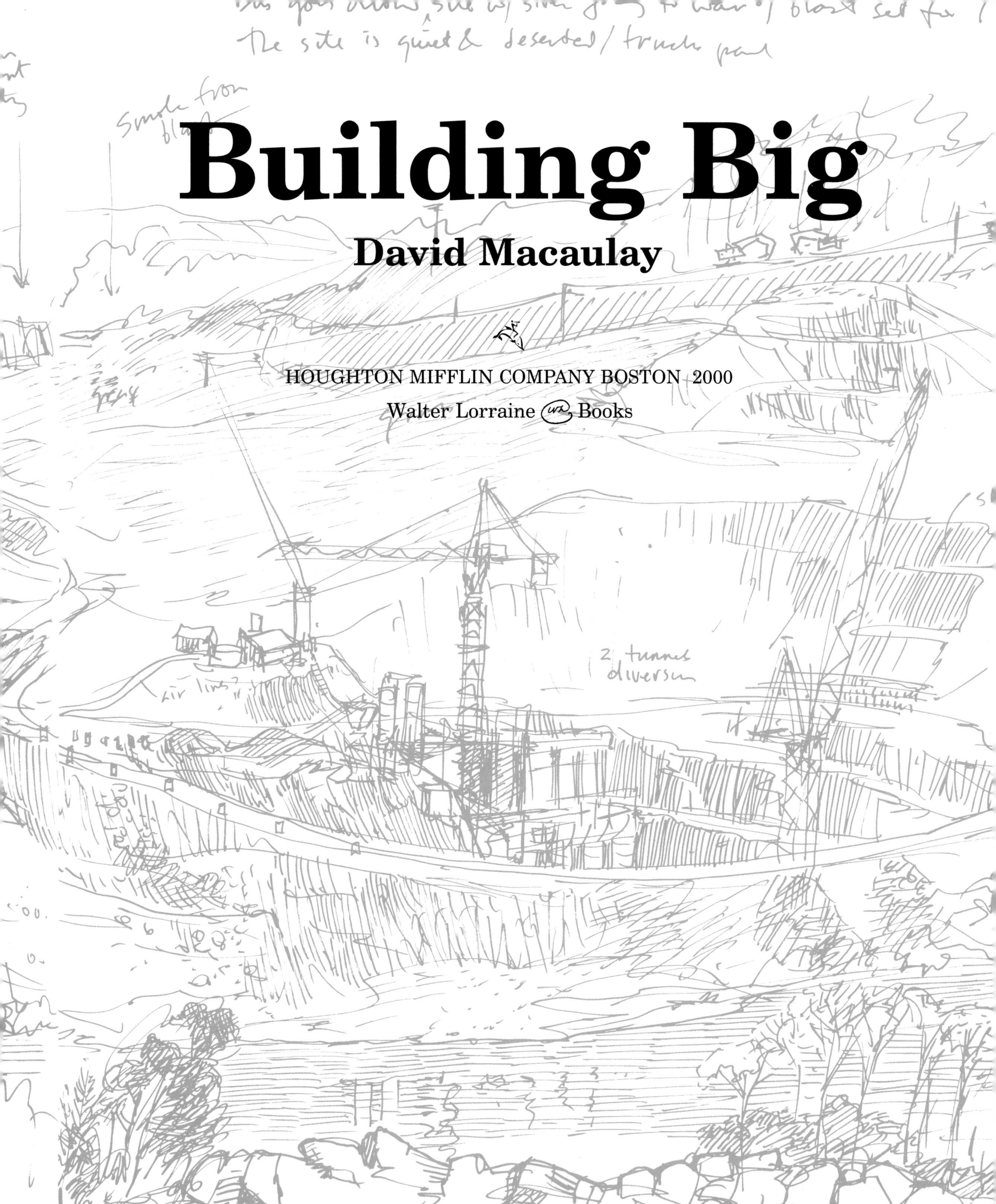

Building Big

David Macaulay

HOUGHTON MIFFLIN COMPANY BOSTON 2000
Walter Lorraine Books

For their willingness to review and comment upon various parts of this book, I would like to thank the following: Chuck Seim, Gary S. Brierley, J. Barry Cooke, William C. Allen, William L. MacDonald, Professor Mark Cruvellier and Executive Producer of the series, Larry Klein, who, unhindered by expertise in any of the subjects, read them all. At Houghton Mifflin, my gratitude as always to my editor, Walter Lorraine and to Donna McCarthy, Margaret Melvin, Liz Duvall and Kathy Black, none of whom ever gave up even as the deadlines came and went. Finally, thank you Ruthie for your unfailing support and for putting up with the absences, the frustration and the endless same-old-conversations with humor and unshakable confidence. This book is for you, love.

Walter Lorraine Books

Library of Congress Cataloging-in-Publication Data
Macaulay, David.
Building Big / by David Macaulay
p. cm.
ISBN 0-395-96331-1
1. Architecture—Juvenile literature. [1. Architecture.] I. Title

NA2555.M24 2000
720—dc21

00-028116

Printed in the United States of America
RMT 10 9 8 7 6 5 4 3 2 1

CONTENTS

PREFACE

Building Big began as five films about the creation of bridges, tunnels, skyscrapers, domes, and dams. Over a period of about two years, various producers, film crews, and I checked in and out of hotels on four continents and talked to a lot of people who design, build, or study these structures. While the filmmakers were concentrating at least as much on the human stories—the ambition, the heartbreak, the triumph—as on the technical, I found myself increasingly intrigued by the nuts and bolts. It's just the kind of person I am. Why this shape and not that? Why steel instead of concrete or stone? Why put it here and not over there? Asking these kinds of questions took me back to the basic design process, which itself begins with questions as engineers and designers struggle to identify and prioritize the problems that must be solved. And it was this particular aspect of building big that finally convinced me there was a role for a so-called companion book.

Knowing that the films would present the big picture—including the larger historical, social, and environmental issues associated with the building of big things—I was free to operate on a much smaller scale. Using some but not all of the examples chosen for the films, this book focuses entirely on the connections between the main planning and design problems that had to be solved and the solutions that were eventually built. There is something reassuring about the fact that whether structures inspire or simply intimidate with their scale, each is generally the result of a logical and therefore accessible sequence of events. Once we recognize that the elements of common sense and logic play at least as important a role in this process as imagination and technical know-how, even the biggest things we build can be brought down to size.

BRIDGES

All the structures in this book willingly reveal important things about why and how they were built if we know what to look for. And of all big pieces of engineering, bridges are probably the most forthcoming. They are in a sense three-dimensional diagrams of the work they do, and this makes them ideal subjects with which to begin.

In large modern bridges, where economy is of the essence, there are very few extra elements to obscure what's going on. What gives these bridges any uniqueness they may have is not some applied decoration but rather their fundamental design and its relationship to the site. Even in the often conservatively built and frequently embellished bridges of old, the way they work can be readily appreciated.

While the specific requirements of every bridge are different, thereby creating an enormous number of variations, there are actually only five basic bridge types—post and beam, arched, cantilevered, suspension, and the newest kid on the block, cable stayed. The bridges included here were not necessarily the largest of their day, but like all bridges, whether dramatic or humble, they all evolved from a similar process. This included defining the problem, establishing the goals, and testing the limits. In the end, each completed structure either reflects the technological understanding of its day or represents a leap in that understanding.

The other thing these bridges have in common is that they were all built to span water—a challenge that seems to have an enduring appeal to those of us with neither wings nor gills. Over the centuries, this problem has been met with ingenuity, common sense, and courage and has resulted in some of the most magnificent pieces of engineering on the surface of the planet.

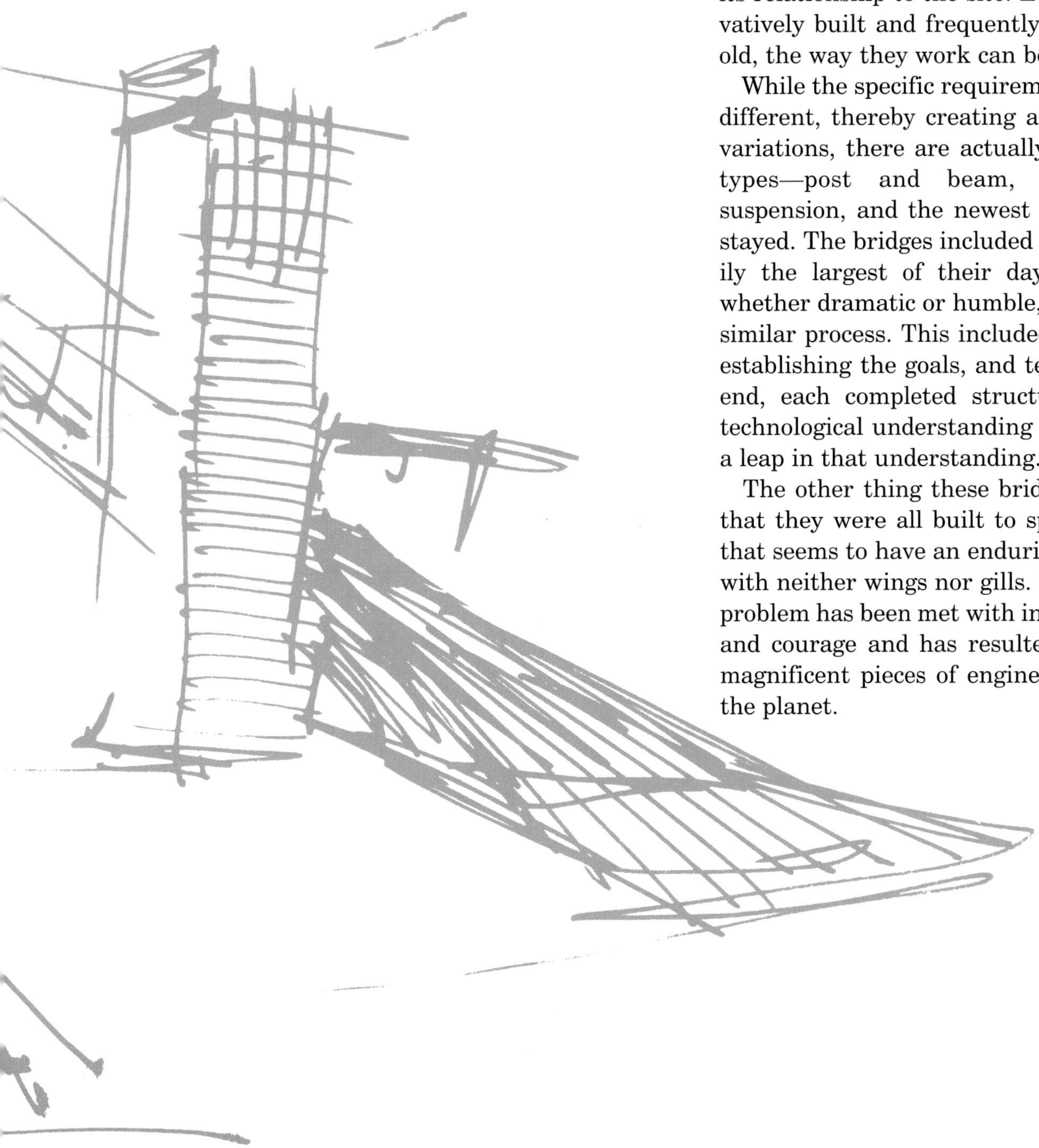

200'
TIBER RIVER

Ponte Fabricio

Rome, Italy, 62 B.C.: The task of the road commissioner and his engineers was to build a bridge linking one bank of the Tiber River with the island in the middle, a distance of approximately 200 feet. Because the island housed medical facilities, it was crucial that people could cross the bridge easily, so the bridge couldn't be too steep. There was a constant stream of boat traffic from the port of Ostia, so the bridge couldn't be too low either.

The kinds of construction materials that may have been considered include an all-wood post-and-beam structure (inexpensive but not fireproof), timber beams on a single stone pier (not entirely fireproof but less of an obstacle to river traffic), and a single stone arch: absolutely permanent, absolutely fireproof, and absolutely unclimbable.

Whether any of these plans was seriously considered is unlikely, given the level of experience the Roman engineers had. The final design was a stone structure with two arches. It offered permanence (in fact, it still stands today), created only one impediment on the river, and was high enough to allow ships to pass underneath yet low enough to provide an easy foot crossing. The three small arches were added to reduce pressure against the bridge during flooding.

The commissioner apparently believed that his engineers had come upon a worthy solution: he had his name carved in four places on the bridge.

FABRICIVS

ICNS·C·F·CVR·VAR
NDVM·COERAVIT

Roman engineers understood that a structure is only as permanent as the foundations upon which it stands. The building of foundations at any site is tedious, but to build them in the middle of a river can be downright treacherous. The builders probably waited until the summer, when the river was low, to begin the Ponte Fabricio. They may have diverted the water using some kind of temporary barrier. Or they might have built a watertight wooden wall, called a coffer dam, around the site of the central pier. Once pumped dry, the enclosed space could be excavated down to the riverbed.

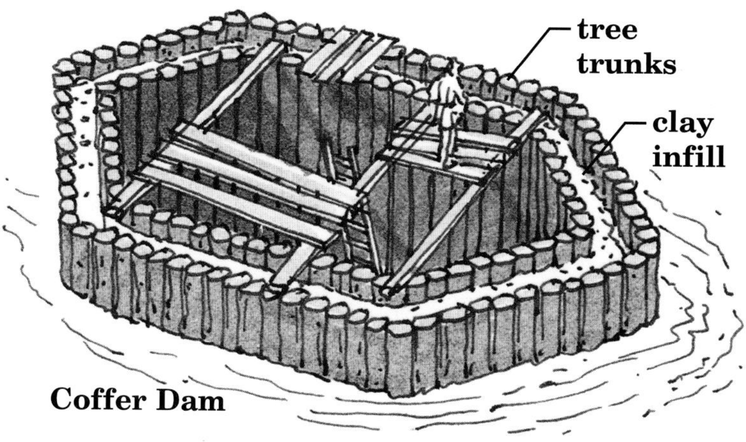

Coffer Dam

Next to the foundations in importance is the pair of arches. These would have been built over a temporary wooden form called a centering. Once the last piece of stone, called the keystone, had been set in place, the arch proper was finished. But if the centering was to be removed at this point, the uppermost stones would want to fall (it's one of the things stones do best), and this in turn would push the sides of the arch outward. To prevent this from happening, more material was built up against the sides of the arch before the centering was removed. This not only prevented movement between the stones but also compressed them together. The more the wedge-shaped stones are compressed, the stronger the arch will become. Thus, it is capable of channeling all the weight from above to the foundations below.

The fact that the bridge is more than 2,000 years old and still in use is a testament to the importance of combining the right shape with the right materials.

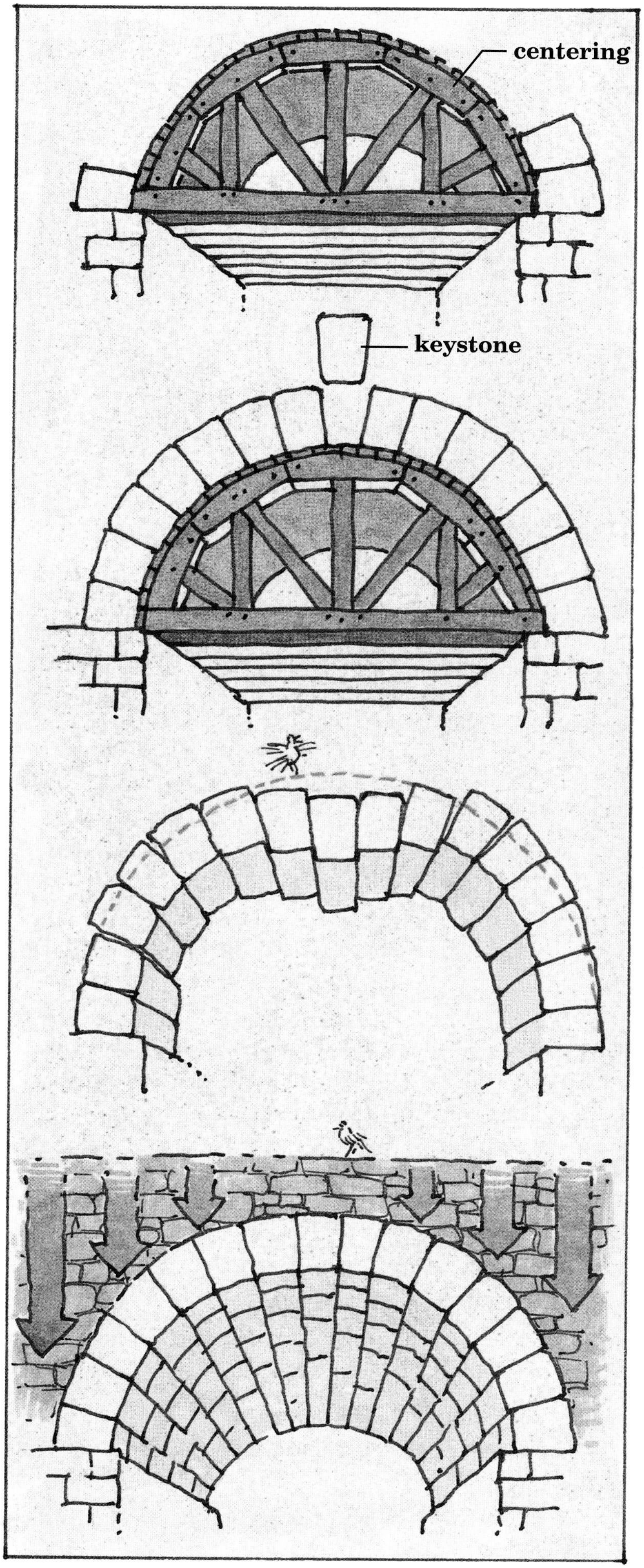

centering

keystone

Iron Bridge

Coalbrookdale, England, 1775: In the second half of the eighteenth century, the Severn River, which runs through Coalbrookdale, England, was a major obstacle to getting raw materials from one side of this industrialized valley to the other. There were very few bridges because of the heavy traffic on the river, so materials were transported on ferries. However, the ferries could not keep up with the increasing productivity of the area.

A new bridge was needed, and it would have to be arched, so as not to block river traffic. Potential builders were asked to think in terms of wood, stone, or brick. But the iron master Abraham Darby III saw the challenge as an opportunity to promote his own skills and foundry. Stone was hard to cut and heavy, which made it expensive to work with and to transport. Iron was more efficient to build with because it could be cast into the exact shapes required and much closer to the building site. Darby built the first all-metal, prefabricated bridge in the world.

Unlike its masonry predecessor, Ponte Fabricio, Iron Bridge was assembled like an oversize Erector® set of about 800 pieces. For each piece a full-size wooden pattern was pressed into a bed of sand and then carefully removed. The resulting cavity was filled with molten iron. Using traditional carpentry joints, such as dovetails, mortises, and tenons, the builders would have put the finished pieces together from a fairly lightweight scaffold instead of a heavy timber centering, which would have brought river traffic to a standstill. While the arch was clearly the best design to span the river, it also turned out to be the best shape for the material. An arch is a compression structure, and cast iron, like stone, is at its happiest when it is compressed. Whether Darby knew this or was simply lucky is anyone's guess. The bridge still stands today because it was designed with the right combination of shape and material. Also, the openness of the structure allows floodwater to pass easily underneath it.

Britannia Bridge

Bangor, North Wales, 1838: The task for railway engineer Robert Stevenson was to build a bridge both strong enough and rigid enough to carry trains back and forth between the Welsh mainland and the island of Anglesey. There was another obstacle besides the 900 feet of water that separates the locations. Because the bridge was to be built over a working shipping channel, the British navy would have to approve Stevenson's design. Arches and piers were forbidden for fear they might constrict the waterway, and there was a minimum height requirement of 100 feet between bridge and water.

After considering various locations, Stevenson chose, not surprisingly, a site that offered the well-placed advantage of a small island near the middle of the strait. Nobody said he couldn't use what was already there. And at least now, he could think in terms of two spans rather than one long one. Since arches were not an option, he designed a bridge based on the post-and-beam structure.

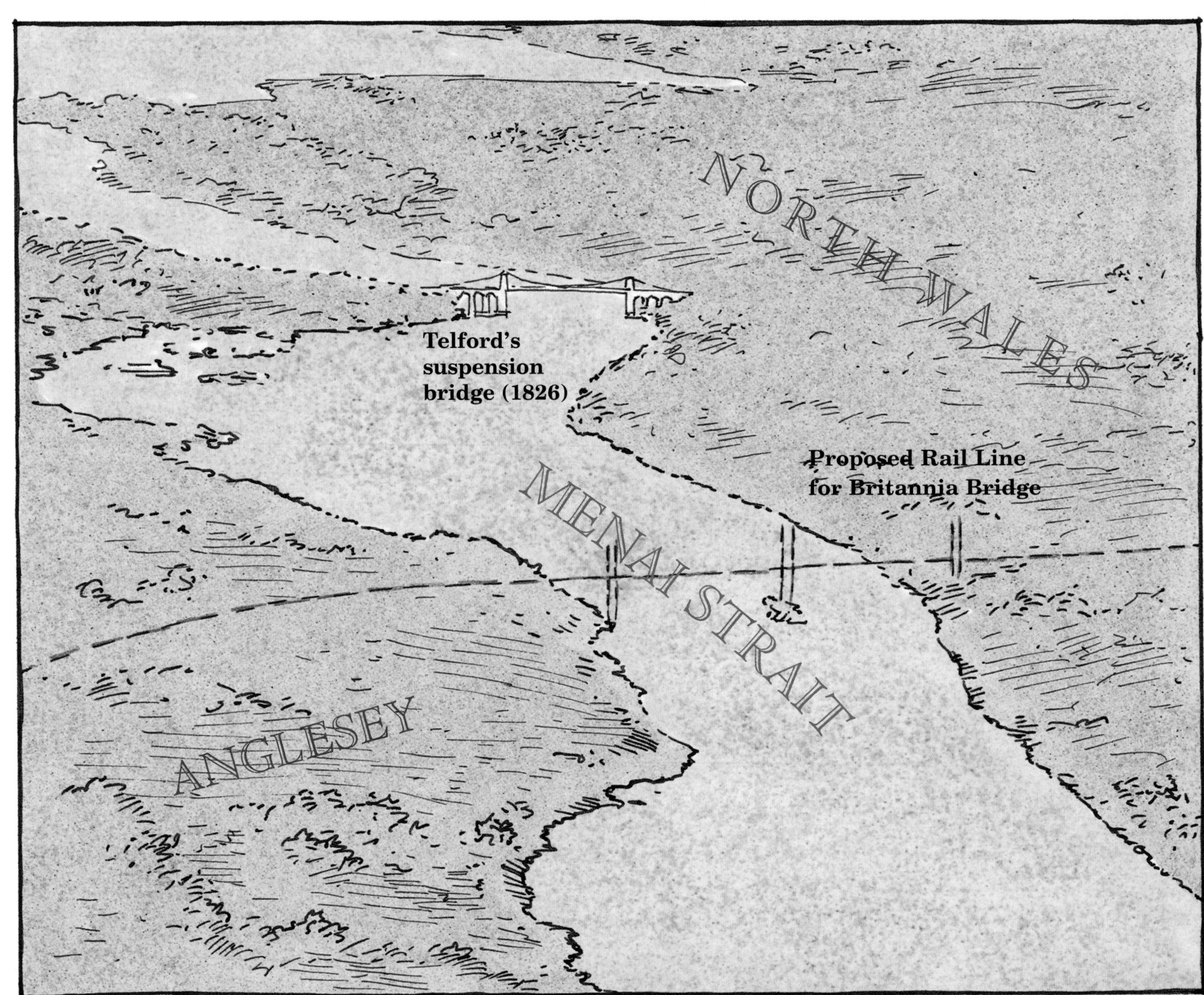

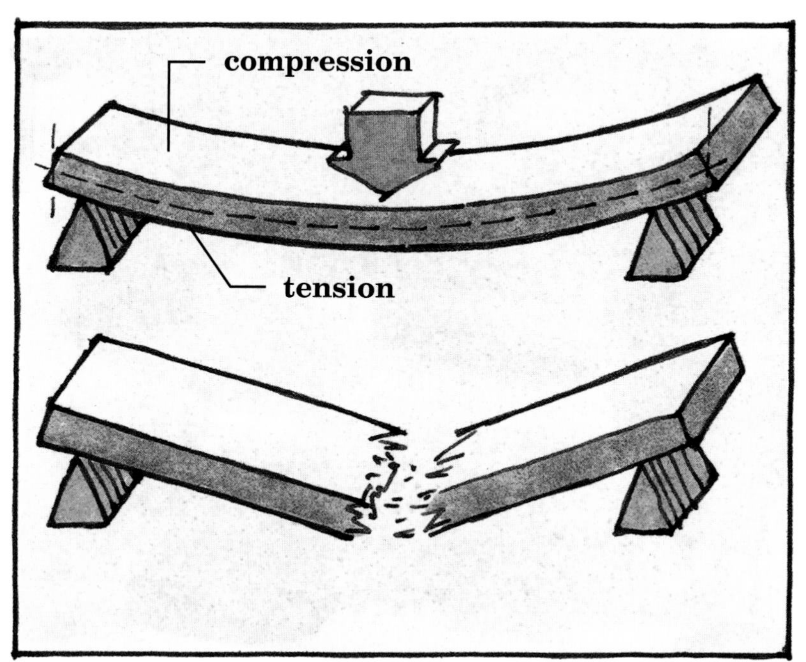

To understand how a beam works, imagine a plank placed over two supports. If you stand on the middle of the plank, it will bend. The top surface of the plank grows slightly shorter because it is being compressed; the bottom surface, on the other hand, is being stretched because it is in tension. If the plank cannot withstand one or both of these forces, it will break.

While the piers of Stevenson's new bridge were under construction, another of his post-and-beam bridges on the same train line collapsed, sending five people to their deaths in the River Dee. The bridge's cast-iron girders were too shallow to resist the bending. They began to twist sideways and quickly buckled. Although this was a very unusual failure, Stevenson and his fellow engineers learned that in addition to bending, beams must also be able to withstand twisting.

The Dee Bridge, May 24, 1847

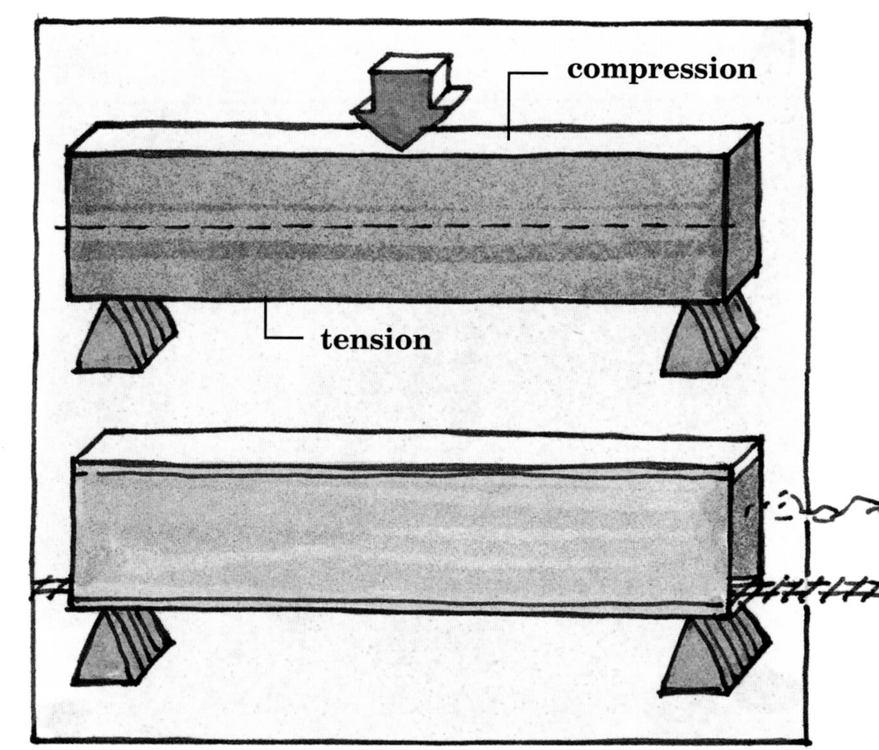

To minimize bending over a 460-foot span, massive beams would have to be used. Wooden beams were out of the question for a variety of reasons, and iron beams would have been too heavy and cumbersome. But now imagine our plank turned on its edge. Again the top surface of the plank will be in compression and the bottom in tension, but there is far less bending, because the bending stress is spread out over a deeper area. Stevenson, working with fellow engineer William Fairburn, solved the problem by making the beam large enough for trains to go through rather than over.

The finished bridge was designed as two parallel tubes, each 30 feet high and 15 feet wide. They were to be made of wrought iron and supported on high stone piers. While the sides were primarily flat plates, the top and bottom were assembled as smaller parallel tubes. All the pieces were riveted together. Because wrought iron, unlike cast iron, works about as well in tension as in compression, more material was used at the top of the beam than at the bottom to help prevent the kind of buckling failure that brought down the Dee Bridge. The four main tubes that spanned the water were fabricated on the banks and floated into position at high tide. Once fitted into the vertical slots of their respective piers, they were slowly and carefully lifted by powerful jacks to the required height.

The Britannia Bridge is the only bridge described in this chapter that is no longer standing. The bridge was constructed of fireproof materials, but a fire in 1970 distorted the metal. The bridge was no longer straight enough to carry trains and therefore was replaced by one with arches!

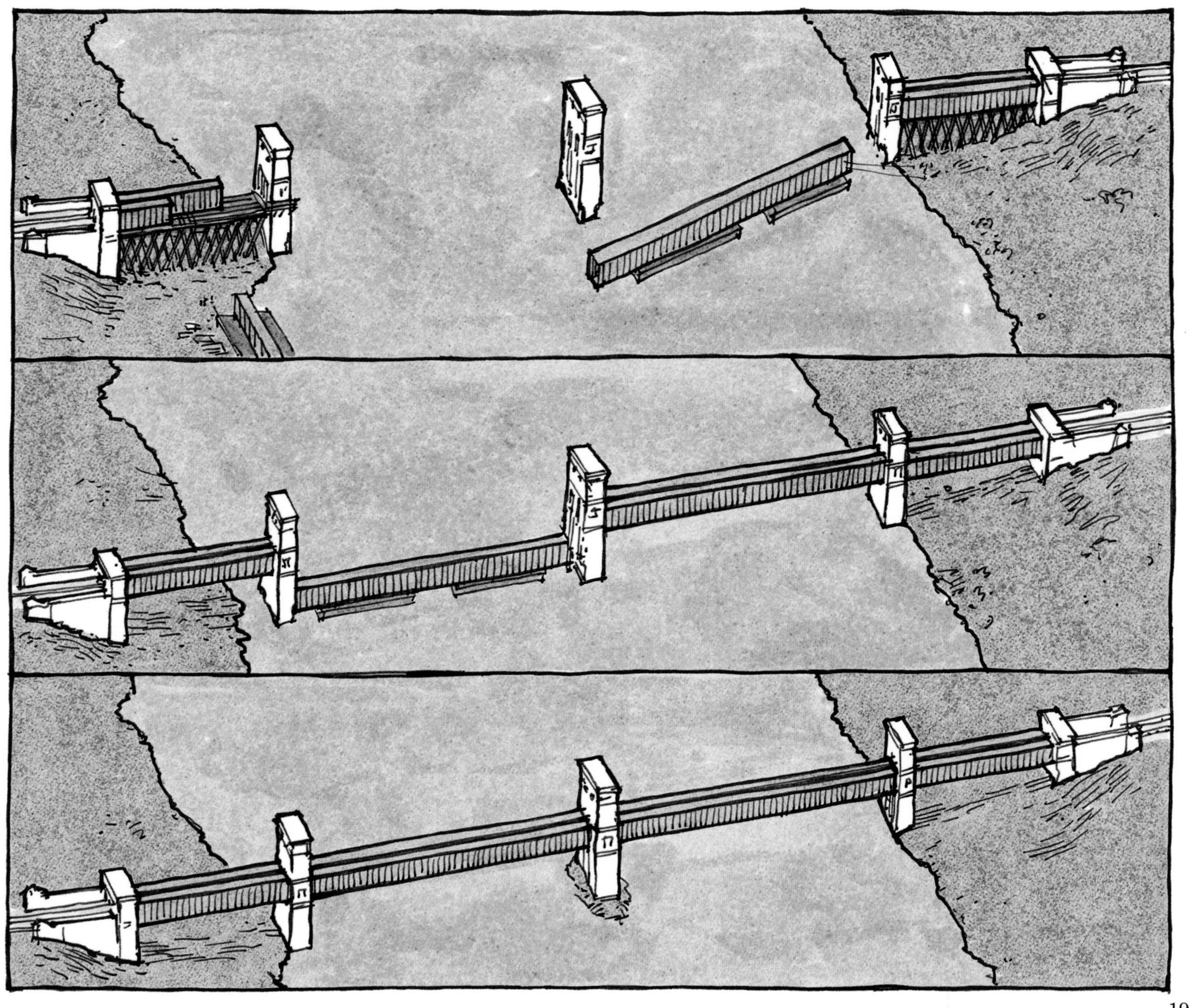

Garabit Viaduct

Saint Flour, France, 1879: Another country, another train bridge over water—this time to carry a freight line through the Massif Central. The body of water to be crossed was a mere stream compared to the Menai Strait, in Wales; however, this stream was 400 feet below the intended line of the track. The engineer was Gustave Eiffel, and Garabit was to be his last bridge. He had designed hundreds of them, including railway bridges in this very region. He understood both the demands of trains and the natural conditions of the area which, in addition to rugged terrain and deep gorges, included very strong winds.

Rather than simply using sheer mass to defeat the wind, Eiffel designed instead to outsmart it. He created open airy structures through which the wind could pass more easily and which required less material to build—another important consideration in these remote locations

The structure of the Garabit viaduct is based on the truss—basically a collection of interconnected triangles the sides of which carry the tension and compression forces.

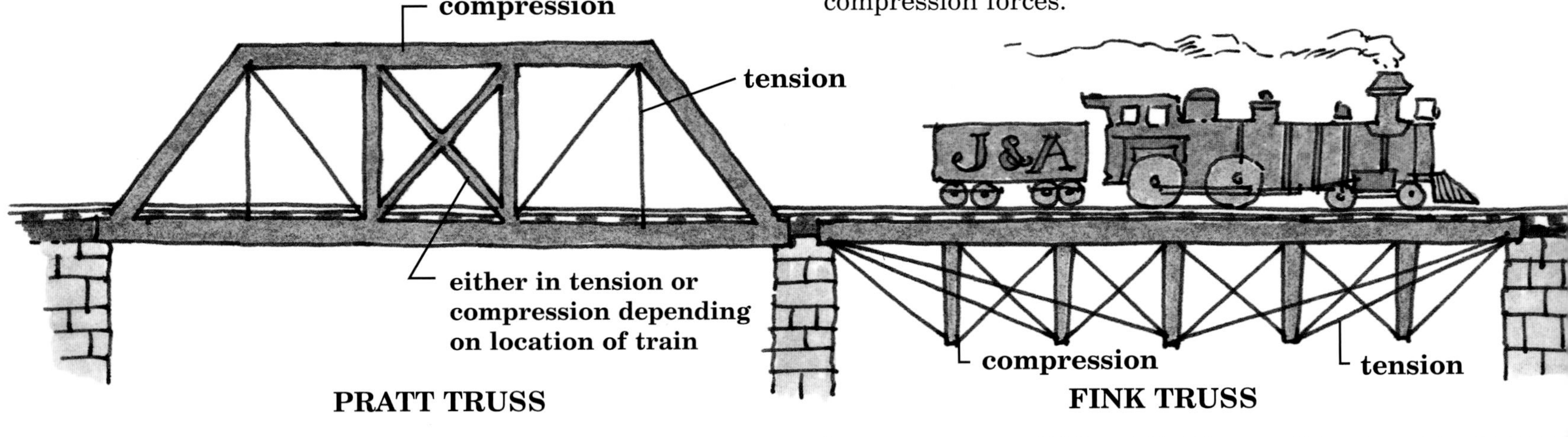

Proposed Rail Line of Garabit Viaduct

Truss bridges were commonly used in nineteenth-century North America to carry trains west. Because wood was plentiful and could be worked with basic carpentry skills, these bridges were quick to build. However, they were also quick to burn. As the workings of the truss became better understood, various timber pieces were replaced by stronger iron. Today, steel trusses are among the most common bridges in North America. They are very strong and can span long distances.

Two of the trusses below are named for their inventors, the other two for their shape. Most trusses are built with a slight upward curvature called camber. When a live load, such as a train, pushes down on a bridge, the truss straightens out but never sags.

BOWSTRING TRUSS

CAMELBACK TRUSS

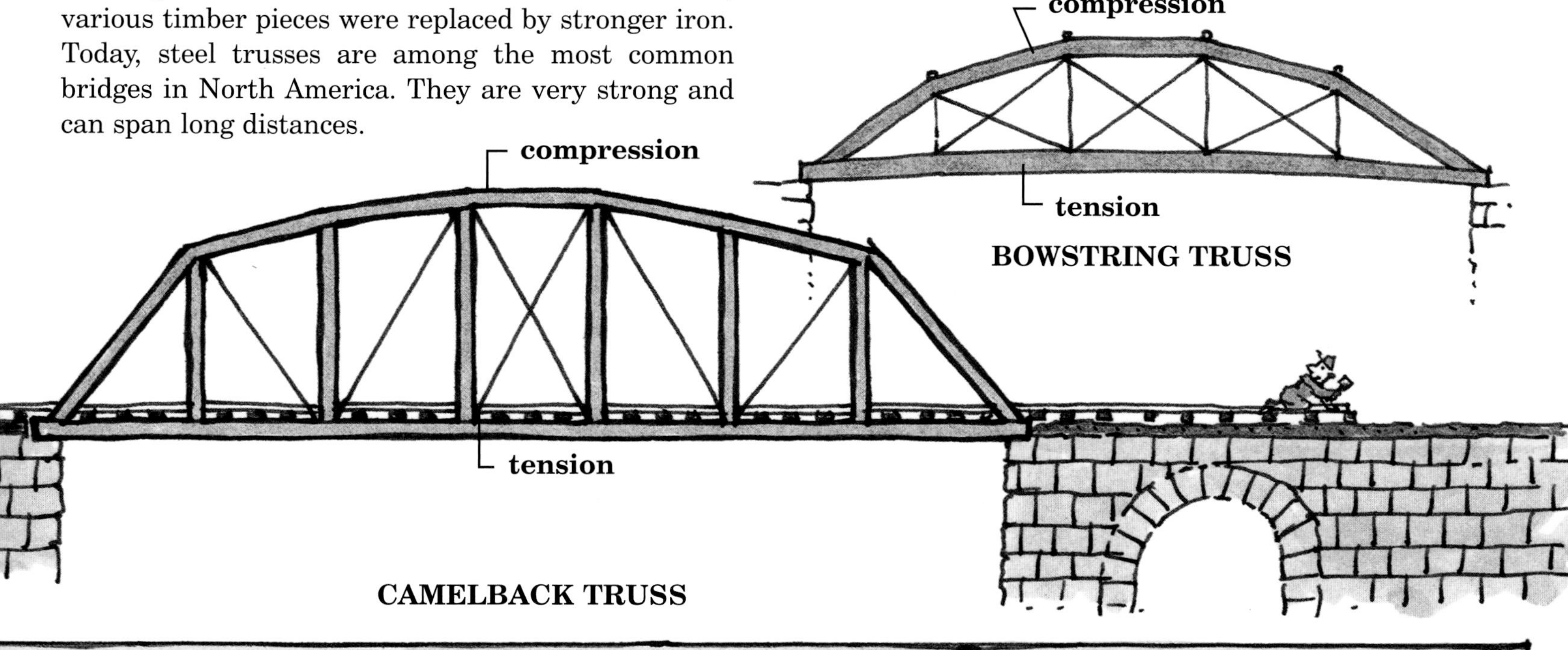

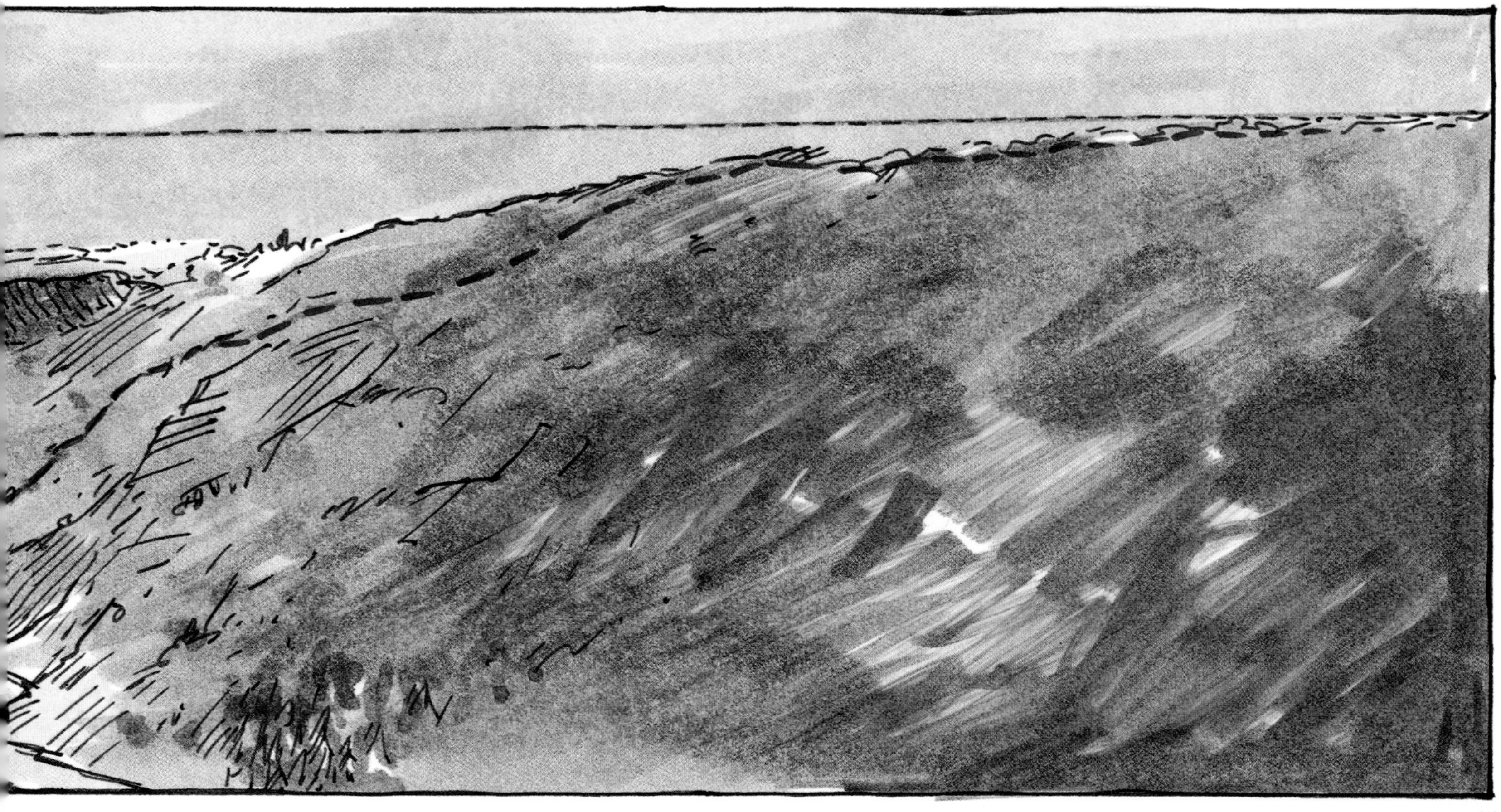

Eiffel's solution is basically a post-and-beam design some 1,850 feet long. As the gorge begins to descend, the track is carried from stone arches to a long straight truss supported on a row of towers. Instead of building three high towers in the center, Eiffel spanned the deepest part of the gorge with a 530-foot-wide arch. Two smaller towers rest on the arch, while its crown serves as the third support.

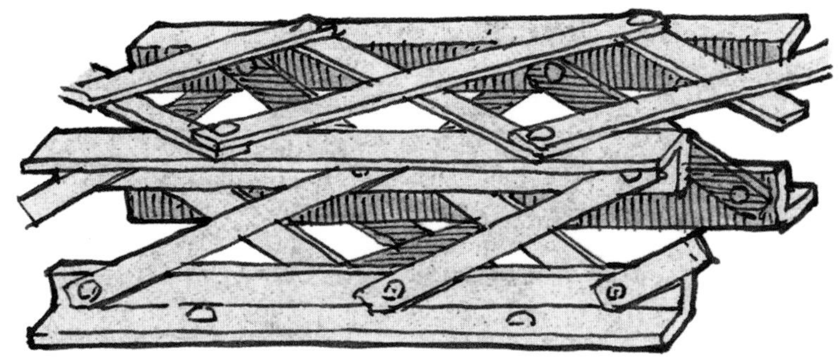

To permit natural expansion and contraction, the ends of the arch are hinged rather than rigidly fixed to their masonry supports. To increase stiffness, the bases of the towers and arch are wider at the bottom than at the top. To minimize wind resistance and to reduce weight, the pieces of the truss are built of even smaller pieces—wrought iron strips and angles all riveted together. The two halves of the arch were built out, or cantilevered, from their hinges and held in place by cables until they met in the center. No centering was needed, but a temporary wooden bridge was built to carry workers and materials more efficiently across the floor of the gorge.

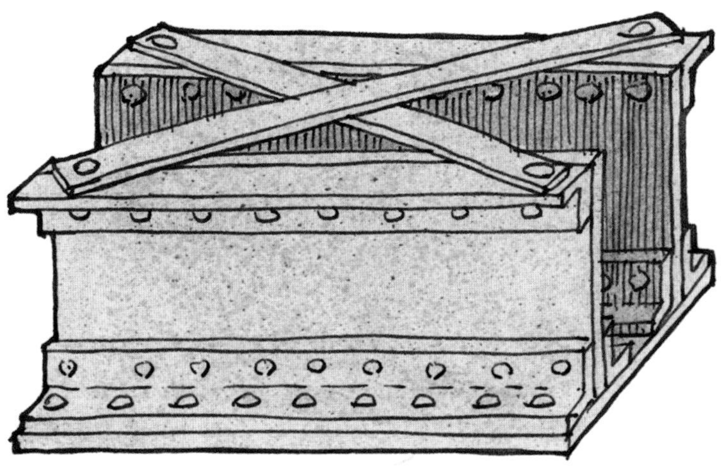

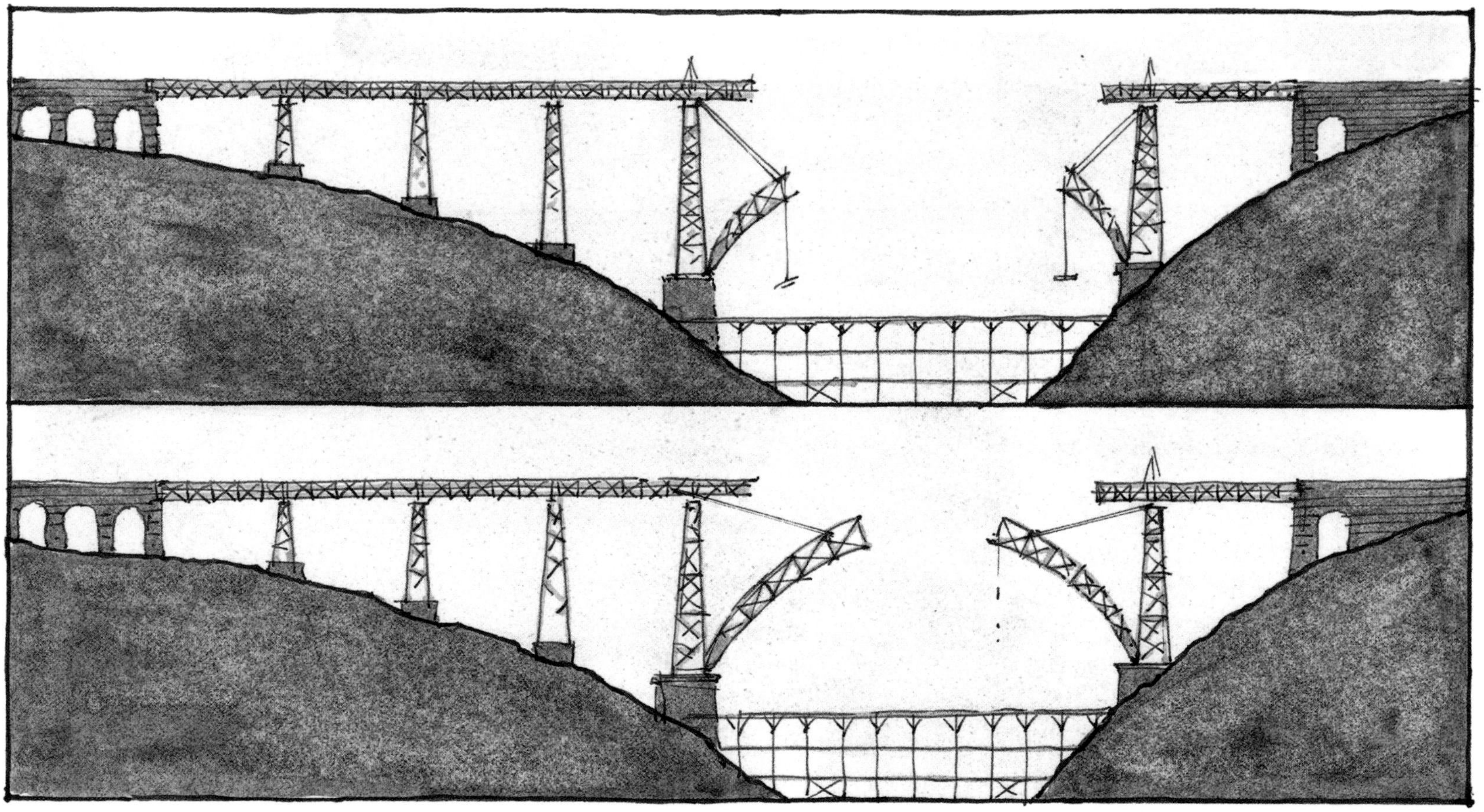

Firth of Forth

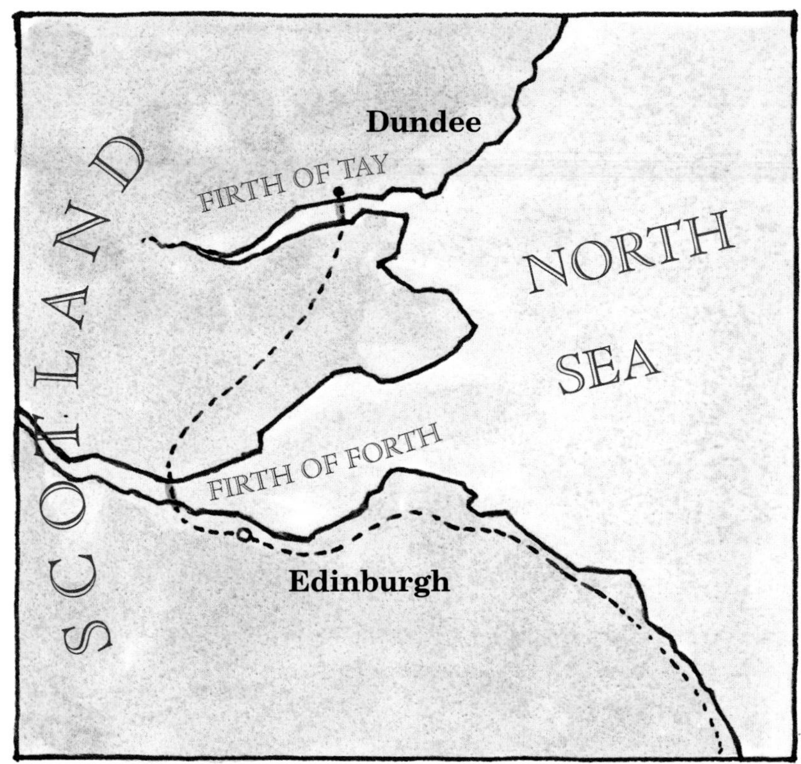

South Queensferry, Scotland, 1880: On the night of December 28, 1879, part of the Tay Bridge, a multi-spanned post-and-beam structure across the Firth of Tay, collapsed during a severe gale, plunging into the water with a loss of 70 lives. The reputation of the bridge's designer was ruined, and his plans for another bridge on the same line were promptly scrapped. The task now fell to two engineers, John Fowler and Benjamin Baker. They were not only to design a bridge that would cross the Firth of Forth but also to rebuild the confidence of train passengers. Their structure had to be strong, and it also had to *look* strong.

After surveying the site to record the configuration of the riverbed, the builders established the line of the bridge across the Firth between North and South Queensferry, a distance of about a mile and a half. Roughly two thirds of that distance was over water. A post and beam bridge was ruled out early. Even if the piers hadn't created a problem for river traffic, the depth of the water, which reached 220 feet at a couple of places, would have made their construction impossible. A suspension bridge was also briefly considered. But while it would have supported the roadbed well above the water, it was not seen as reliable enough to satisfy the demands of either trains or passengers.

The engineering team finally settled on a design that would employ three enormous cantilevered sections and two smaller suspended sections. The center cantilever would stand on the small island of Inchgarvie, in the middle of the estuary. The southern cantilever would be located as close to the center one as the depth of the water would allow. That specific distance would then be used between the center cantilever and the northern cantilever.

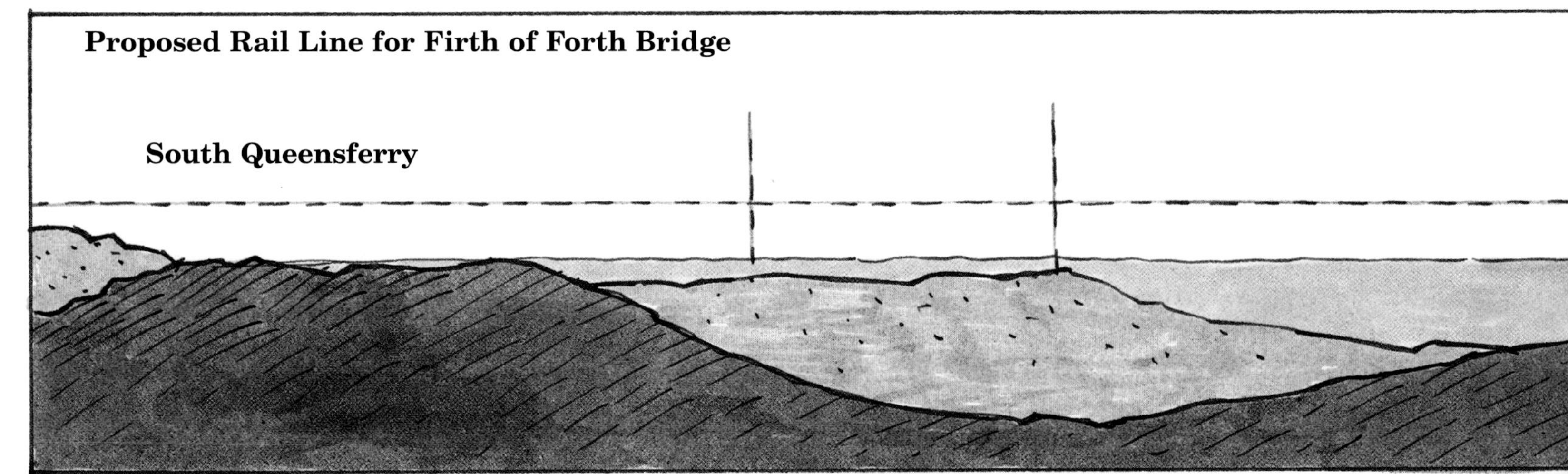

A cantilever is a horizontal beam fixed at only one end. Generally, two cantilevers face each other to support a suspended span. Stevenson's Britannia Bridge illustrated how by increasing the depth of a beam it is possible to reduce the bending. Since most of this bending happens in the center of the beam, that is where the depth should be greatest. In the cantilevers of the Forth Bridge, it's as if the supports of the beam have been moved into the center below the heaviest and hardest working part of the beam. With less weight at the points farthest from the supports, there is less bending and therefore, less building material is required. Here the cantilevered beams extend in opposite directions from each of the three towers to maintain a balance. If we link these three structures together by suspending two smaller bridges between them, we have a continuous beam. The separate sections are actually hinged together so that the largest forces will still be channeled directly to the foundations.

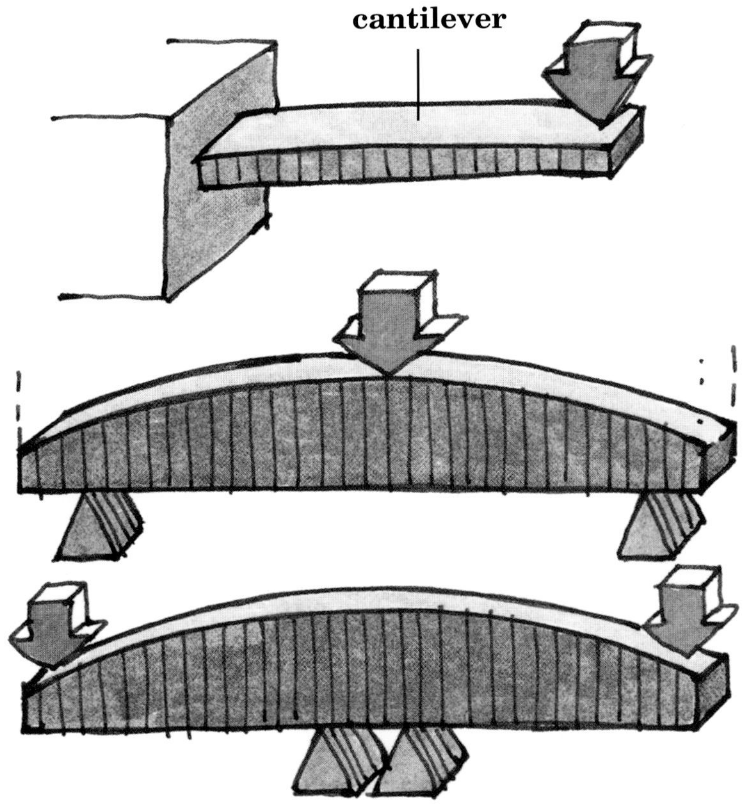

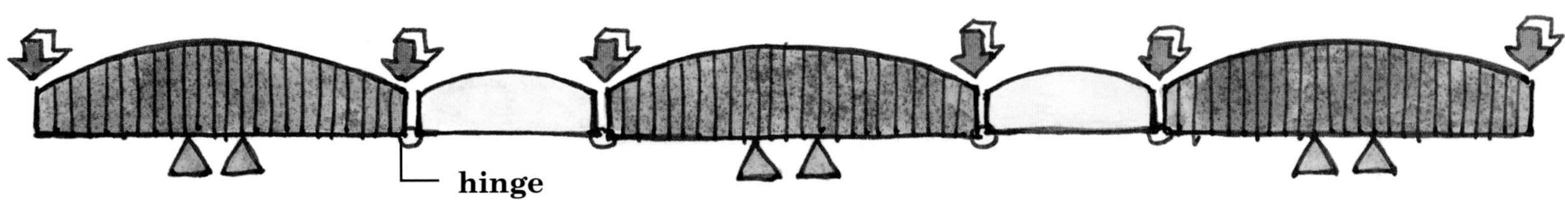

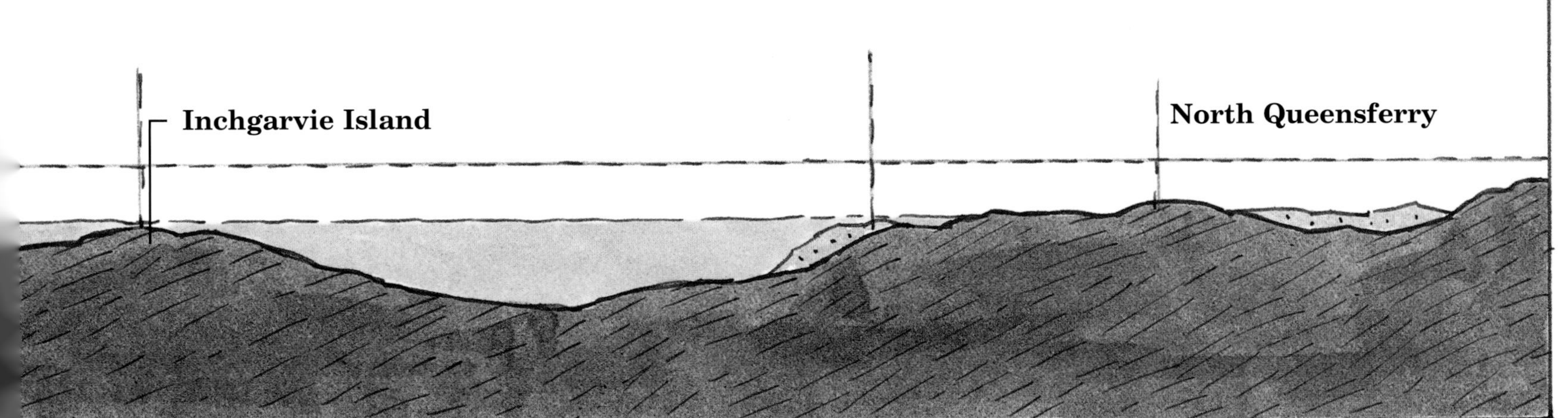

Each tower has four tubular steel legs, and each leg stands on its own massive pier. Of the twelve legs needed, six had to be built in water so deep that pneumatic caissons were required. These wrought-iron cylinders were 70 feet in diameter and roughly 70 feet high. They were brought to the site in pieces and reassembled on the beach before being towed to their final locations and sunk. The work chamber at the bottom of the caisson and the work platforms at the top were linked by three tubular shafts—two were used to transport materials and one was used by workers. Each was accessed through an airlock. Water at the bottom of the work chamber was forced out as compressed air was pumped in.

Men could now work reasonably safely on the riverbed. As they excavated muck and loose rock, sending it up one of the shafts, the space above them was filled with concrete. This increased the weight of the caisson, which slowly sank on its wedge-shaped base. Once a firm footing had been reached, the work chamber too was filled with concrete. Now there was a secure base on which to build the masonry piers that would support the steelwork. Half of the construction time for the entire bridge was spent building the foundations. Fabricius would have approved.

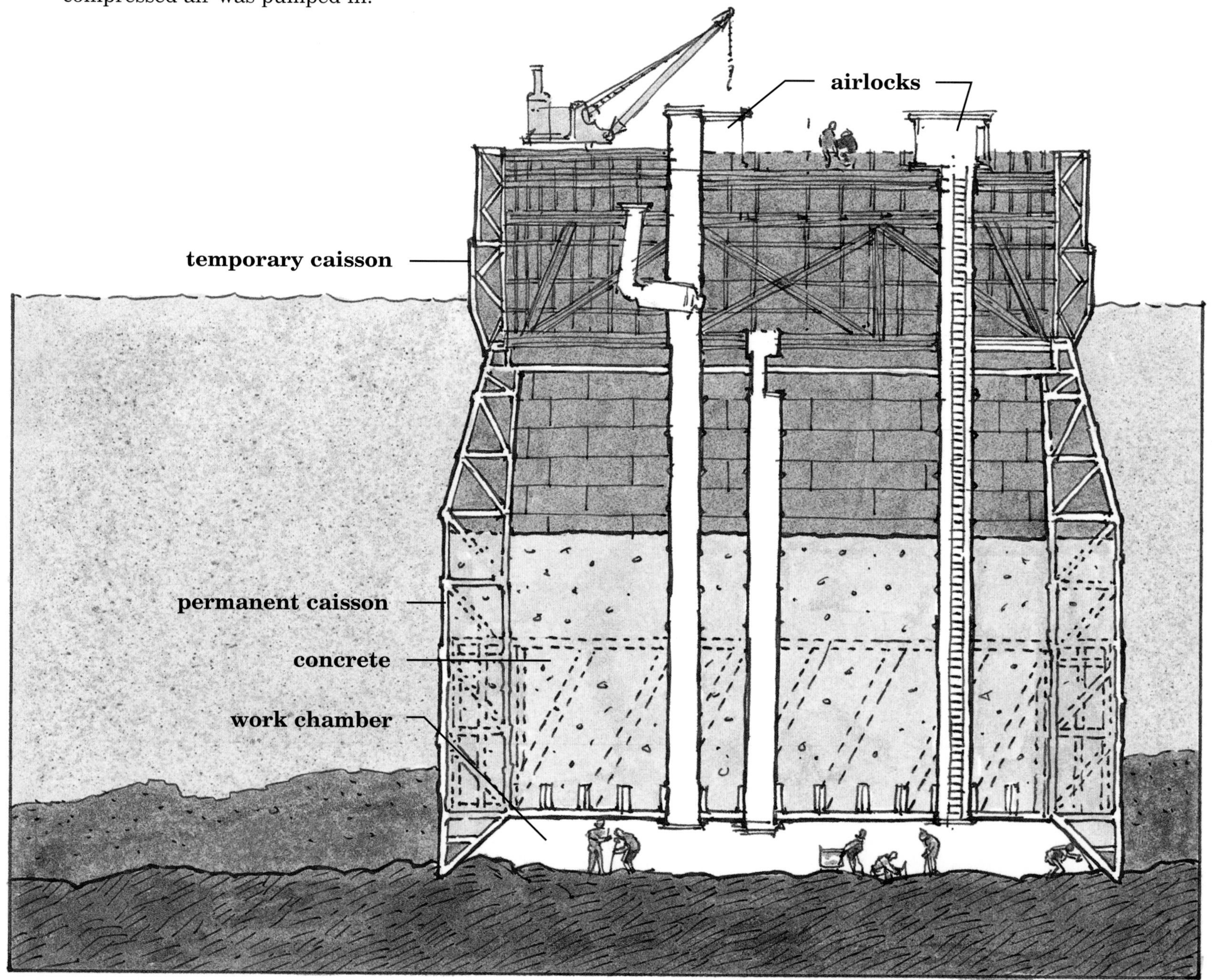

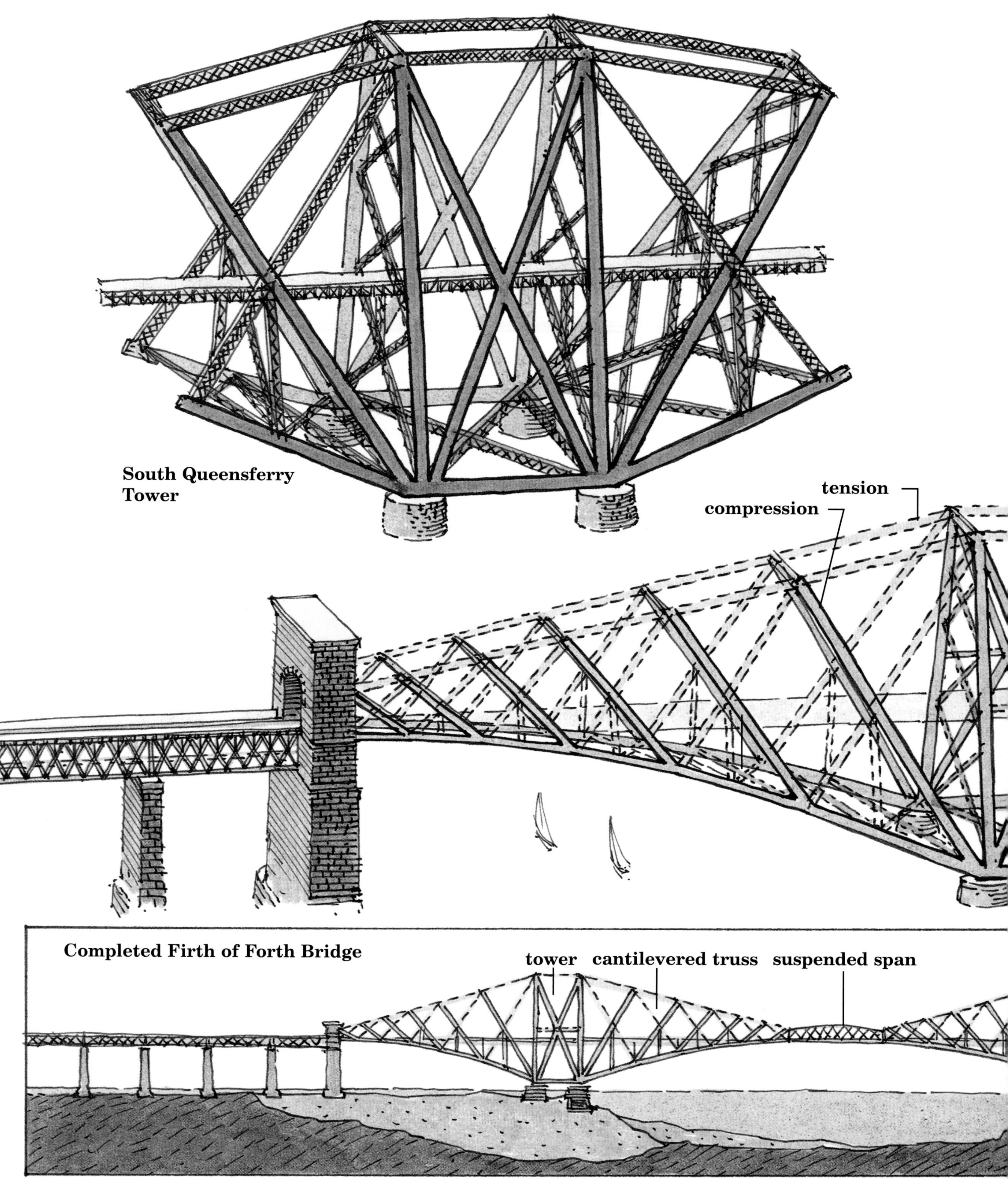
South Queensferry
Tower
tension
compression
Completed Firth of Forth Bridge
tower
cantilevered truss
suspended span

The forces of the wind as well as those created by a crossing train are carried through the cantilevered trusses to the three huge towers, the main tubes of which are twelve feet in diameter. The five tubes that meet at each corner of a tower are riveted together and tied into the pier below. As at Garabit, the entire structure is wider at the bottom than at the top for greater stability.

Fowler and Baker created a structure so strong that the wind could never blow it down. And one only needs see how totally dwarfed a train is by the bridge to imagine the reassuring psychological impact it must have had on even the most skeptical passengers. But Fowler and Baker also created a structure so incredibly expensive that it has rarely been copied, particularly at this scale. The only cantilever bridge larger than the Forth is a visually inferior imitation built in Quebec in 1917.

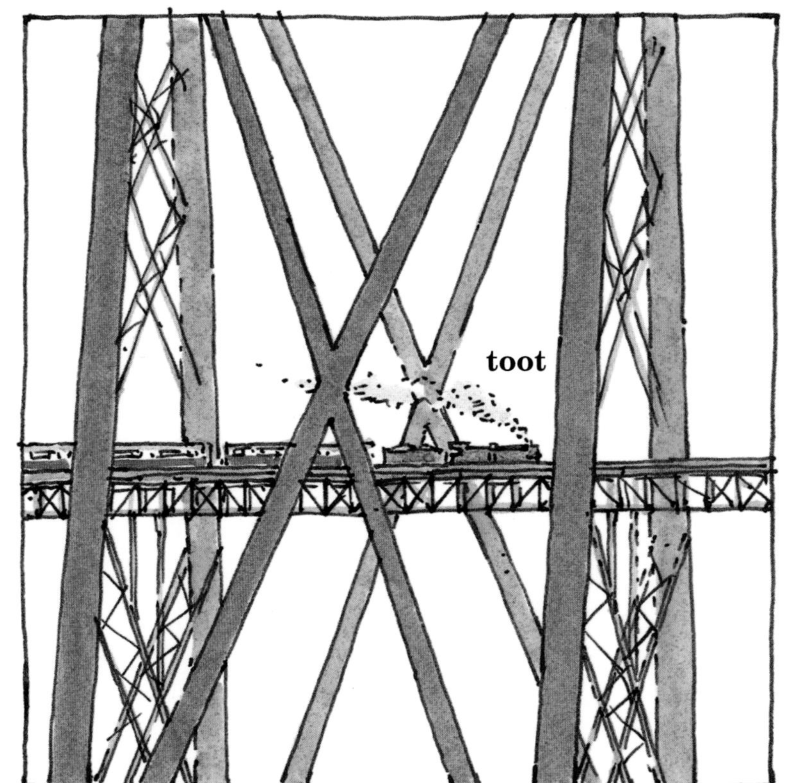

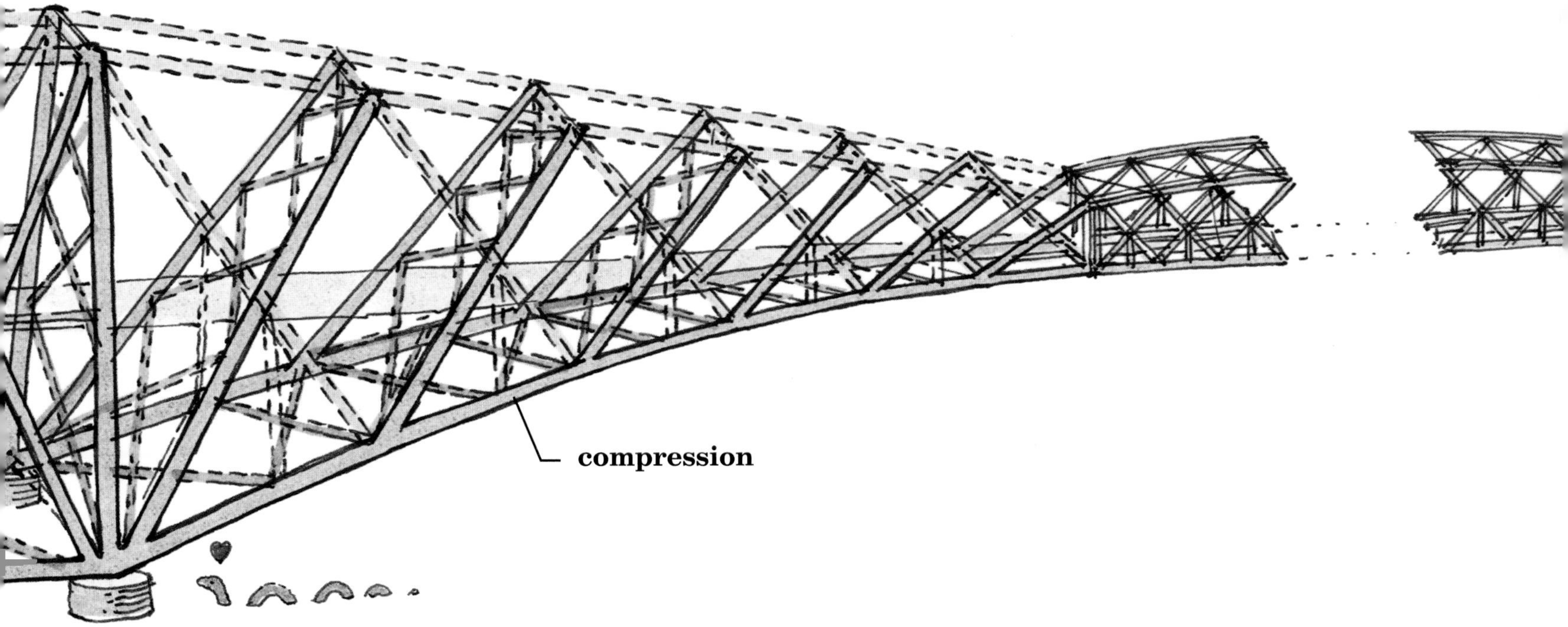

Golden Gate Bridge

San Francisco, California, 1930: The problem was too many cars and not enough ferries to get them from the city to the spectacular countryside of Marin County and Northern California. People were waiting in line for hours—sometimes even days. The solution was a bridge. A number of locations were scouted, but the Golden Gate site was chosen because it would require a shorter span and a less extensive network of approach roads than any of the others. Still, the span would have to be longer than anything built before it. An engineer by the name of Joseph Strauss was eager to take on the challenge, although his first proposal was an ungainly combination of cantilever and suspension bridge. By the time the funding was in place to build the bridge, it had evolved into a pure suspension design.

The main parts of a suspension bridge, other than the roadway, are the towers, the cables, and the cable anchorages. The roadway itself actually hangs from the cables. If the cables stopped at the tops of the towers, their own weight in addition to the weight of the roadway and that of the traffic would bend the tops of the towers toward each other. To prevent this from happening, the cables pass over the tops of the towers and are connected to concrete anchorages cast into solid rock. The action of the cables pulling down on both sides of a tower creates a strong vertical force that must be carried to the foundations.

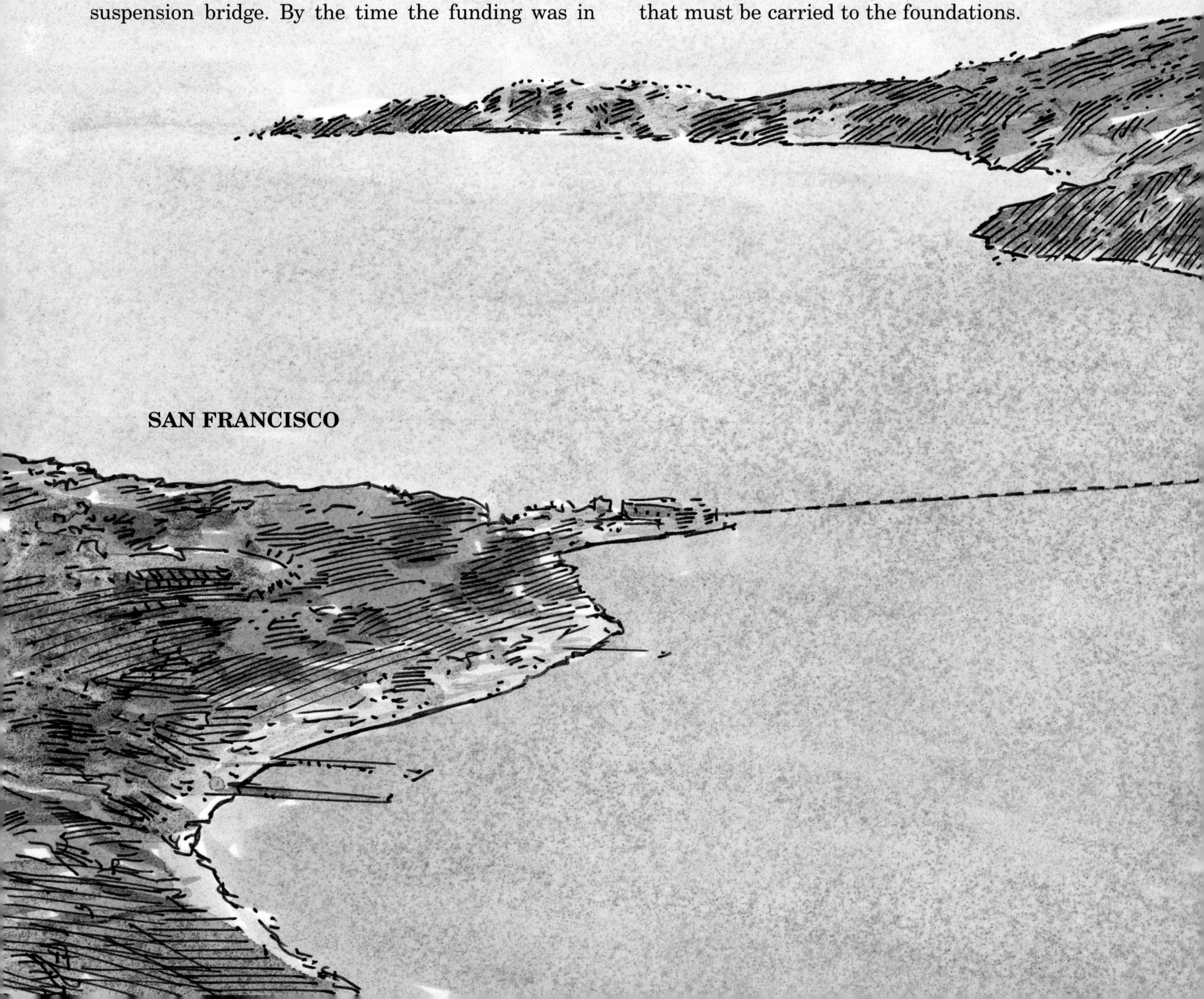

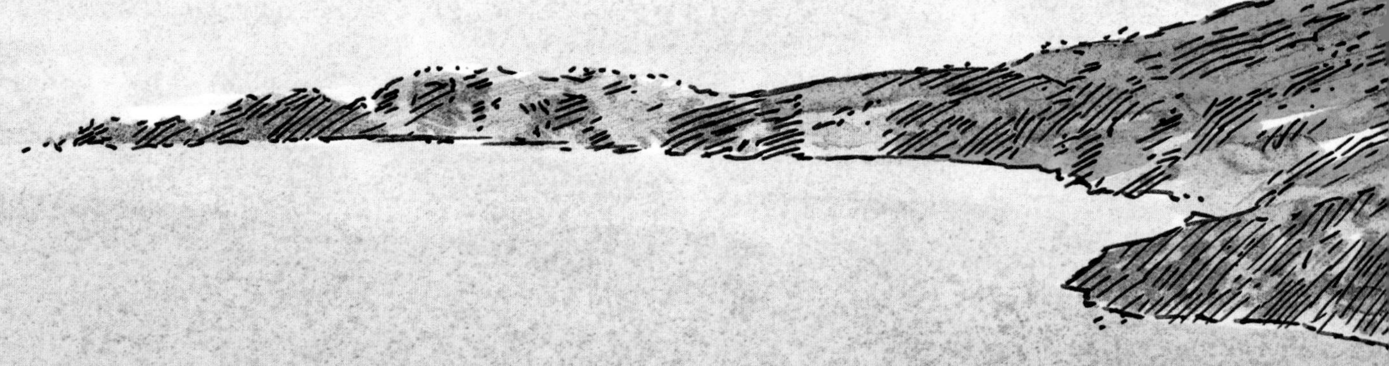

SAN FRANCISCO

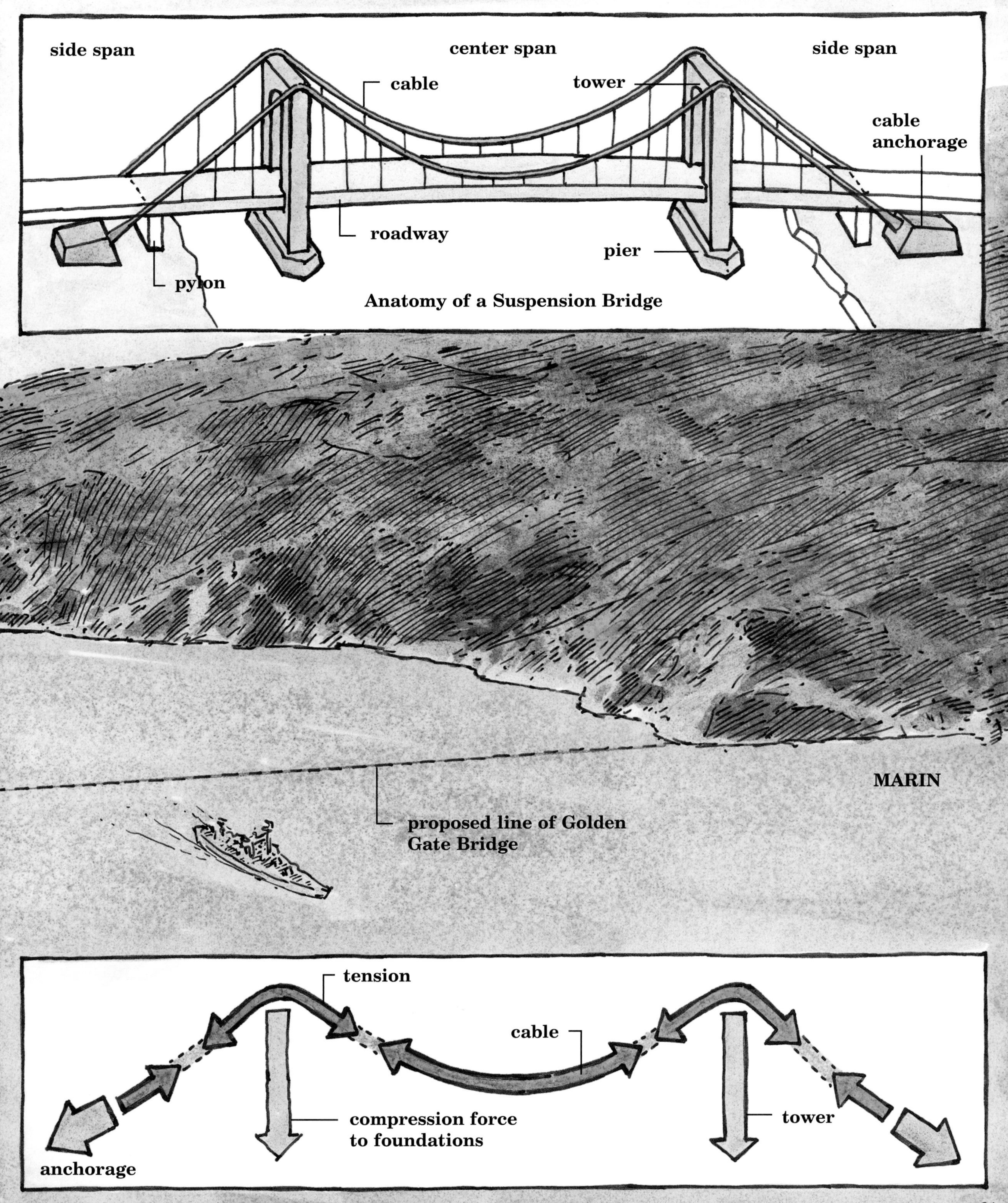
side span
center span
side span
cable
tower
cable anchorage
roadway
pier
pylon
Anatomy of a Suspension Bridge
MARIN
proposed line of Golden Gate Bridge
tension
cable
compression force to foundations
tower
anchorage

Initially, the Golden Gate Bridge seemed to design itself. After the line of the roadway was established, the towers were located. They needed to be as close to each other as possible to keep the center span as short as possible. On the Marin side, the floor of the bay descends rapidly; therefore, the tower was situated very close to the shore. Because the foundations of the San Francisco tower would need to be sunk 20 feet into bedrock and divers could not work more than 100 feet down, that tower was situated where the water was 80 feet deep. The length of the main span turned out to be 4200 feet.

To avoid unnecessary and expensive underwater work, the San Francisco pylon—the support between the ends of the side span and the approach road—was placed on the closest dry land, about 1100 feet from the tower. That distance was simply matched on the other side to make the bridge symmetrical. The cable anchorages could then be located behind the pylons along the same axis.

The height of the bridge at the center of the midspan (220 feet) and at the two towers (210 feet) was determined by the U.S. Navy to ensure clearance for its fleet. The approximate depth of the roadway structure was to be 30 feet. The lowest point of the main cable would be approximately 10 feet above that. The optimum curvature of the cable for the most even distribution of forces over a 4200-foot span would require a sag of about 470 feet. Add these dimensions to the height above the water and you have the approximate height of the towers. Finally, a width of 90 feet was chosen for the road. A smaller width would have seemed visually disproportionate for a structure of this magnitude.

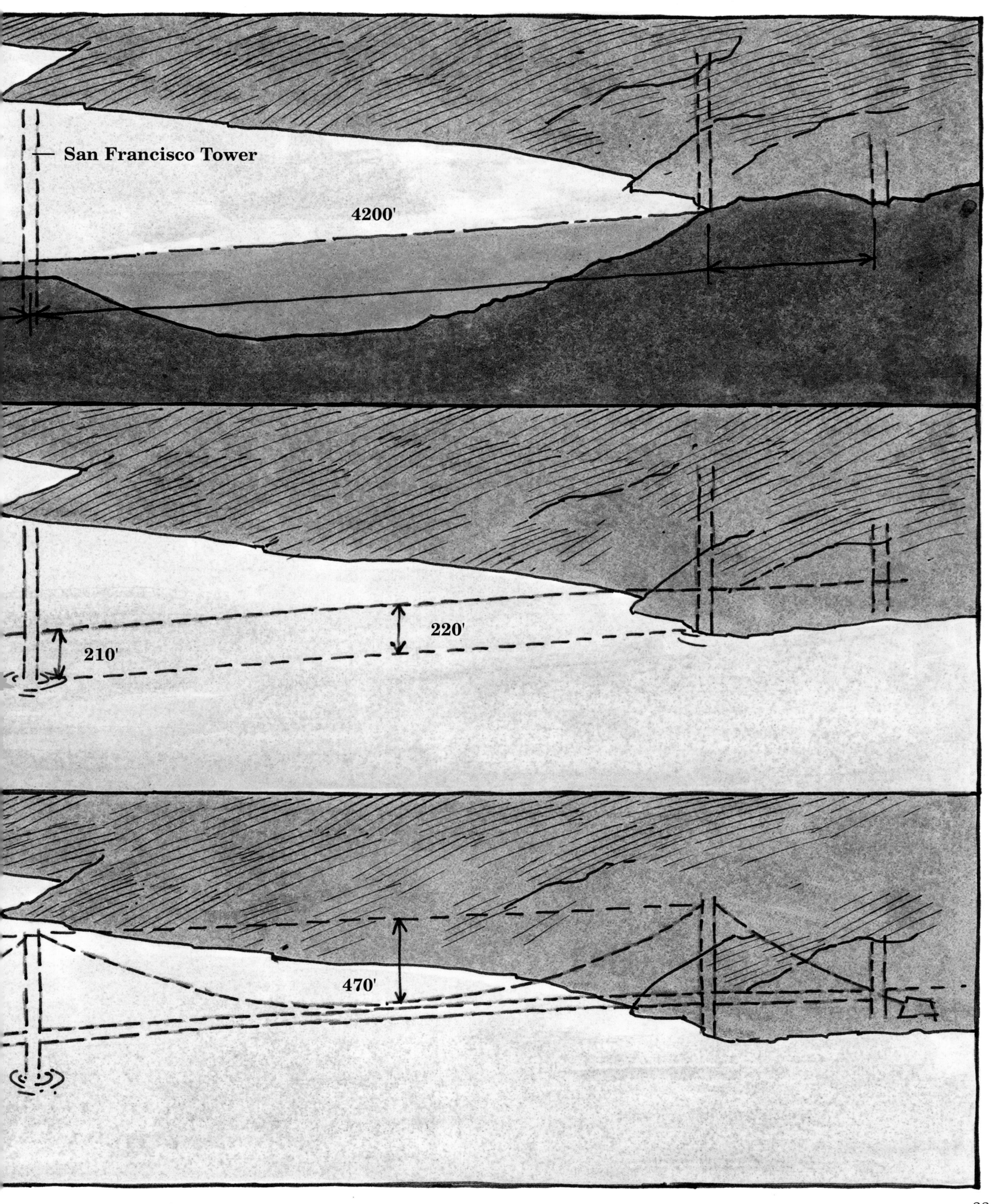
San Francisco Tower
4200'
220'
210'
470'

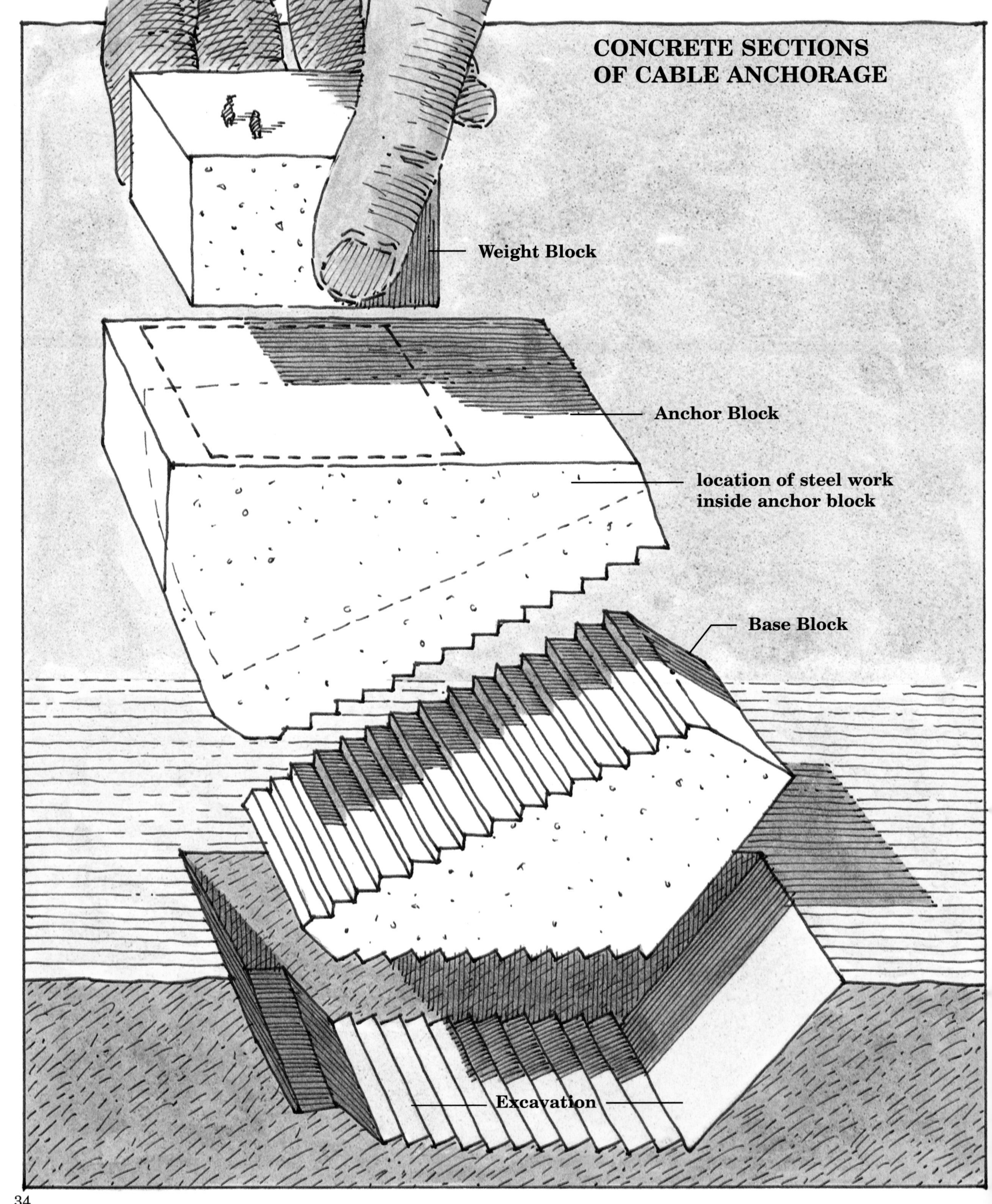
CONCRETE SECTIONS
OF CABLE ANCHORAGE
Weight Block
Anchor Block
location of steel work
inside anchor block
Base Block
Excavation

Once the design of the bridge had been finalized, work began on the anchorages. Each is composed of three main pieces: the base block, which is keyed into the bedrock; the anchor block itself, which is keyed into the base block; and a weight block, which simply rests on top of the anchor block. It is the tremendous weight of the anchorage pushing down that counteracts the pull of the cable. The ends of the cables were attached to a series of enormous eye bars that were in turn fastened to heavy girders at the back of the anchor block. The girders and the eye bars were to be embedded in concrete.

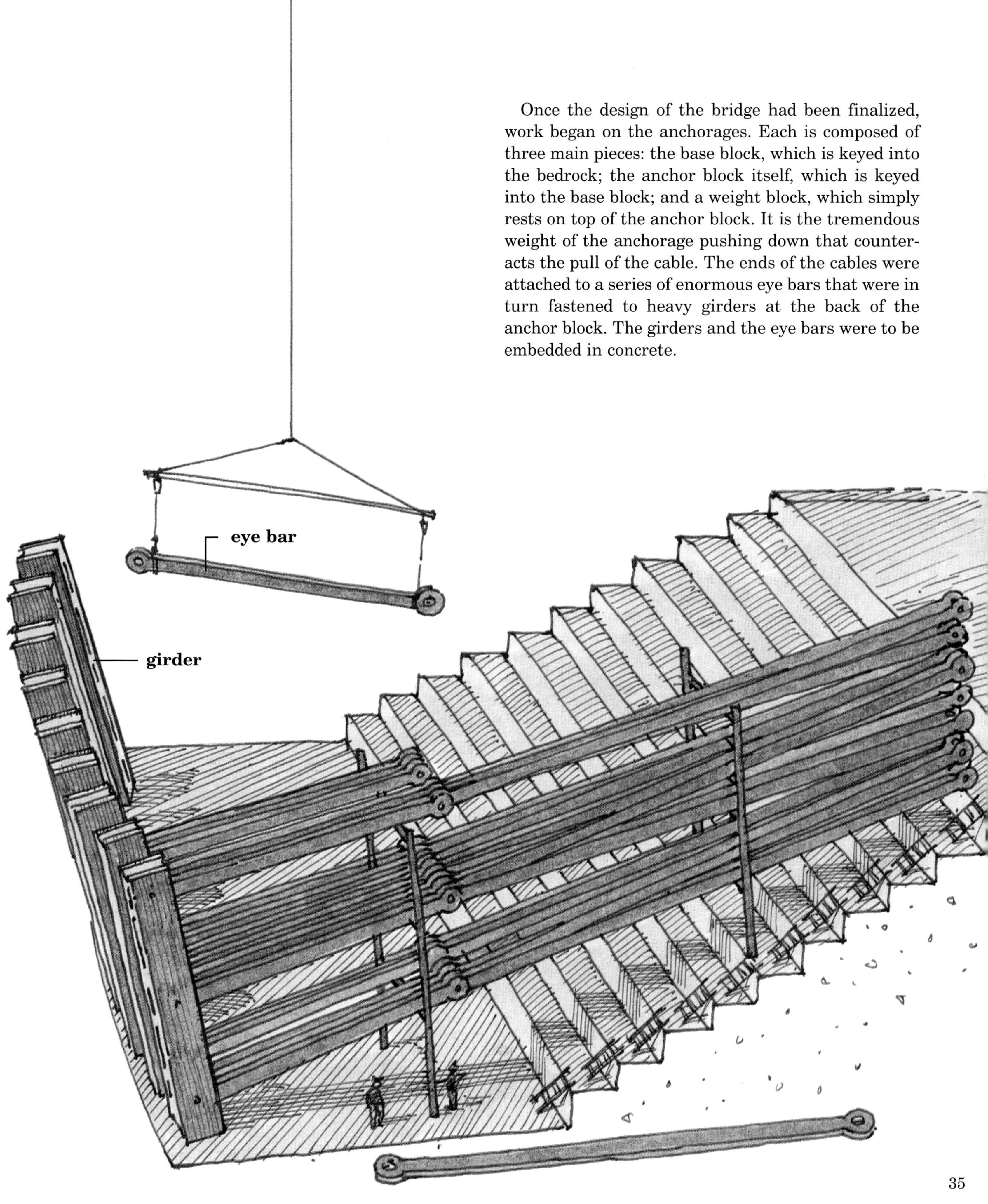

The two steel towers stand on massive concrete piers. Because the San Francisco pier is 1100 feet off shore, a jetty was first built for the delivery of materials, equipment, and workers to the site. After blasting away much of the rock at the end of the jetty, the workers built an enormous elliptical concrete ring called a fender. Its base went down 20 feet into the bedrock and its rim stood 15 feet above the water. This not only served as a coffer dam during construction but also provided permanent protection for the finished pier.

Because most of the concrete was needed only beneath the two legs of each tower, the central section could be left hollow. This space and the area between the fender and the pier were eventually flooded for added weight. Steel angle irons that extended some 50 feet into the concrete would eventually be tied to the legs of the tower for additional stability.

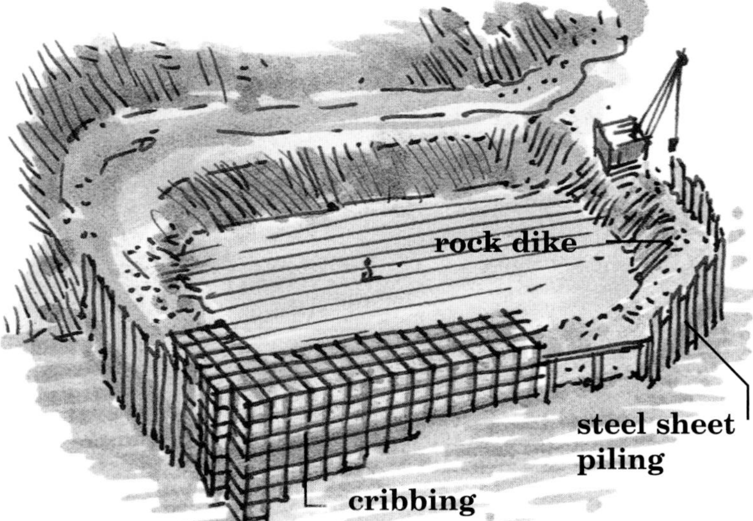

Site of Marin Pier

The pier for the Marin tower was to be built in shallow water near the shore; therefore, construction was less complicated. A coffer dam was first built around the site. The part that extends into the water is built with cribbing—heavy timber boxes that are filled with rock and sunk into position. The ends of the cribbing are connected to land with a simple rock dike. The entire structure is then sheathed on the outside with steel sheet piling—interlocking pieces of steel that are driven into the ground. Once complete, the area was pumped dry and the site was excavated to expose a solid footing for the pier.

water hole to flood center cavity

Cross section—San Francisco Pier

pier
fender

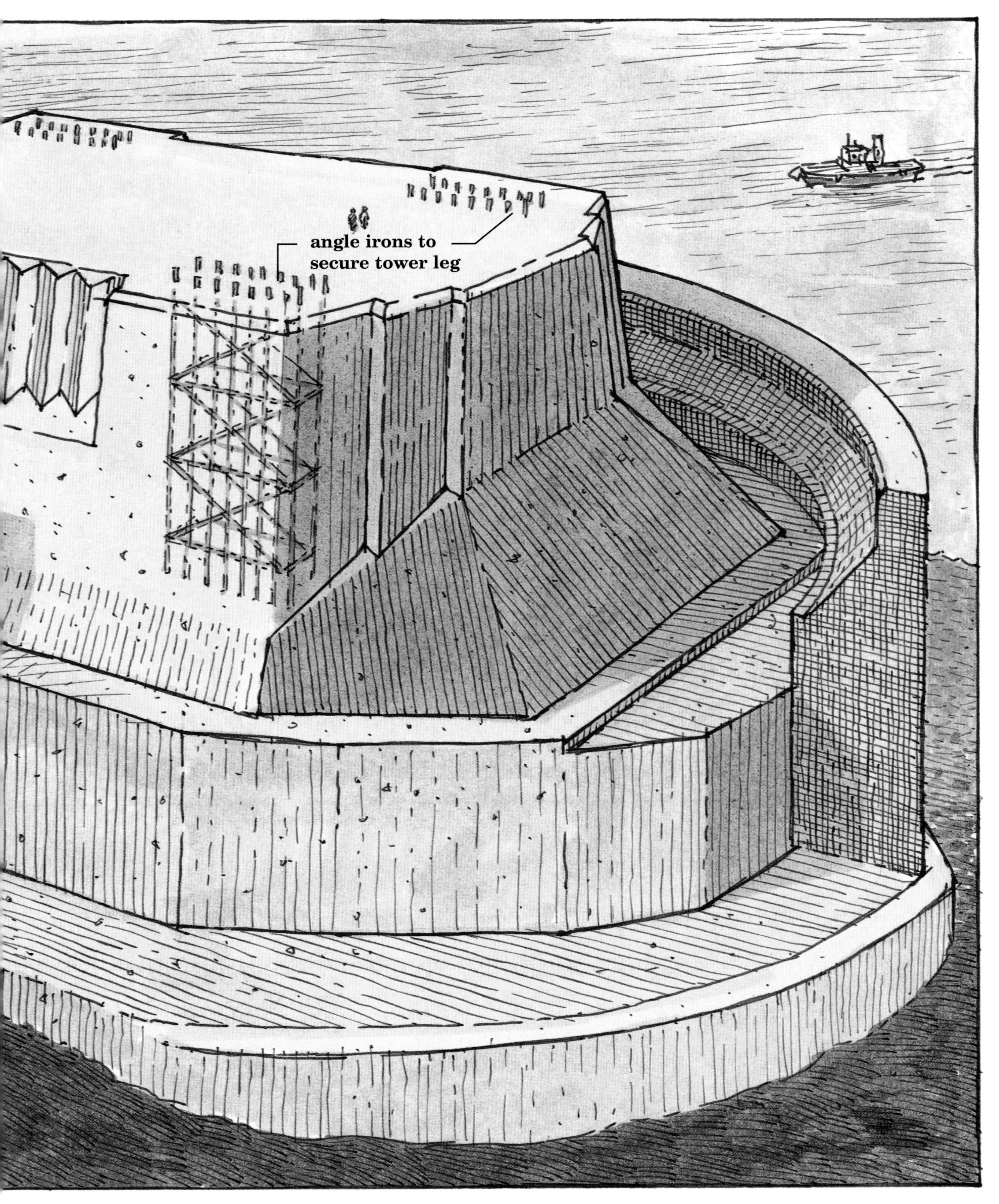
angle irons to
secure tower leg

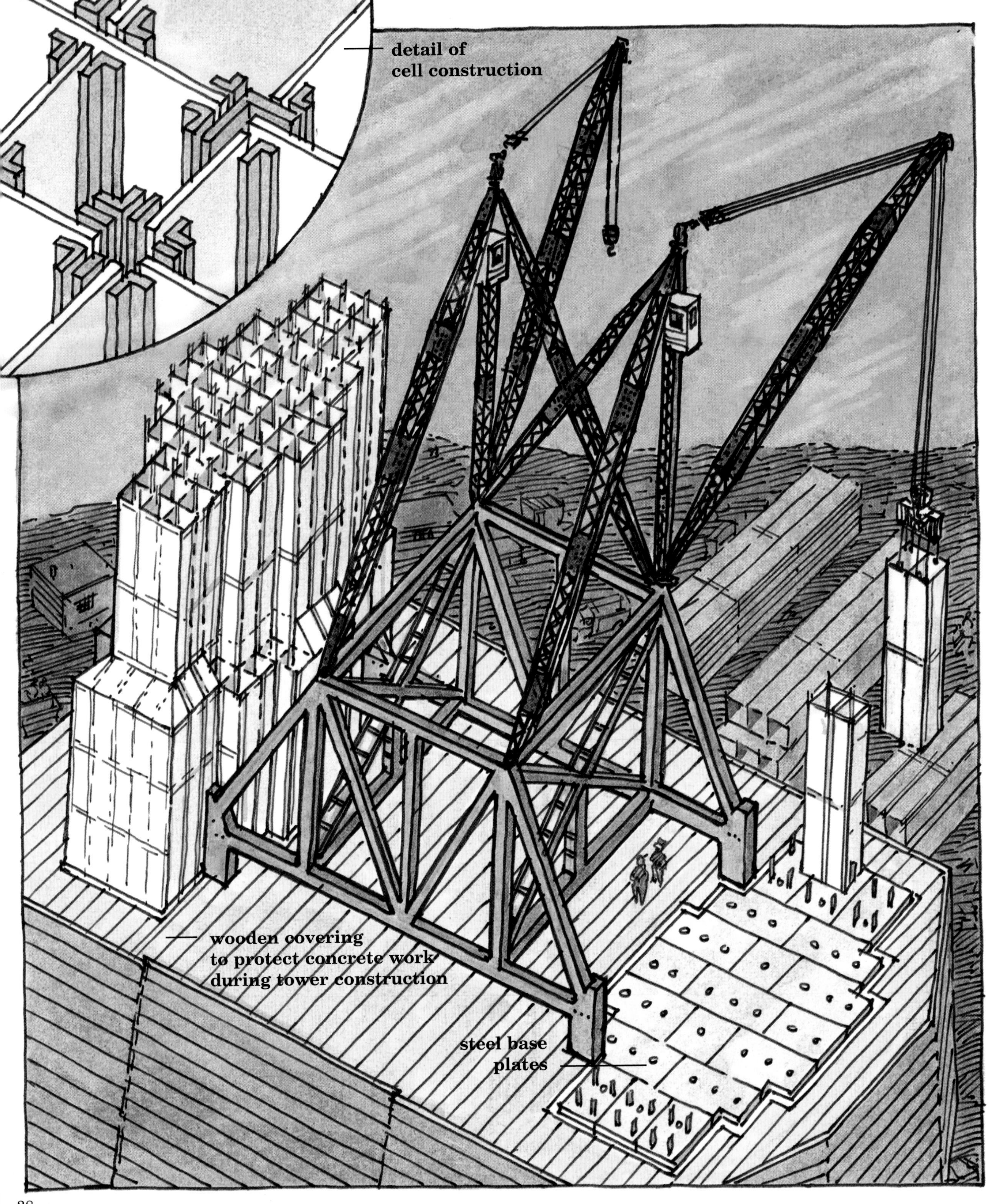
detail of
cell construction
wooden covering
to protect concrete work
during tower construction
steel base
plates

The two towers of the bridge are identical. Each has two legs connected with cross-bracing to stiffen the structure against the considerable force of the wind. The legs are built up from clusters of steel tubes called cells. The cells are 3½ feet square and approximately 45 feet tall. These are made of angles and plates riveted together. To help distribute the weight of the legs and prevent them from crushing the concrete immediately below, they sit on thick plates that are pinned in place with long dowels.

The cell clusters are lifted into place by a creeper derrick (a truss bridge), on top of which two stiff-legged derricks have been placed. Once the legs of the towers reach a certain height, the creeper derrick is hoisted up between them. Since the pier for the Marin tower was a far simpler undertaking than that of its counterpart across the gate, the Marin tower was completed well ahead of its partner.

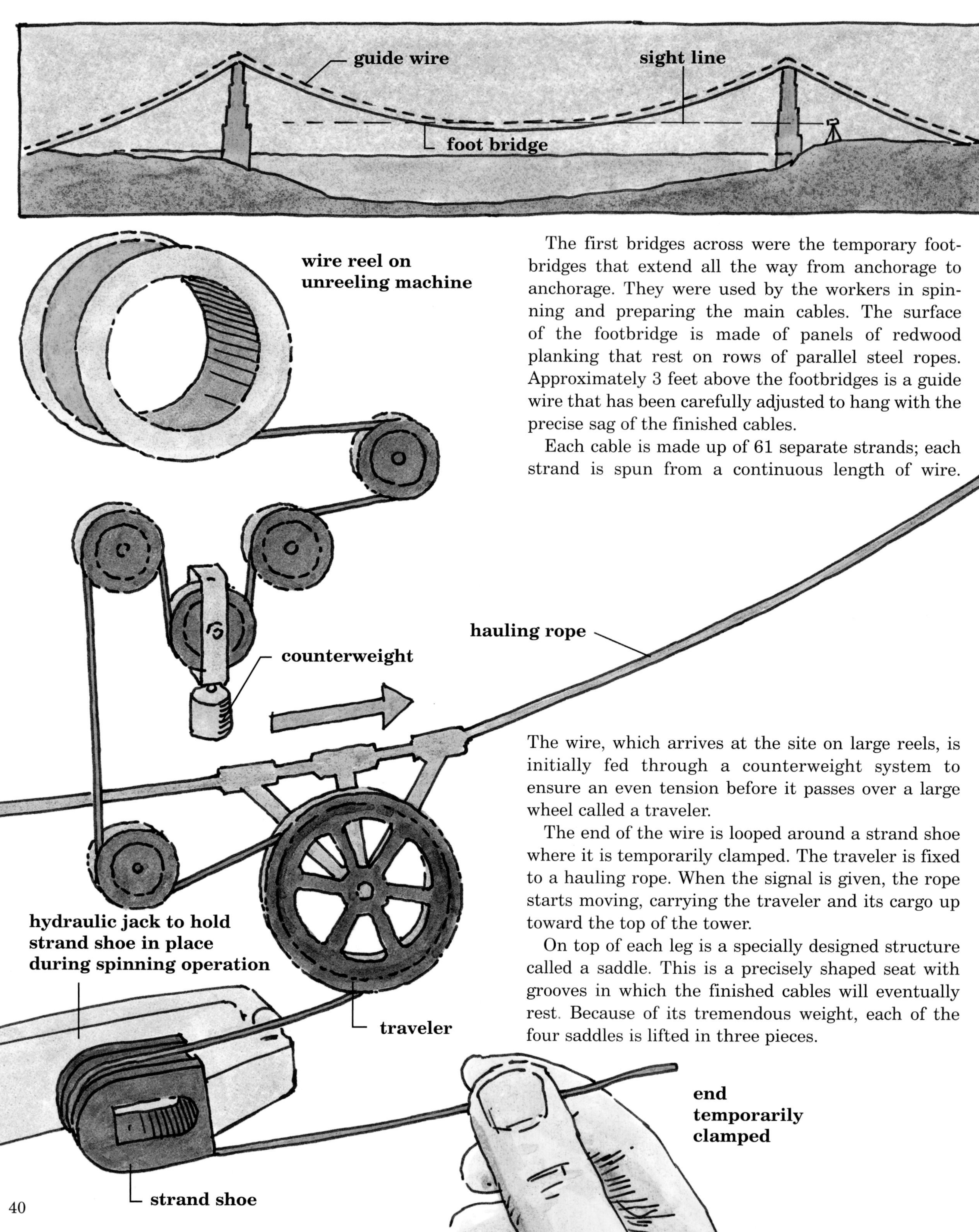

The first bridges across were the temporary footbridges that extend all the way from anchorage to anchorage. They were used by the workers in spinning and preparing the main cables. The surface of the footbridge is made of panels of redwood planking that rest on rows of parallel steel ropes. Approximately 3 feet above the footbridges is a guide wire that has been carefully adjusted to hang with the precise sag of the finished cables.

Each cable is made up of 61 separate strands; each strand is spun from a continuous length of wire. The wire, which arrives at the site on large reels, is initially fed through a counterweight system to ensure an even tension before it passes over a large wheel called a traveler.

The end of the wire is looped around a strand shoe where it is temporarily clamped. The traveler is fixed to a hauling rope. When the signal is given, the rope starts moving, carrying the traveler and its cargo up toward the top of the tower.

On top of each leg is a specially designed structure called a saddle. This is a precisely shaped seat with grooves in which the finished cables will eventually rest. Because of its tremendous weight, each of the four saddles is lifted in three pieces.

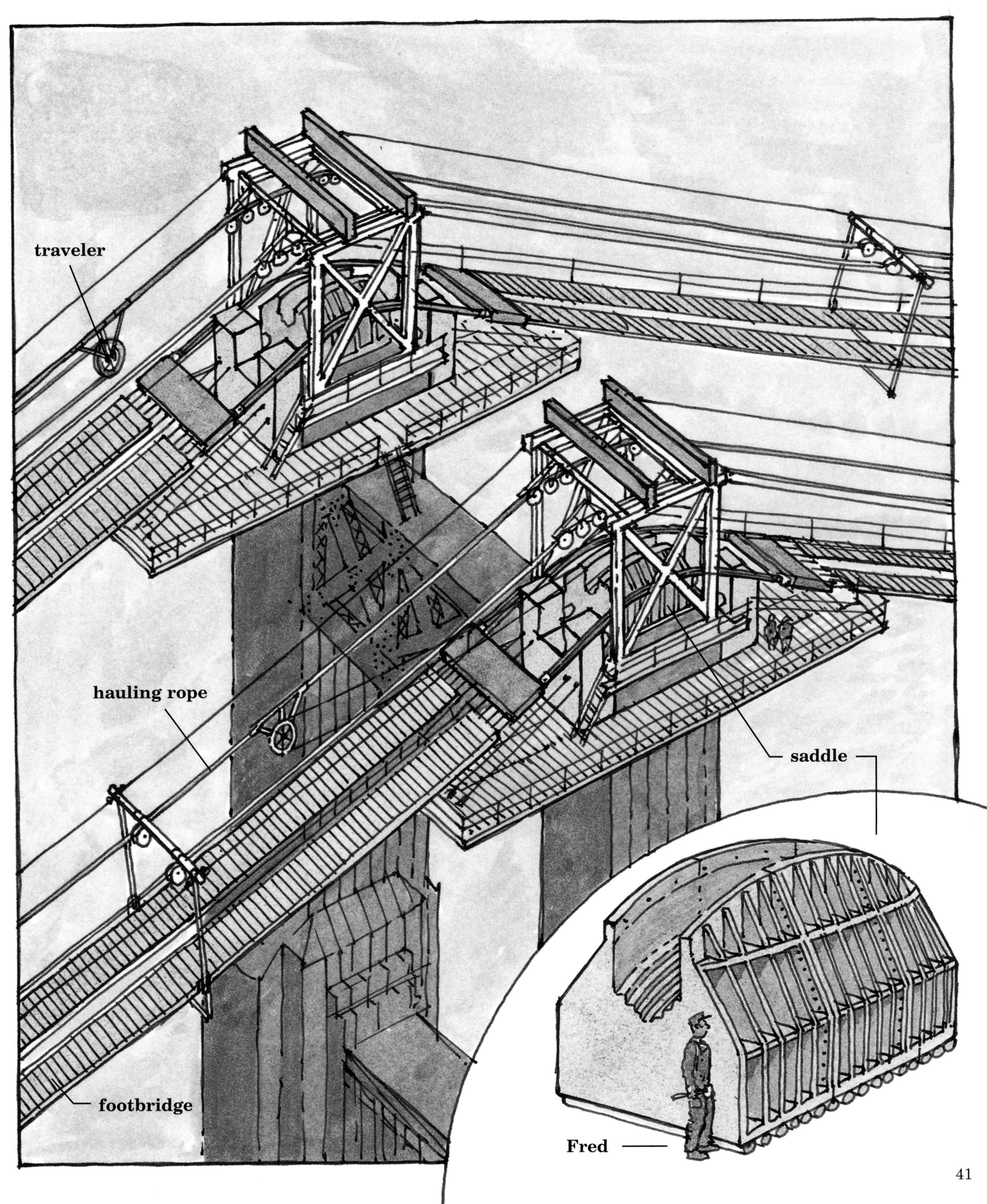
traveler
hauling rope
footbridge
saddle
Fred

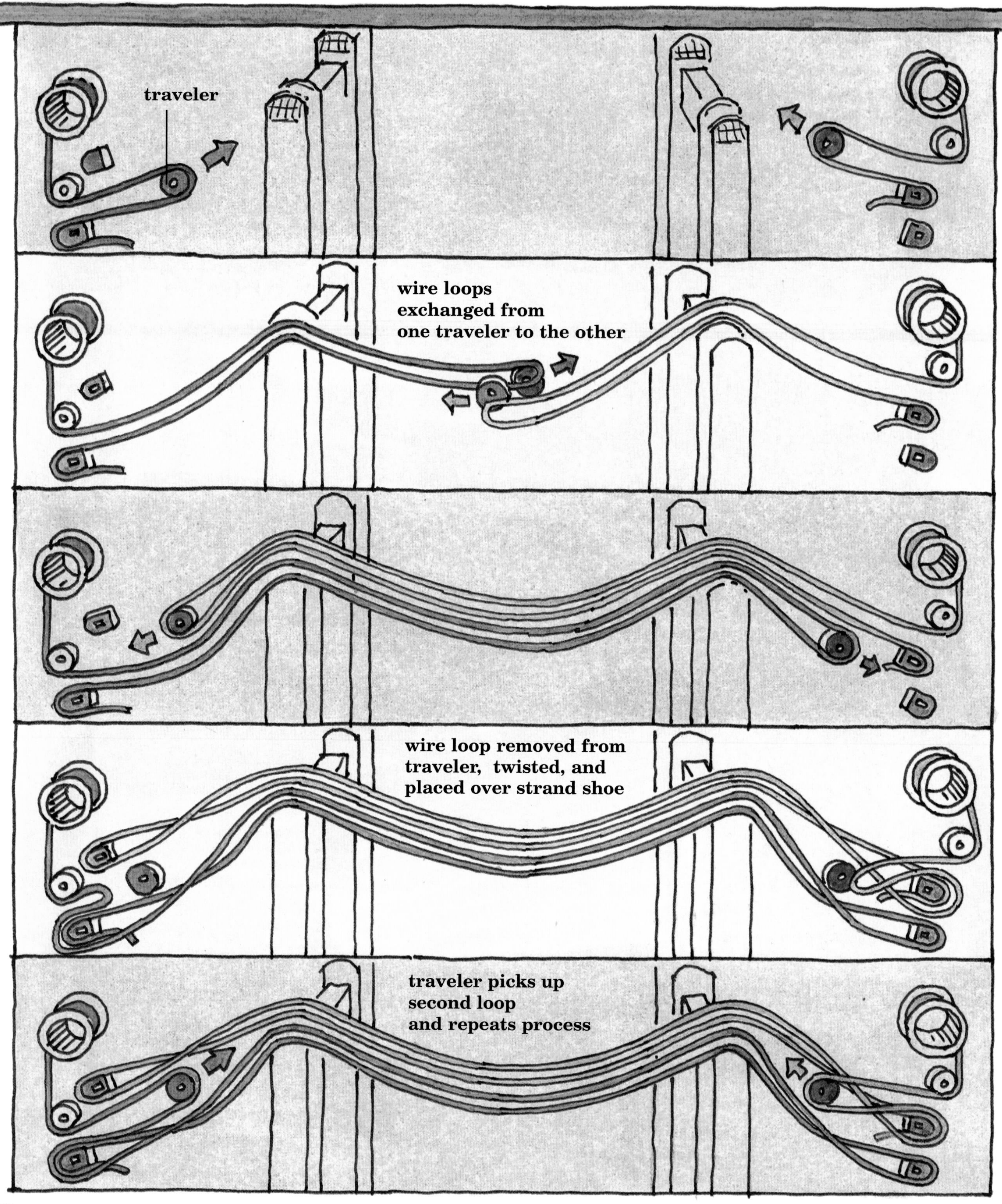
traveler
wire loops
exchanged from
one traveler to the other
wire loop removed from
traveler, twisted, and
placed over strand shoe
traveler picks up
second loop
and repeats process

Every traveler first carried four wires. Eventually they carried six wires to hurry the pace of the construction. Only two wires are shown here.

Two separate travelers, each spinning a different strand, move toward each other. When they meet in the middle of the center span, the wires are slipped from one wheel to the other.

Each traveler now returns to its starting point to complete the journey of the wire from the opposite side.

Upon arrival, each loop of wire is removed and wrapped around its own strand shoe.

The empty wheel then picks up a new loop from its original reel and begins the journey all over again.

Each strand is made up of more than 400 lengths of wire that lie side by side. That is about 500 miles of wire per strand. When a spool runs out, a new wire is connected to the end of the old with a tubular sleeve that is designed to prevent the wires from pulling apart. As the travelers move back and forth, the growing strands are continually checked against the guide wire to ensure that the exact curvature is maintained.

As work begins on a strand, the last pieces of eye bar are installed at each anchorage, linking those already embedded in concrete with a particular strand shoe. Once a strand is completed, the shoe (which has been held in a temporary position in front of the eye bars so that loops can be wrapped around it) is pulled back and pinned in place between the eye bars.

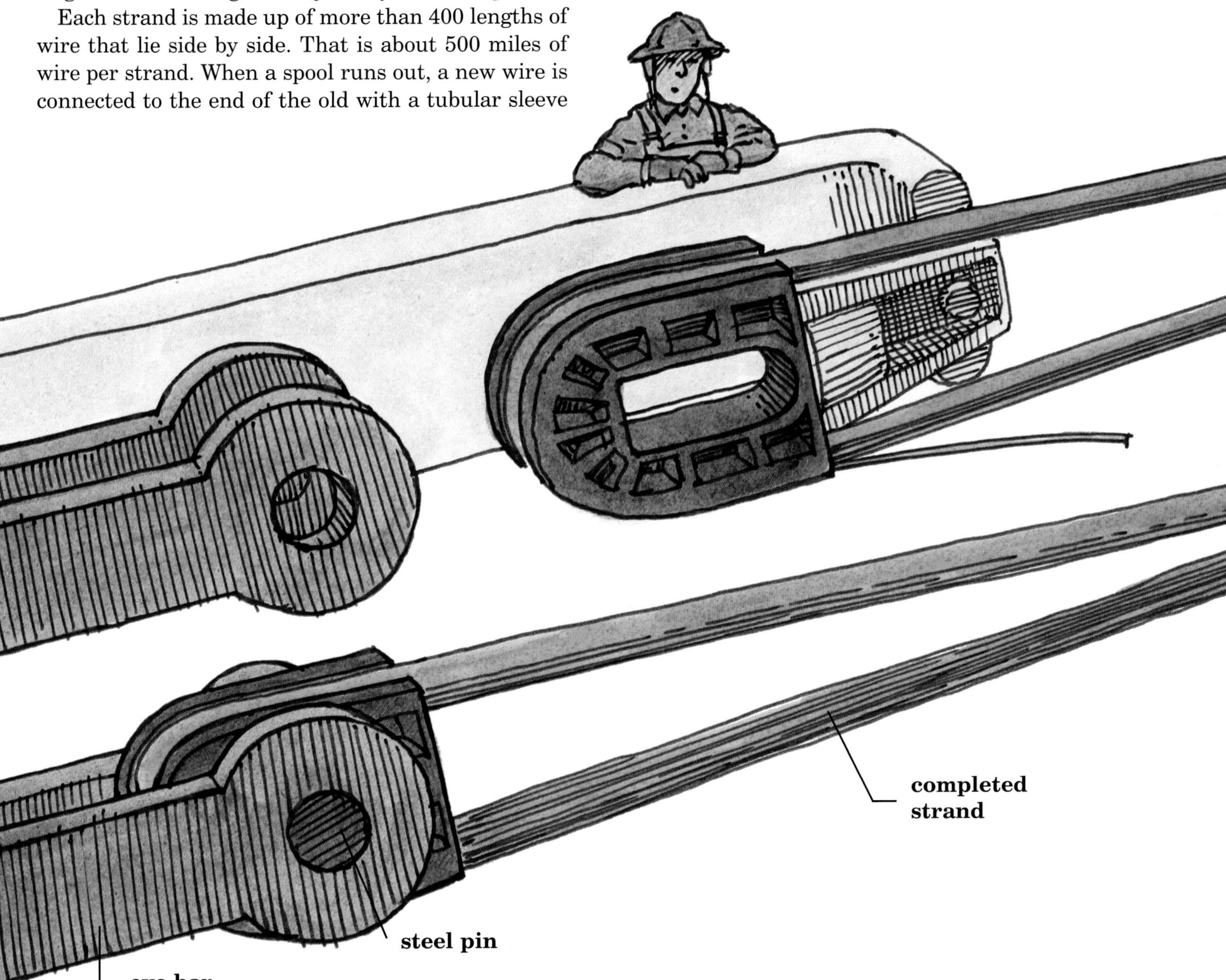

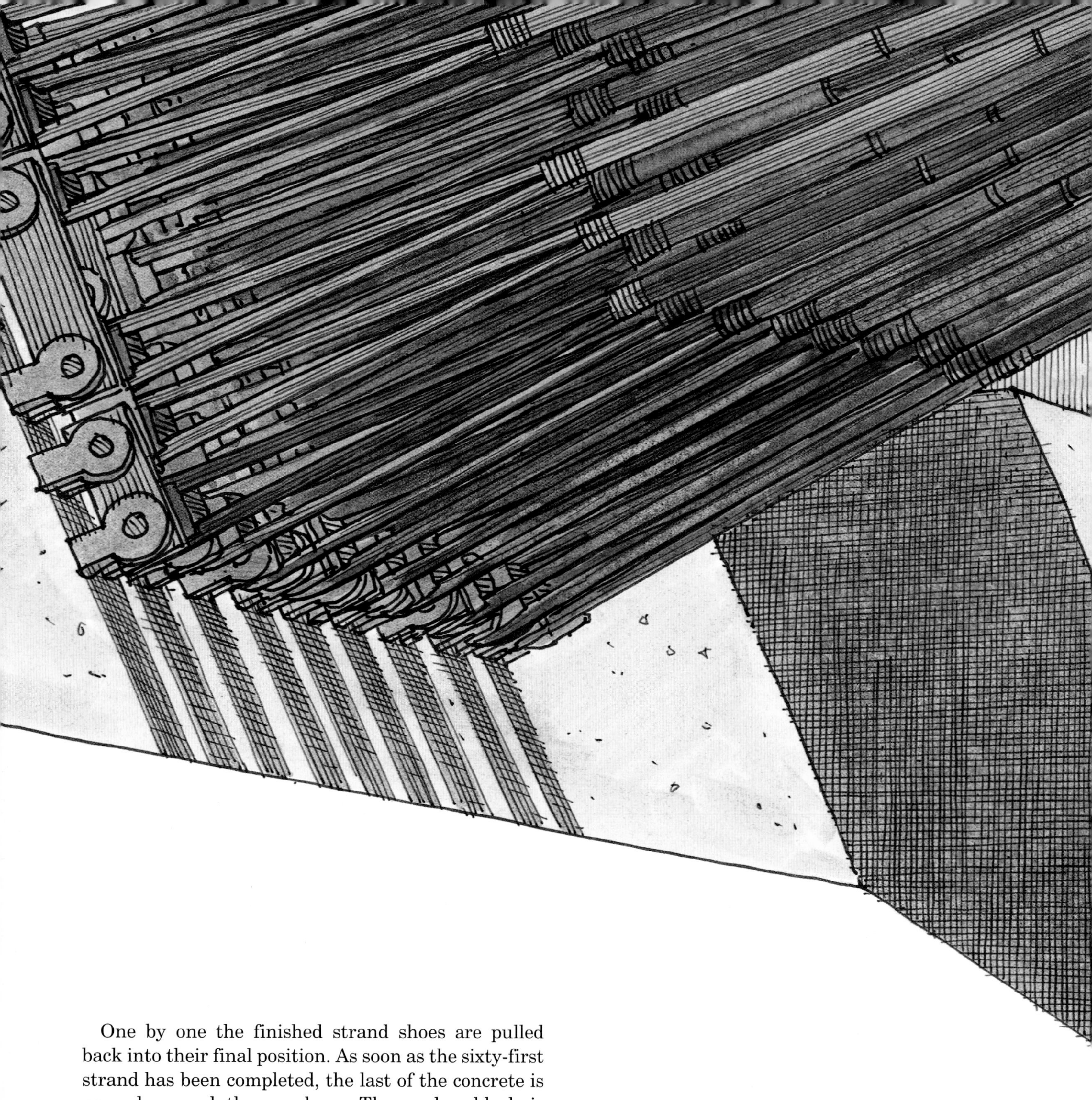

One by one the finished strand shoes are pulled back into their final position. As soon as the sixty-first strand has been completed, the last of the concrete is poured around the eye bars. The anchor block is finished. Eventually, both pairs of anchorages will be enclosed by high walls and a concrete roof.

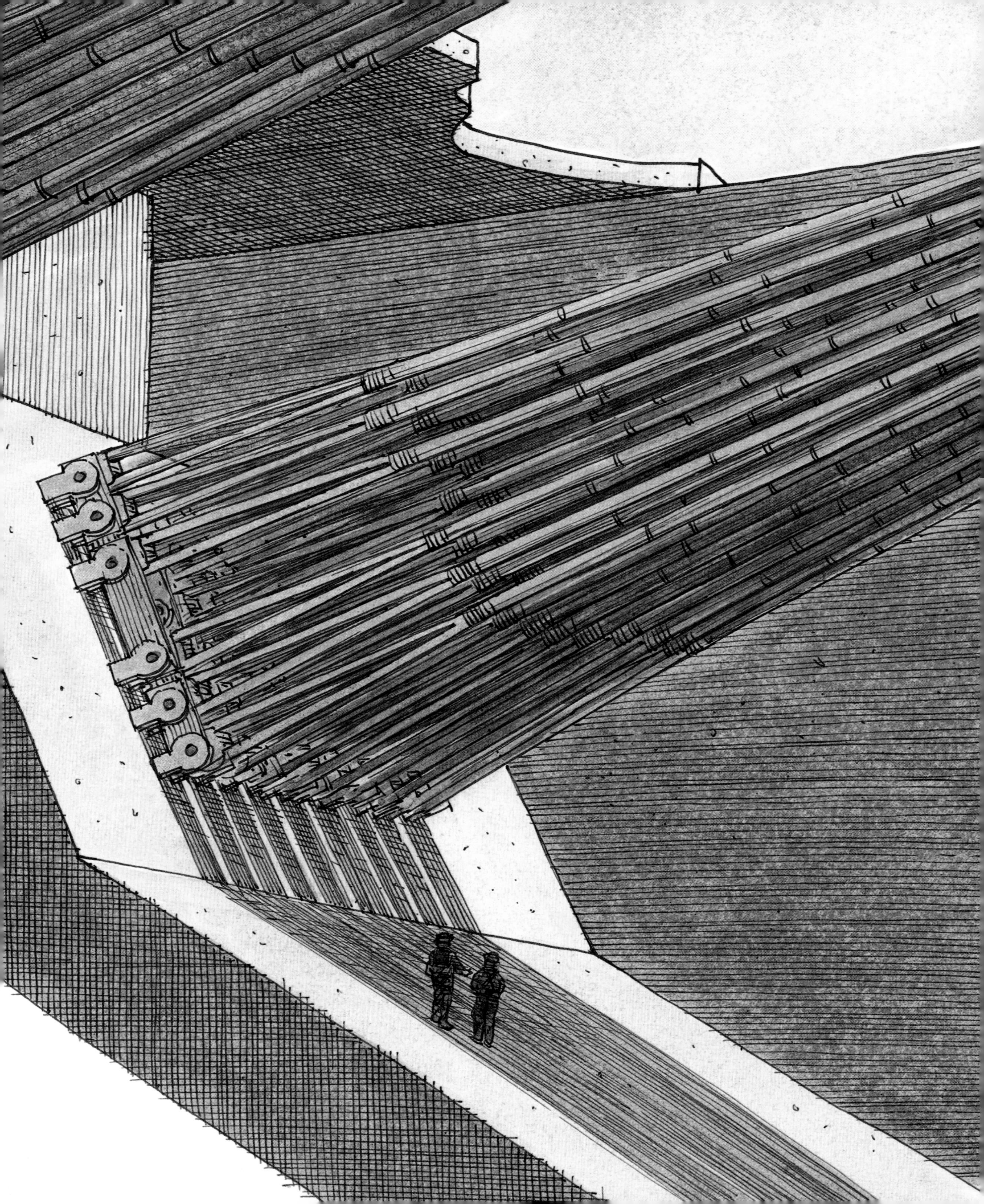

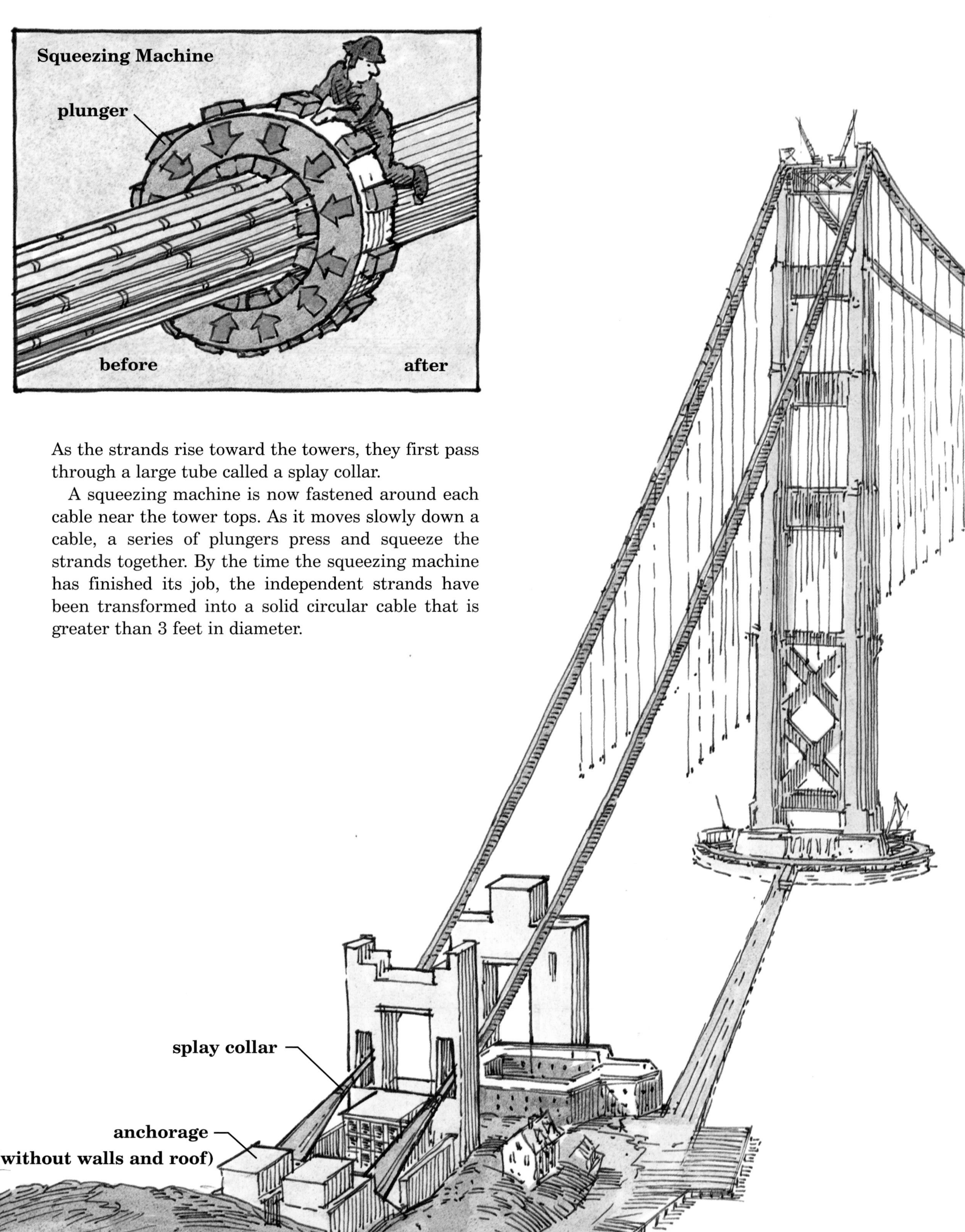

As the strands rise toward the towers, they first pass through a large tube called a splay collar.

A squeezing machine is now fastened around each cable near the tower tops. As it moves slowly down a cable, a series of plungers press and squeeze the strands together. By the time the squeezing machine has finished its job, the independent strands have been transformed into a solid circular cable that is greater than 3 feet in diameter.

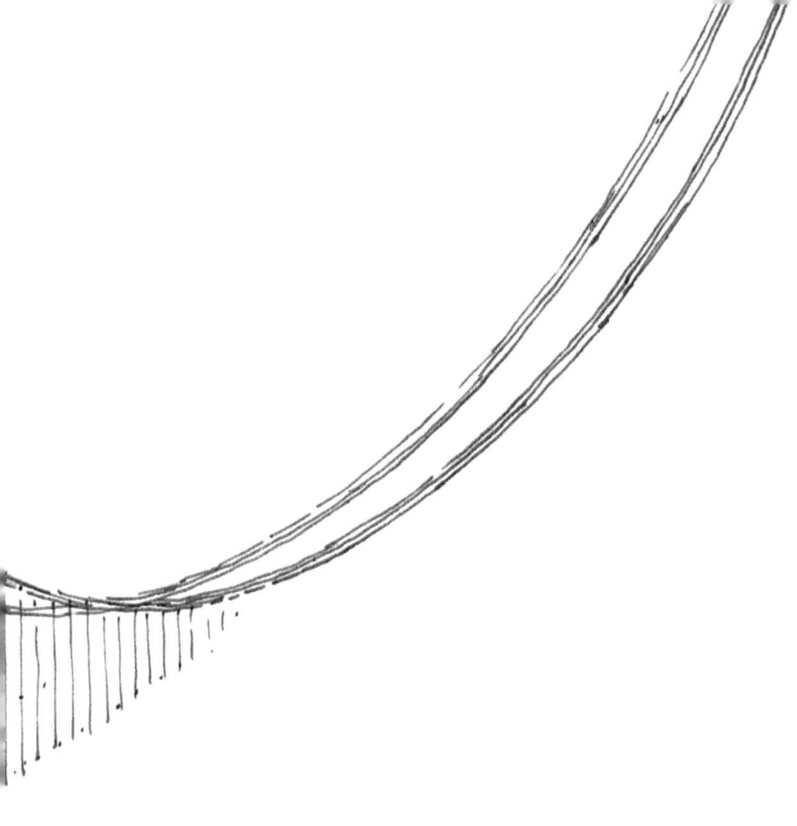

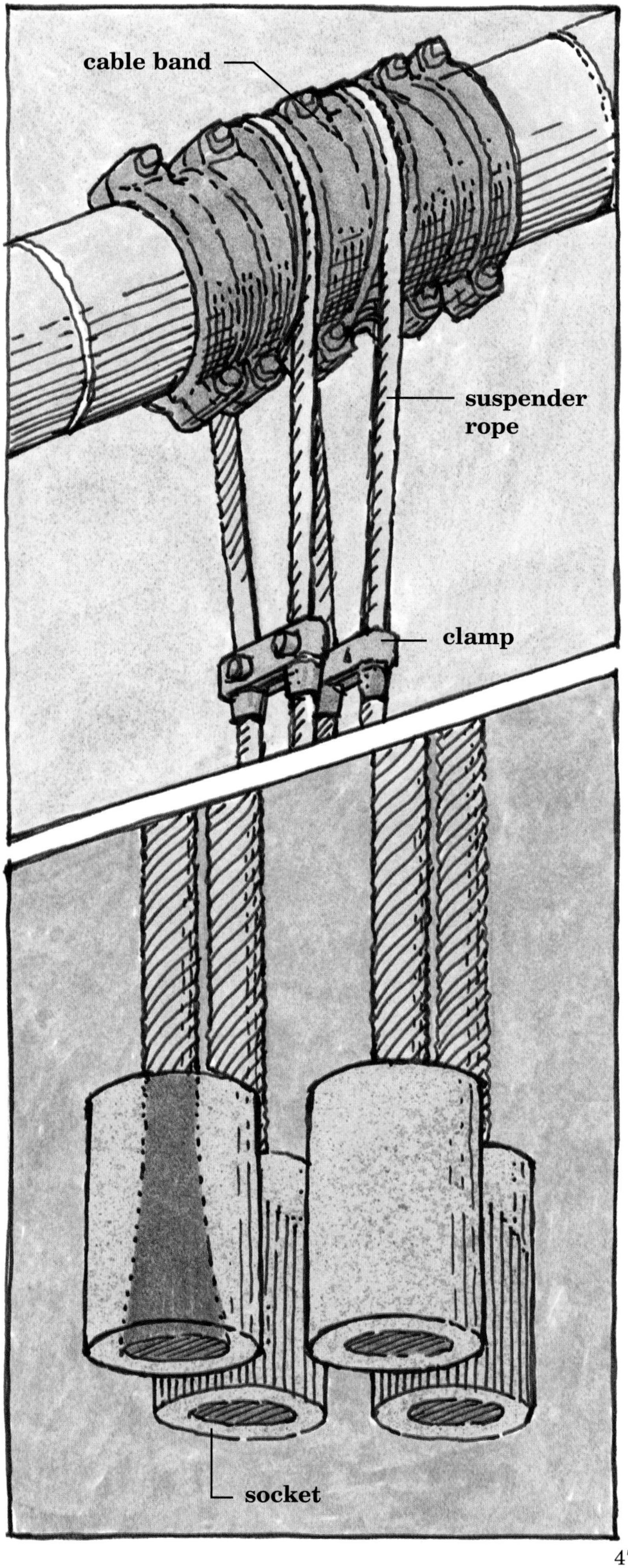

A cable band is clamped every 50 feet along the finished cable. Suspender ropes, each approximately 2 inches in diameter, are then hung over the cable bands. These steel ropes support the road itself. Each suspender rope has been cut to a specific predetermined length to ensure that the finished road will hang at exactly the correct height and camber.

All the suspender ropes are delivered to the site with their ends embedded in steel cylinders called sockets. Each rope enters a cone-shaped cavity within a socket, where its individual wires are untwisted to look something like a wire brush. The socket is then inverted and filled with molten liquid zinc, which permanently fuses rope and socket together.

Each cluster of four sockets disappears into a 25-foot-high post. In fact, the post rests on the tops of the sockets. It is neither bolted nor welded to the sockets—it simply rests on top of them. Each post is connected to its counterpart on the opposite side of the roadway by a deep floor beam. The floor beams support smaller beams called stringers; stringers eventually support the roadway itself. The only connections between the road and the cables are those sockets.

cable band
suspender rope
clamp
socket

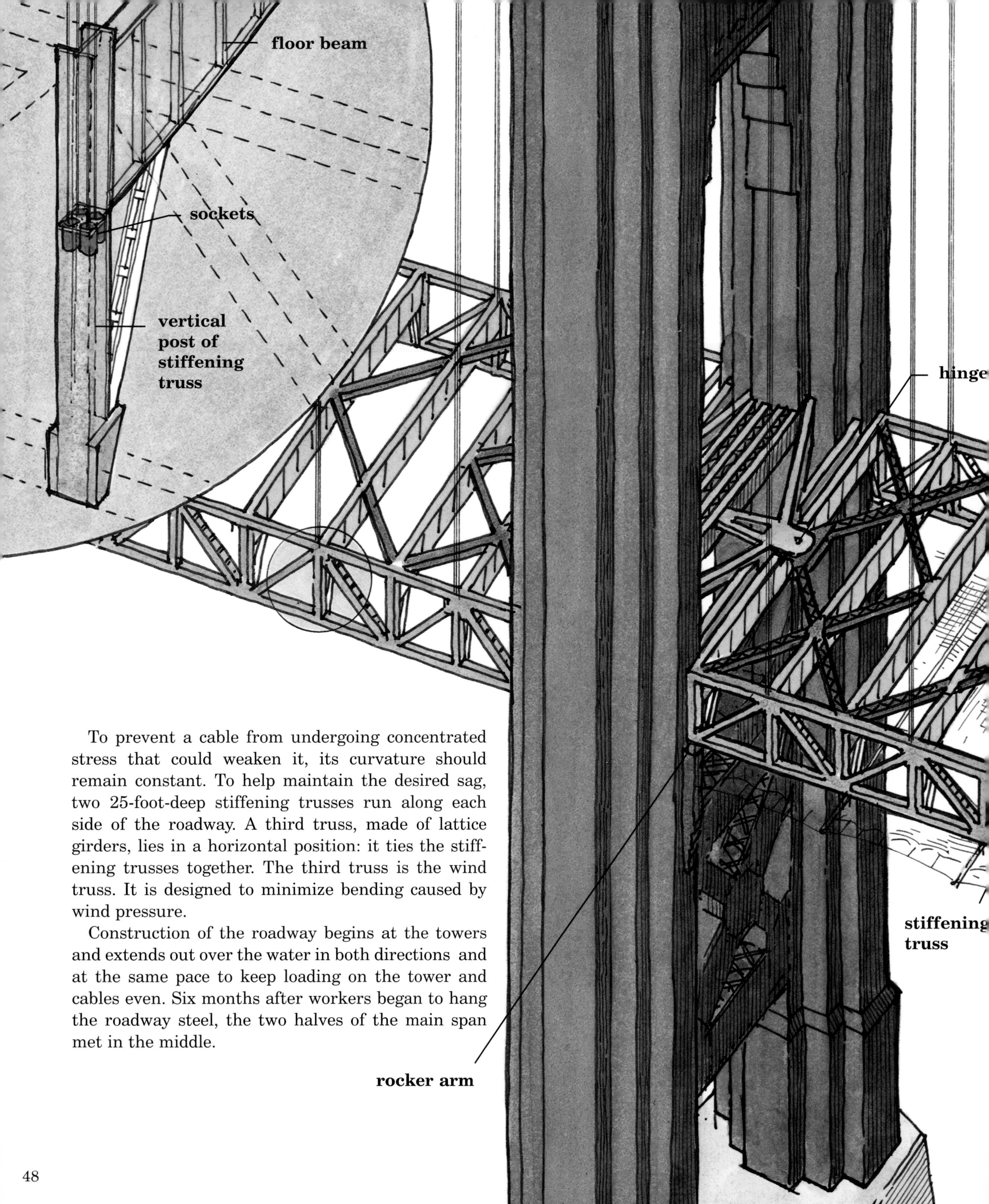

To prevent a cable from undergoing concentrated stress that could weaken it, its curvature should remain constant. To help maintain the desired sag, two 25-foot-deep stiffening trusses run along each side of the roadway. A third truss, made of lattice girders, lies in a horizontal position: it ties the stiffening trusses together. The third truss is the wind truss. It is designed to minimize bending caused by wind pressure.

Construction of the roadway begins at the towers and extends out over the water in both directions and at the same pace to keep loading on the tower and cables even. Six months after workers began to hang the roadway steel, the two halves of the main span met in the middle.

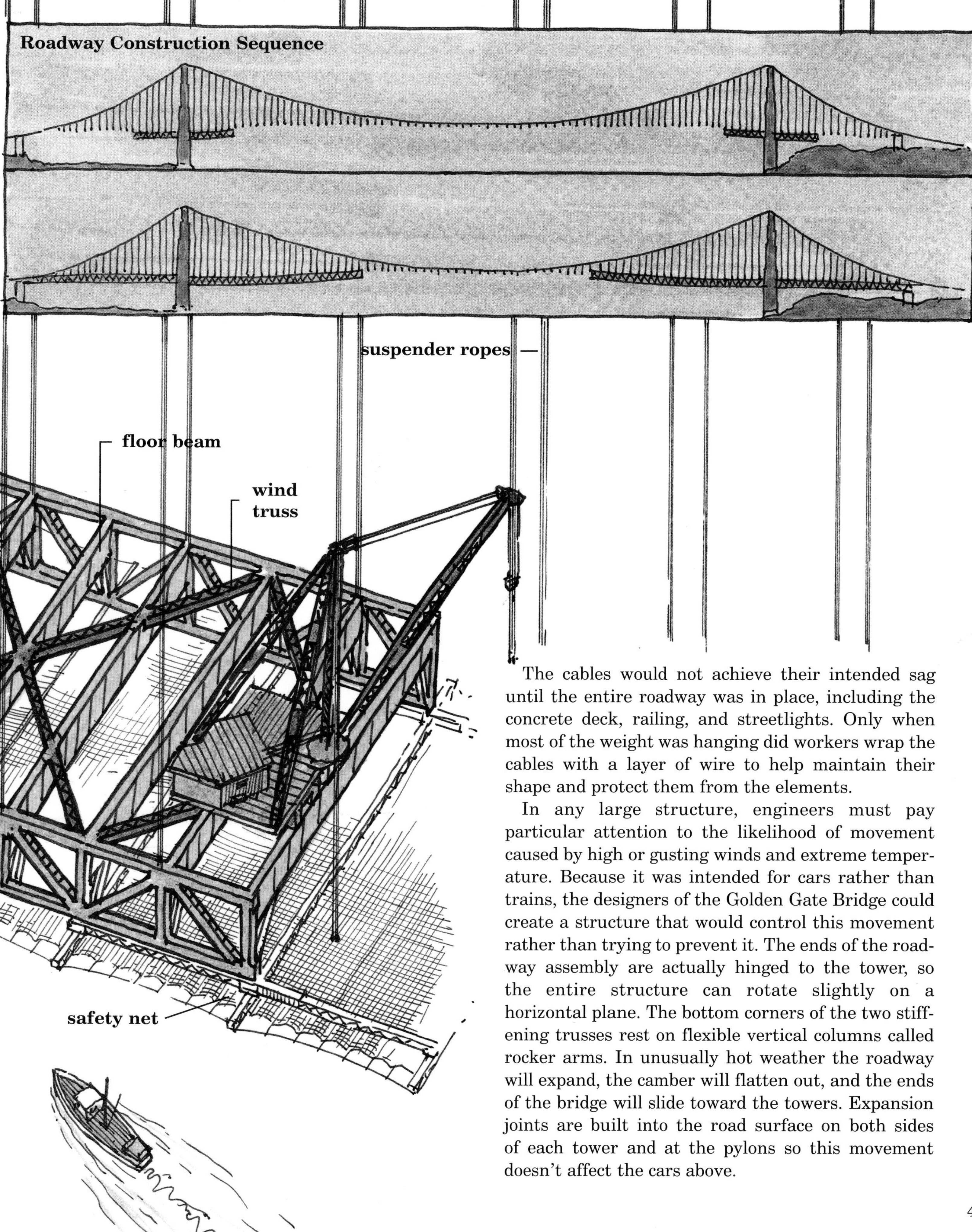

The cables would not achieve their intended sag until the entire roadway was in place, including the concrete deck, railing, and streetlights. Only when most of the weight was hanging did workers wrap the cables with a layer of wire to help maintain their shape and protect them from the elements.

In any large structure, engineers must pay particular attention to the likelihood of movement caused by high or gusting winds and extreme temperature. Because it was intended for cars rather than trains, the designers of the Golden Gate Bridge could create a structure that would control this movement rather than trying to prevent it. The ends of the roadway assembly are actually hinged to the tower, so the entire structure can rotate slightly on a horizontal plane. The bottom corners of the two stiffening trusses rest on flexible vertical columns called rocker arms. In unusually hot weather the roadway will expand, the camber will flatten out, and the ends of the bridge will slide toward the towers. Expansion joints are built into the road surface on both sides of each tower and at the pylons so this movement doesn't affect the cars above.

In its day, this bridge created by Strauss and Clifford Paine was a masterpiece of engineering technology and building efficiency. Construction took less than five years. But while the Golden Gate may be the most famous bridge in the world, it has long since relinquished its claim as the longest bridge in the world. This title currently belongs to the Akashi Kaikyo bridge in Japan, shown below for comparison.

Not only are larger and larger suspension bridges being built today, new ideas and technologies are being explored. Because large bridges are expensive undertakings, engineers continue to seek ways to

build them more efficiently. New aerodynamically shaped prefabricated roadways are replacing the older stiffening trusses, reducing construction time as well as the impact of the wind. It is now possible to prefabricate cable strands to eliminate air-spinning time (if there is a vehicle large enough to transport the mile-and-a-half-long strands to the site). While some towers are made of concrete, heavy but very stiff, others are using much less steel than those of the Golden Gate Bridge. Rather than simply restricting movement with thick walls, builders are now installing sophisticated devices inside their towers to dampen it.

Ponte de Normandie

Honfleur, France, 1990: The French highway administration decided to build a new bridge across the river Seine with a clear span of 2800 feet. It would need to rise 165 feet above the water so as not to obstruct ship traffic. They considered a suspension bridge but eventually rejected the idea after looking more closely at the geology of the area. Because there was no solid rock into which anchorages could be cast, each would have had to do the job entirely with its own weight. This would have required massive and therefore prohibitively expensive structures. So instead they settled on a kind of bridge that needs no such anchorages. These are called cable-stayed bridges, and at the time of its completion in 1994, Ponte de Normandie was the longest one in the world.

In a cable-stayed bridge, the roadway is supported by a series of cables extending in one or two planes from the tower or towers. Unlike the main cable of a suspension bridge, cable stays are straight and anchor directly into the roadway itself. Each forms the third leg of a triangle. The cable stays are in tension while the road and tower are in compression.

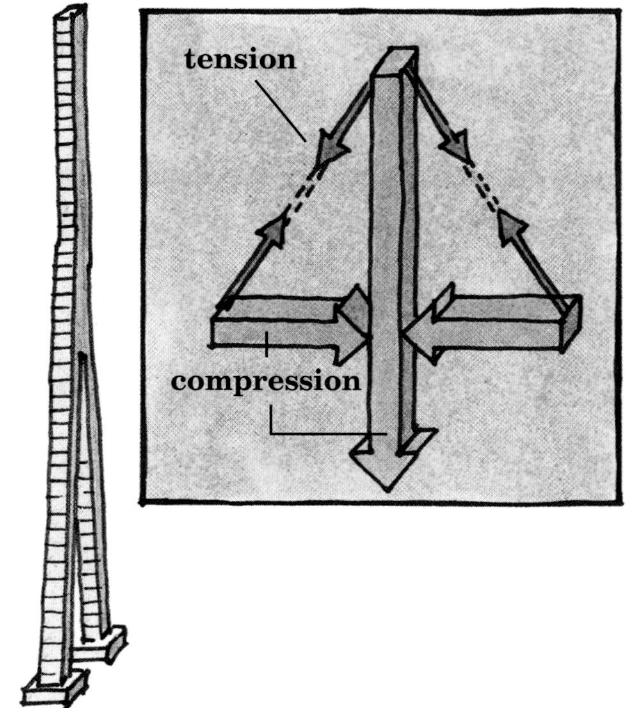

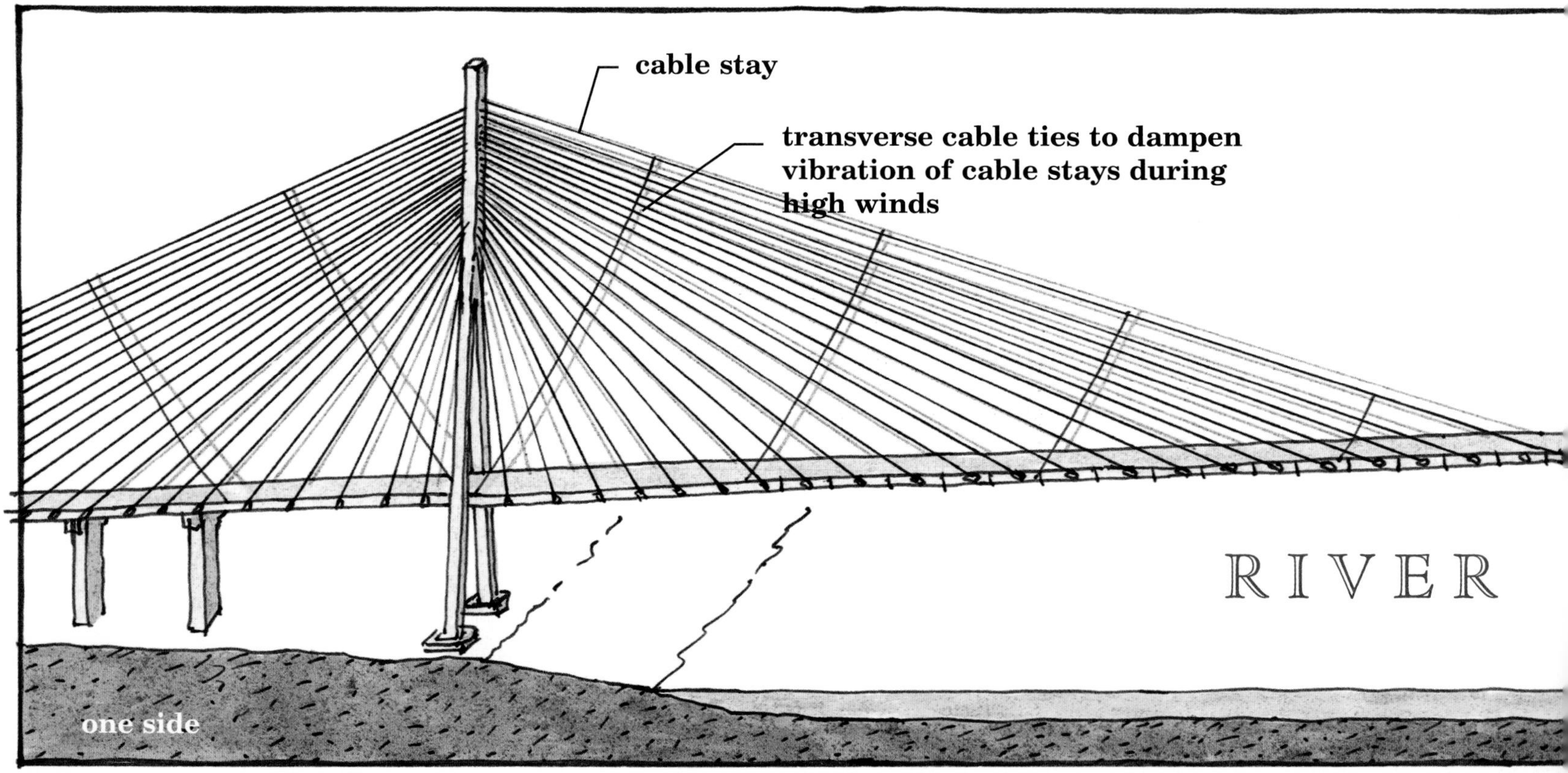

cable stay

transverse cable ties to dampen vibration of cable stays during high winds

RIVER

one side

Once the foundations were in place, two 700-foot-high concrete and steel towers were then erected. The roadway was built of prefabricated sections. Those of the side spans as well as that part of the main span closest to the towers were made of concrete. One section of concrete roadway was cantilevered out from opposite sides of a tower simultaneously to maintain balance. As each new section was fixed to the one before it, two cable stays were attached—one on each side of the roadway.

Those sections making up the bulk of the main span were steel. These were floated out and lifted into place. The cross-section of the roadway, whether of concrete or steel, is basically a shallow box aerodynamically designed to minimize wind resistance.

Concrete was used nearer the towers and between them and the approach roads to give the structure more rigidity. Steel was used for most of the main span because it is lighter yet still very strong.

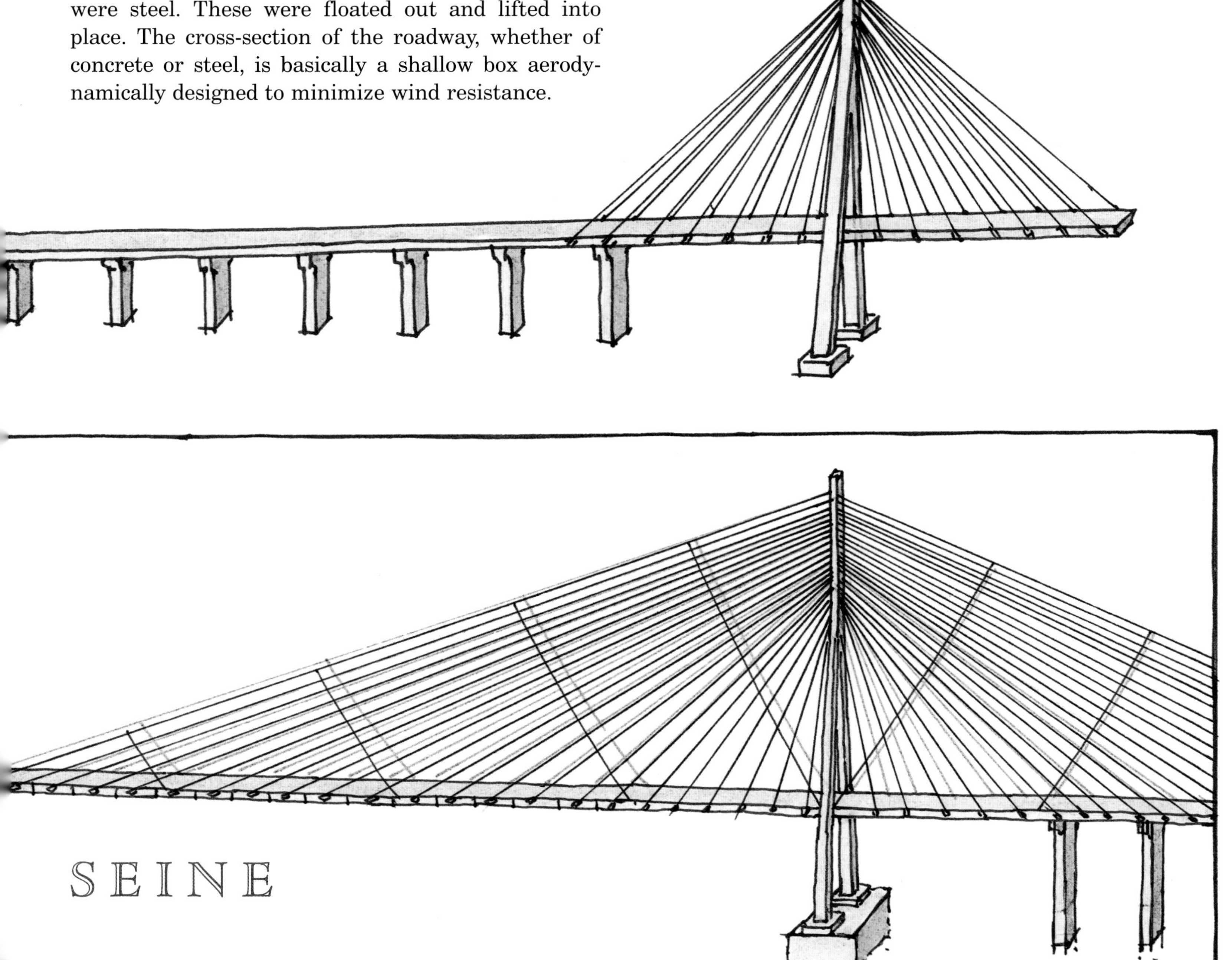

Double-plane cable-stayed bridge

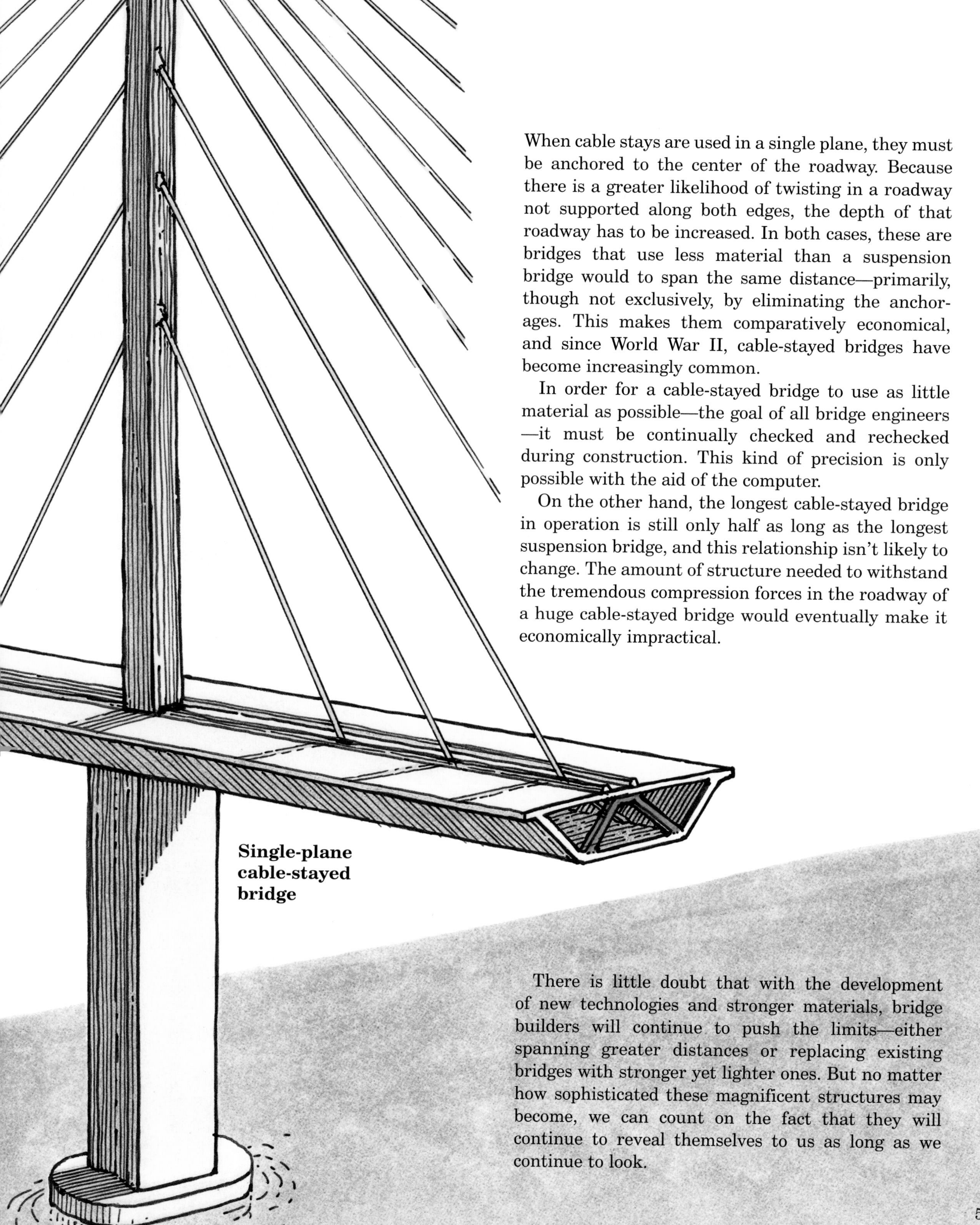

When cable stays are used in a single plane, they must be anchored to the center of the roadway. Because there is a greater likelihood of twisting in a roadway not supported along both edges, the depth of that roadway has to be increased. In both cases, these are bridges that use less material than a suspension bridge would to span the same distance—primarily, though not exclusively, by eliminating the anchorages. This makes them comparatively economical, and since World War II, cable-stayed bridges have become increasingly common.

In order for a cable-stayed bridge to use as little material as possible—the goal of all bridge engineers—it must be continually checked and rechecked during construction. This kind of precision is only possible with the aid of the computer.

On the other hand, the longest cable-stayed bridge in operation is still only half as long as the longest suspension bridge, and this relationship isn't likely to change. The amount of structure needed to withstand the tremendous compression forces in the roadway of a huge cable-stayed bridge would eventually make it economically impractical.

Single-plane cable-stayed bridge

There is little doubt that with the development of new technologies and stronger materials, bridge builders will continue to push the limits—either spanning greater distances or replacing existing bridges with stronger yet lighter ones. But no matter how sophisticated these magnificent structures may become, we can count on the fact that they will continue to reveal themselves to us as long as we continue to look.

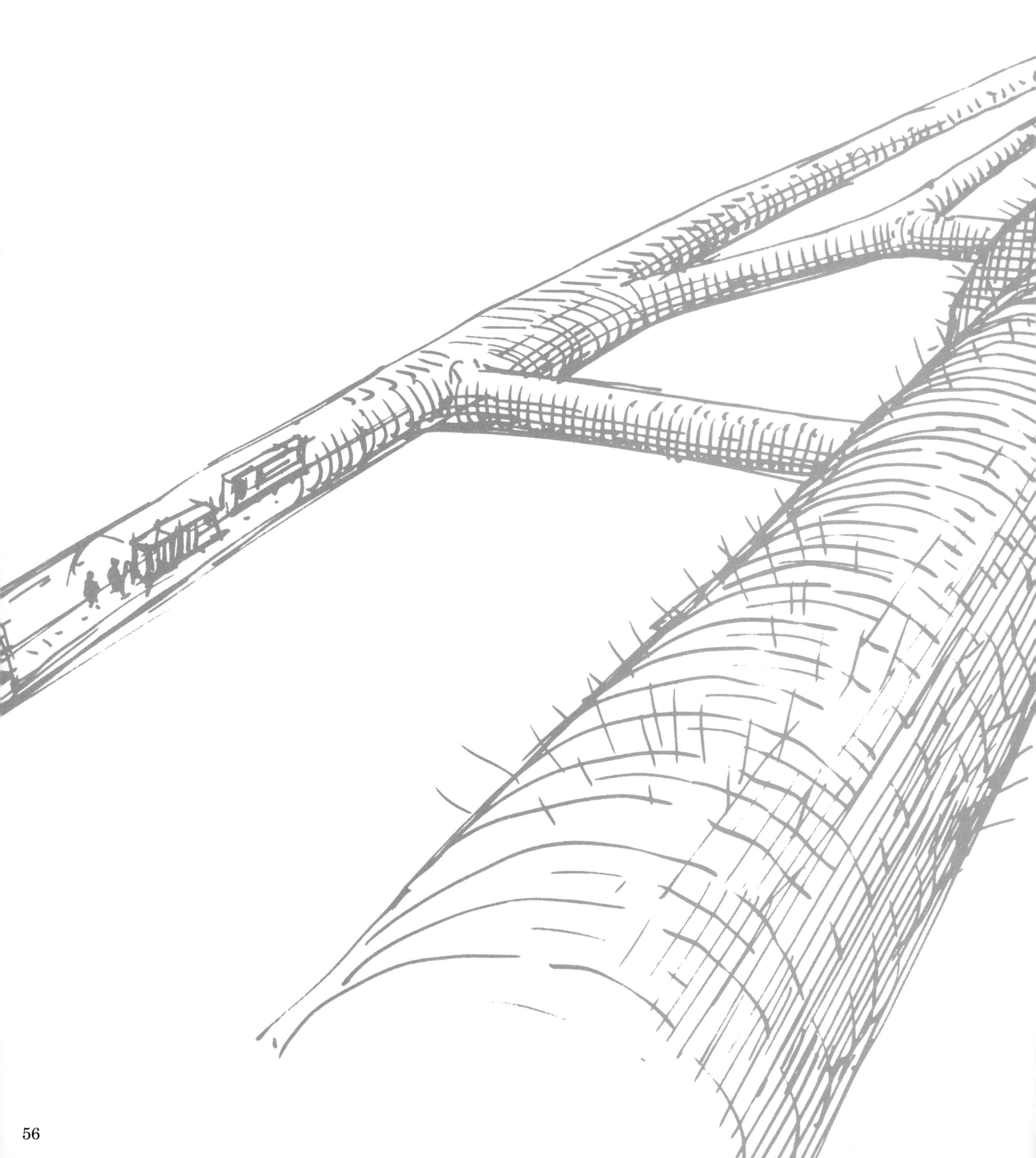

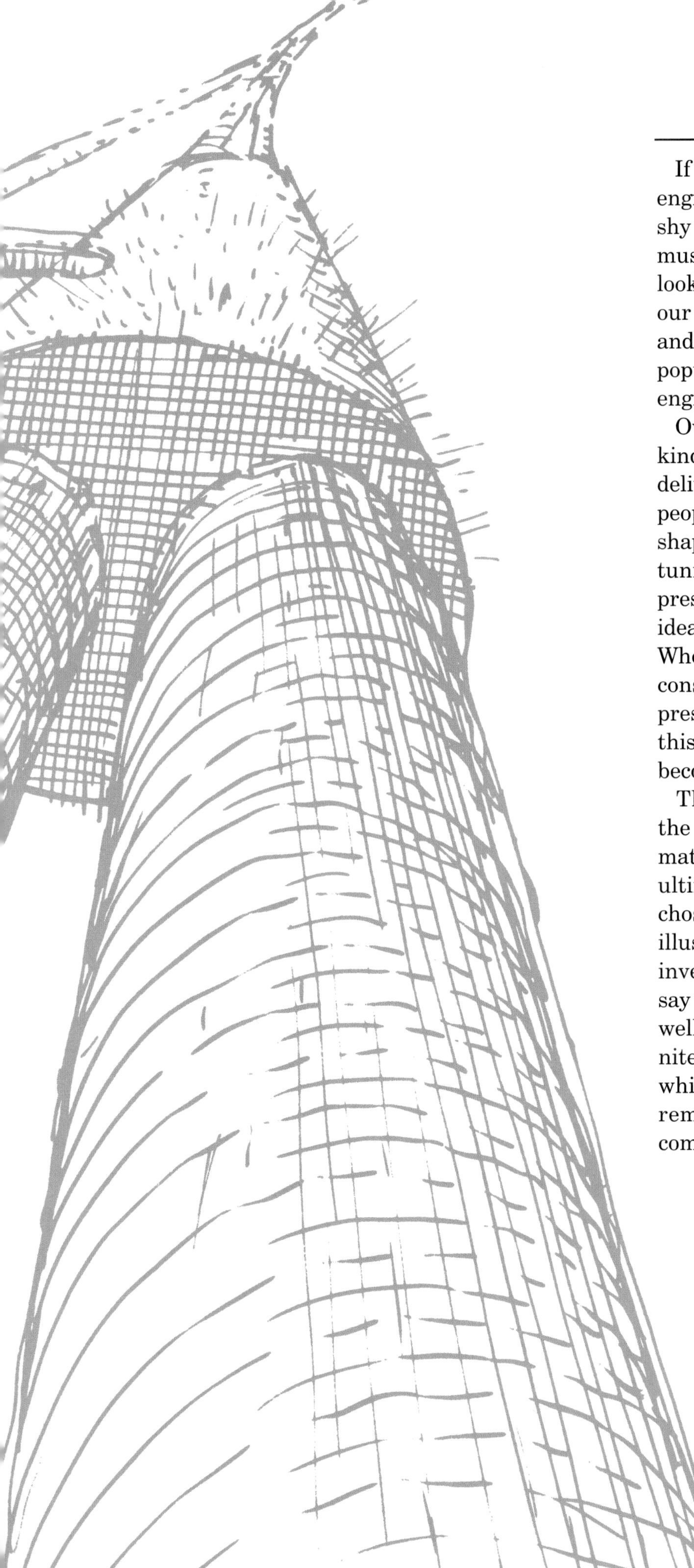

TUNNELS

If bridges are the most forthcoming examples of engineering in this book, tunnels are their painfully shy cousins. They live only to serve, and to serve they must hide. Very few things about the way tunnels look as we pass through them are even likely to catch our attention. So while bridges, skyscrapers, domes, and even a few dams enjoy varying amounts of popularity, I think it's fairly safe to say that only an engineer could love a tunnel.

Over the centuries, tunnels have been built for all kinds of reasons, from burying mummified bulls and delivering drinking water to mining salt and moving people. But regardless of their different uses, the shape or geometry of tunnels is quite similar. All tunnels have weight on top of them, and most receive pressure from the sides, which makes the arch the ideal shape.

When a tunnel is bored through a mountain or constructed under water, it may have to withstand pressure from every direction, including below. In this case, the arch is simply made continuous, so it becomes more or less cylindrical.

The way tunnels are built depends primarily on the technology available, the type and condition of material through which they must pass, and their ultimate length. The examples that follow have been chosen not only to show various possibilities but to illustrate the builders' level of determination and inventiveness, about which the finished structures say so little. While their initial costs may be high, well-designed and well-built tunnels can last indefinitely and require relatively little maintenance—all of which makes it that much easier to take these remarkable and often indispensable structures completely for granted.

Two Ancient Tunnels

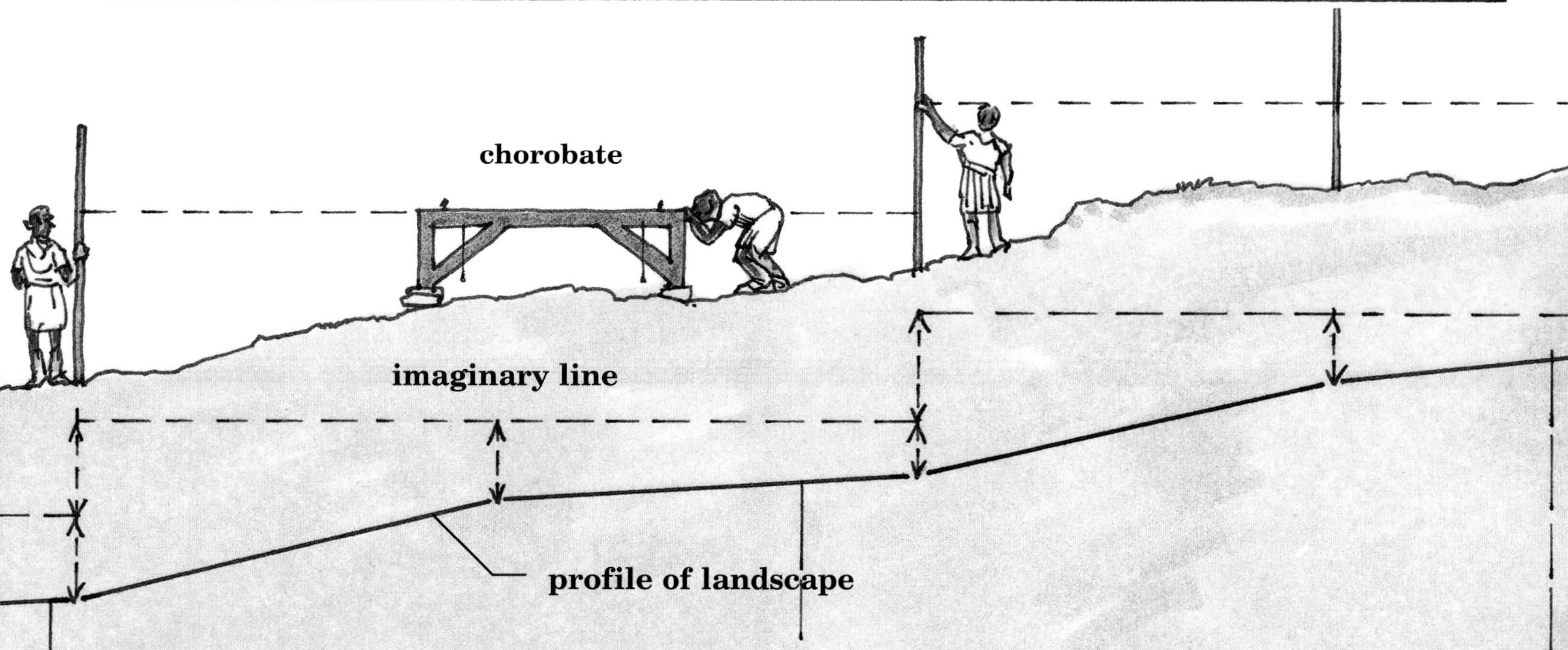

Central Italy, A.D.41: To increase his land holdings in the vicinity of Lake Fucinus, the emperor Claudius I had his engineers drain the lake. This required the planning and digging of a three–and-a-half-mile-long tunnel through soft limestone. Once the engineers had chosen a likely path for the tunnel, they created a profile map of the terrain along its route. Using a leveling instrument called a chorobate as well as measuring sticks and strings, they translated the landscape into a set of precise but imaginary steps. At specific intervals they recorded the distance between the top of each step and the ground. These vertical measurements and the horizontal distances between them were then drawn out, creating an accurate picture of the mountain on which the tunnel and its portals could be located.

Some time in the sixth century B.C. on the Greek island of Samos, a tunnel, 3400 feet long, had been cut in similar conditions to carry water pipes. Perhaps to speed up construction, it was dug from both ends at the same time. Unfortunately, the two halves missed each other by about fifteen feet and had to be connected with a sharp S curve. Over the following centuries, engineers began using closely spaced vertical shafts along the line of a tunnel to avoid this problem. If diggers didn't run into a shaft, they knew they were off course and could make adjustments. And since the engineers could determine the length of each shaft precisely from the profile map, the shafts helped establish the desired grade, which is particularly important for tunnels meant to carry water.

line of tunnel floor

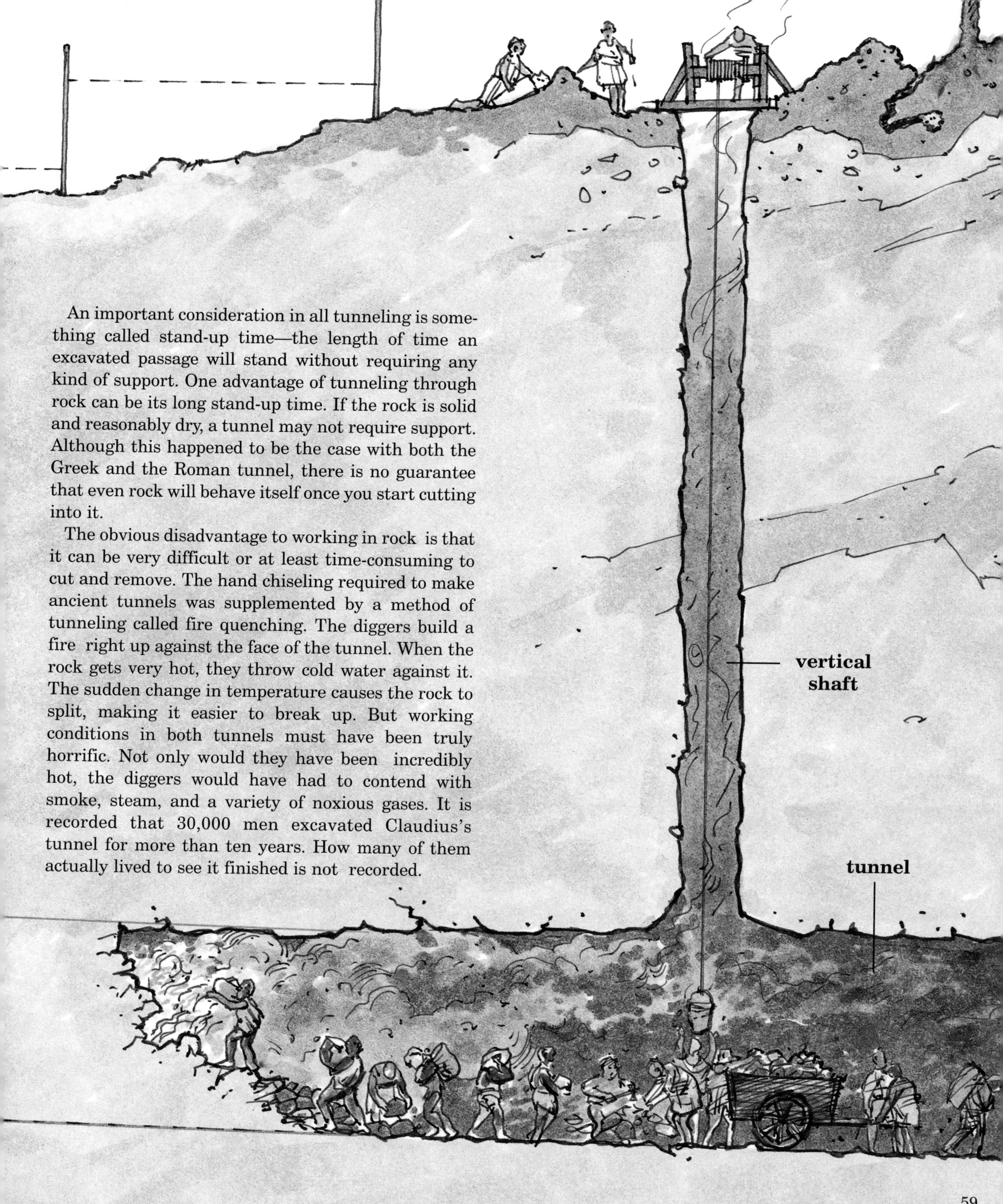

An important consideration in all tunneling is something called stand-up time—the length of time an excavated passage will stand without requiring any kind of support. One advantage of tunneling through rock can be its long stand-up time. If the rock is solid and reasonably dry, a tunnel may not require support. Although this happened to be the case with both the Greek and the Roman tunnel, there is no guarantee that even rock will behave itself once you start cutting into it.

The obvious disadvantage to working in rock is that it can be very difficult or at least time-consuming to cut and remove. The hand chiseling required to make ancient tunnels was supplemented by a method of tunneling called fire quenching. The diggers build a fire right up against the face of the tunnel. When the rock gets very hot, they throw cold water against it. The sudden change in temperature causes the rock to split, making it easier to break up. But working conditions in both tunnels must have been truly horrific. Not only would they have been incredibly hot, the diggers would have had to contend with smoke, steam, and a variety of noxious gases. It is recorded that 30,000 men excavated Claudius's tunnel for more than ten years. How many of them actually lived to see it finished is not recorded.

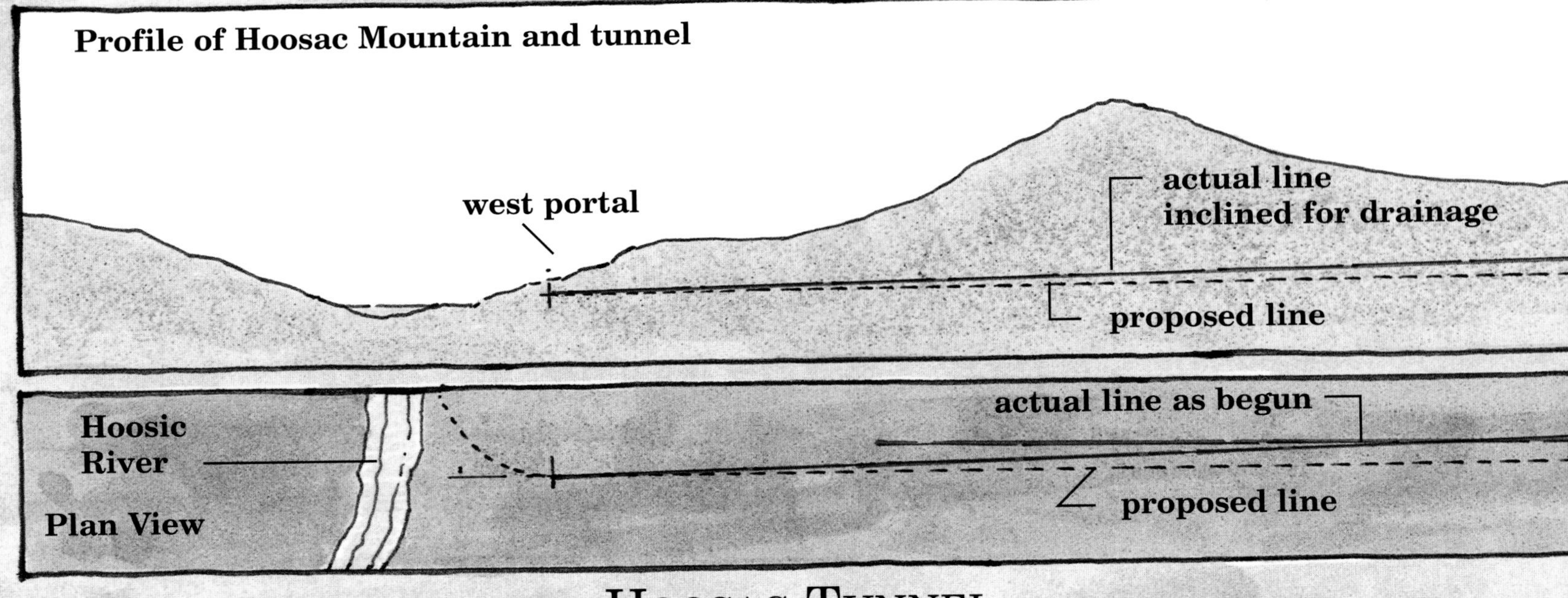

Hoosac Tunnel

North Adams, Massachusetts, 1855–1876: When the Troy and Greenfield Railway Company was chartered in 1848, its goal was to create a link between Vermont, Massachusetts, and the city of Troy, New York. Unfortunately, the most efficient route for the new line ran through a mountain range in north western Massachusetts, specifically over a mountain called Hoosac. Because tracks can't be too steep or their curves too abrupt, train travel over mountainous terrain always takes longer than it does over flatter ground. Tunneling, in spite of the difficulties involved, is often the best alternative. In fact, the idea of tunneling through Hoosac had already been proposed for an earlier canal scheme and it soon became the preferred choice of the railroad company.

With assurance from the state geologist that the mountain rock would behave in a uniform and predictable way, have excellent stand-up time, and present no serious water problems, the engineer optimistically began his project. The tunnel was to be arch shaped for additional stability, approximately twenty feet wide and twenty-one feet high, and would carry a single four-and-a-half-mile-long track. According to the chief engineer, it would take about four and a half years to build—less if the workers dug a couple of shafts to increase the number of headings, or locations from which the tunnel could be excavated.

The first two years were spent surveying the mountain. Once an accurate profile had been produced, the builders could locate the two entrances and establish

crown
top heading
first bench
second bench
West face

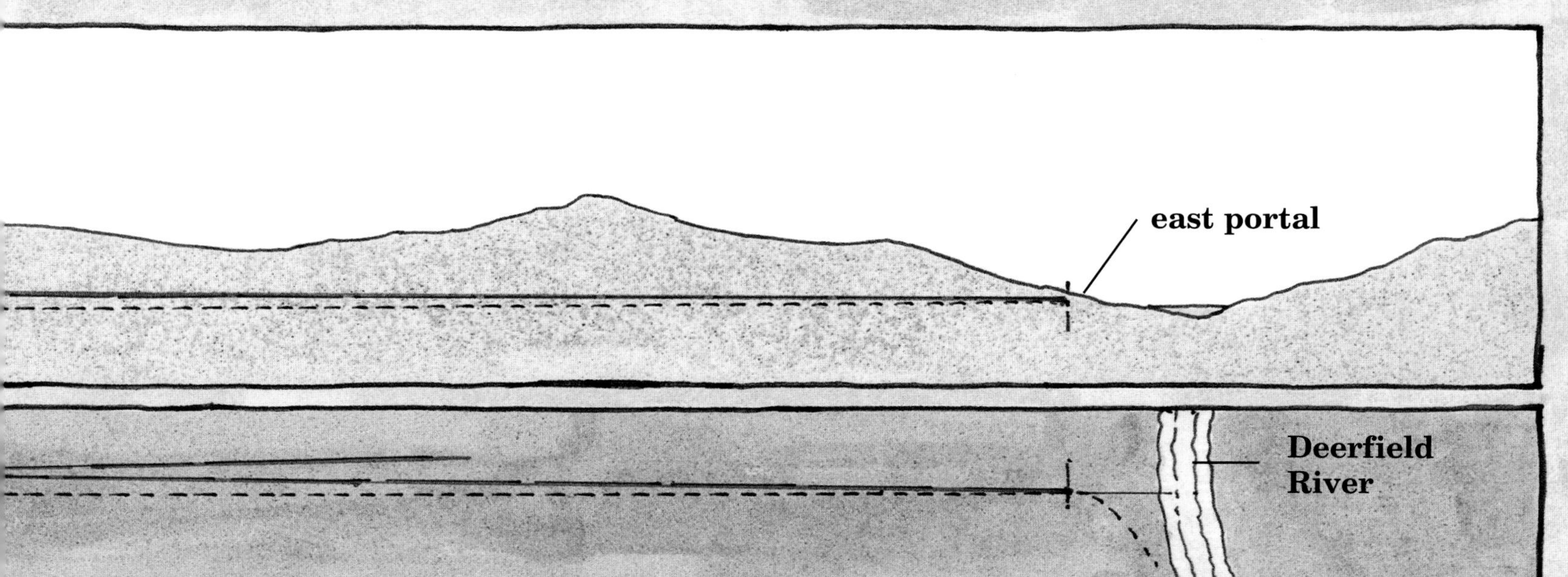

the line between them. Since the two portals ended up more or less on the same level, the tunnel was to rise slightly toward its center to ensure adequate drainage, if any water was encountered. Also, instead of approaching each other on the same line, both halves of the tunnel would enter the mountain at a slight horizontal angle, the idea being that when they eventually met, only a gentle curve would be required to connect them. The engineer wasn't taking any chances. The drastic S curve of Samos may have been fine for water pipes, but it would have caused a huge locomotive to derail, ripping up the tracks in the process—which is not conducive to maintaining a schedule.

When construction finally began, the workers excavated both faces in sections. At the west end, they began by digging at the top or crown of the tunnel. By excavating what is called a top heading first, they could determine whether or not the rock right above the tunnel was stable. If not, they would support it with heavy timbers as they went. Once the top heading had been carried some distance into the mountain, other workers began removing the six-foot layer of rock immediately below the floor of the top heading. This is called a bench. Eventually a second six foot bench was excavated down to track level. Staggering construction in this way meant that not all the workers would be up against the same face at the same time. At the east end, the contractor decided to dig a bottom heading instead of a top heading. Once the tunnelers had gone a certain distance, a second team working behind them began removing the upper layer of rock, called the stope.

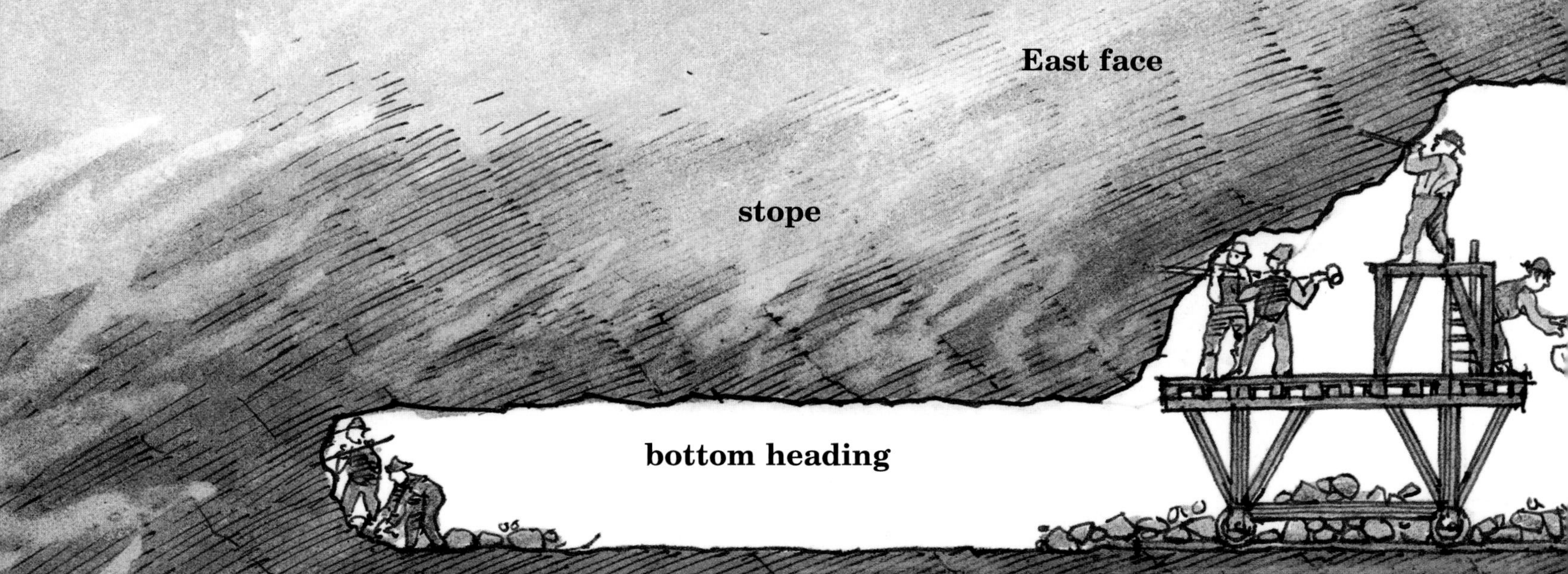

drilling the rock

loading the powder

Like most hard-rock tunnels, Hoosac was to be dug by the "drill and shoot" method. First, eight or ten holes were drilled up to three feet into the rockface. This was done by one man with a drill and a hammer or by a team in which one man would hold the drill while the others took turns hammering.

In either case, the holder would rotate the drill slightly after each hit. Once several holes had been drilled, they were filled with gunpowder. Everyone then got as far from the face as possible, except for the man whose job it was to light the fuse. Presumably, he was either the fastest or the newest member of the team. When the smoke cleared, the group returned and began breaking up and removing the shattered rock, called spoil, in a process known as mucking. This same tedious and dangerous sequence would be repeated over and over until the job was done.

running

blasting

mucking

Eventually a number of important changes put Hoosac literally at the cutting edge of hard-rock tunneling. Pneumatic drills, which had only recently been perfected, replaced the old hand-drill process. Several of them could be clamped to a movable carriage, which would be pushed right up against the face. The compressed air that ran them was piped in from either steam- or water- powered compressors at both entrances. Now the workers could drill holes three or even four times as deep in a fraction of the time. Powder was replaced by a fairly new invention called nitroglycerin. It was far more powerful, and if delivered in a frozen state, relatively safe. An electrical detonation system was also now available. To these technological improvements was added the center cut method–a sequence of drilling and shooting from the center of the face out toward the sides—and the labor was divided into specialized groups so that every worker no longer tried to do everything.

The rock at the east end was, as the geologist had promised, solid—so solid, in fact, that a couple of steam operated boring machines were brought in to pick up the pace. Unfortunately, they both failed.

The west end was a different story. Almost immediately diggers ran into a large area of rock that behaved more like soil. It was loose and porous. No sooner was a space excavated than it would fill up with this "demoralized rock" and water. After six years of struggle, the project was way behind schedule and quickly heading over budget. The contractor was replaced, new engineers were hired, and the state of Massachusetts, hoping to protect its investment, took over.

Center Cut Method

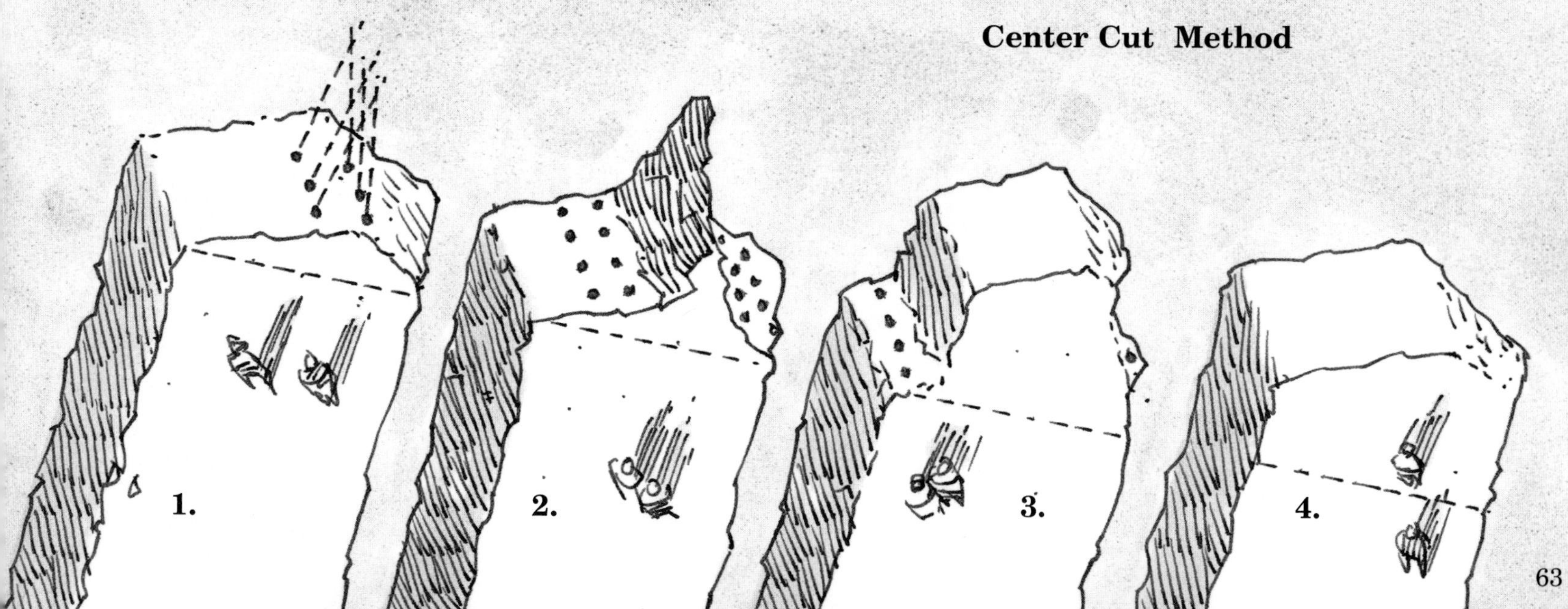

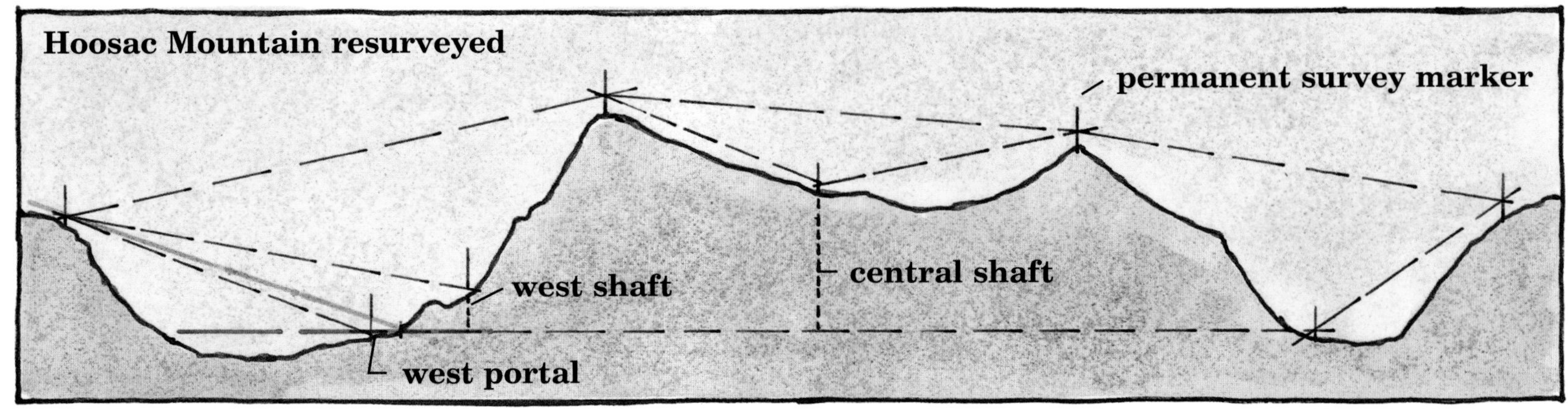

To speed things up even more, the new engineer took the daring step of putting the east and west headings back on the same line rather than having them enter the mountain at different angles. First, he resurveyed the entire path of the tunnel, extending it up the sides of the hills facing each portal. All the surveying was done with a transit—basically a powerful telescope mounted so that it can be rotated vertically and horizontally degree by degree. A compass below the telescope indicates the orientation, and several spirit levels keep the instrument horizontal. As the survey was being carried out, eight permanent markers were erected at key locations along the route.

The real challenge was to carry the line surveyed along the top of the mountain accurately through it. Standing in front of a portal and looking though his transit, the surveyor could locate the exact center line of the tunnel by using the marker immediately in front of him and the one across the valley as a guide. Once he had them in line, he simply flipped the telescope vertically 180 degrees until he was looking straight into the tunnel. A worker inside held a plumb bob—a pointed weight on the end of a string—and someone else held a lantern behind it so the surveyor could see what he was doing. When the point of the plumb bob was exactly in line with the crosshairs of the transit, the workers secured it to a wooden stake driven into the crown of the tunnel. Fifty feet or less into the tunnel, a second plumb bob was hung. It too was moved around until its point lined up exactly with the point of the first one. As the tunnel slowly moved into the mountain, so did the procession of plumb bobs.

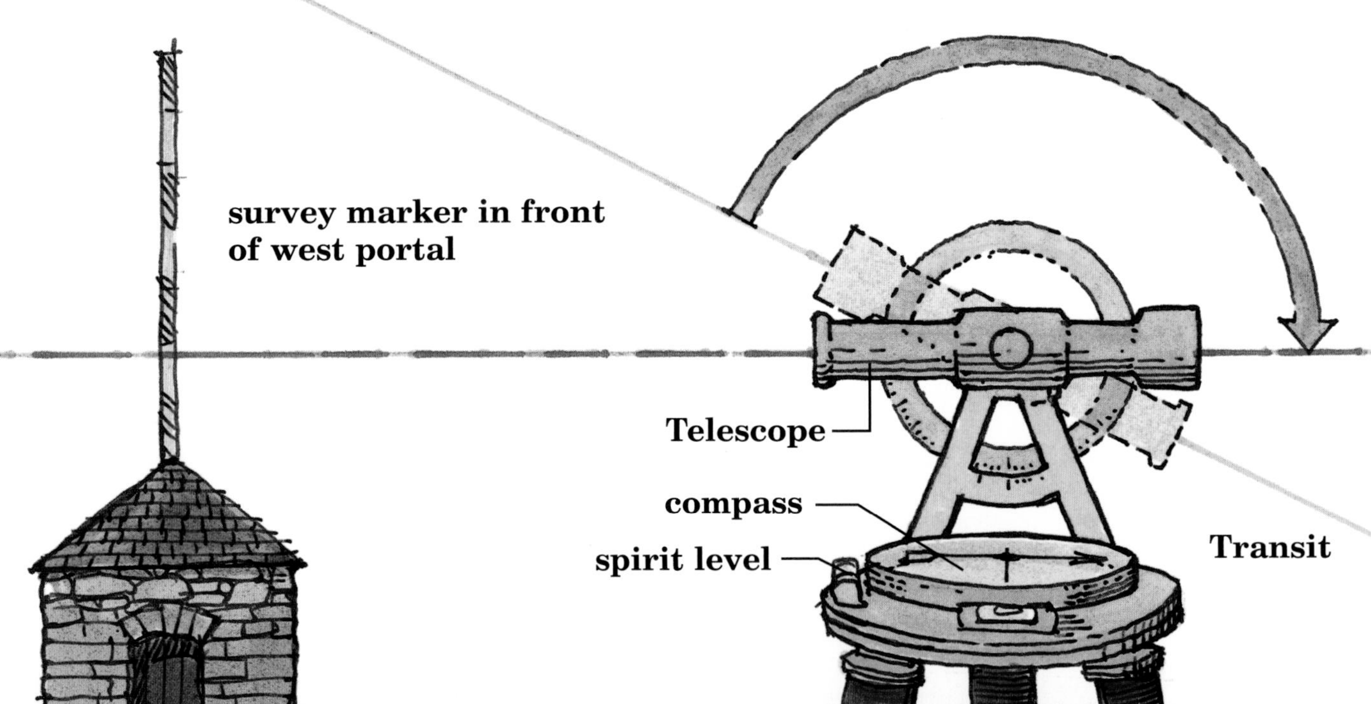

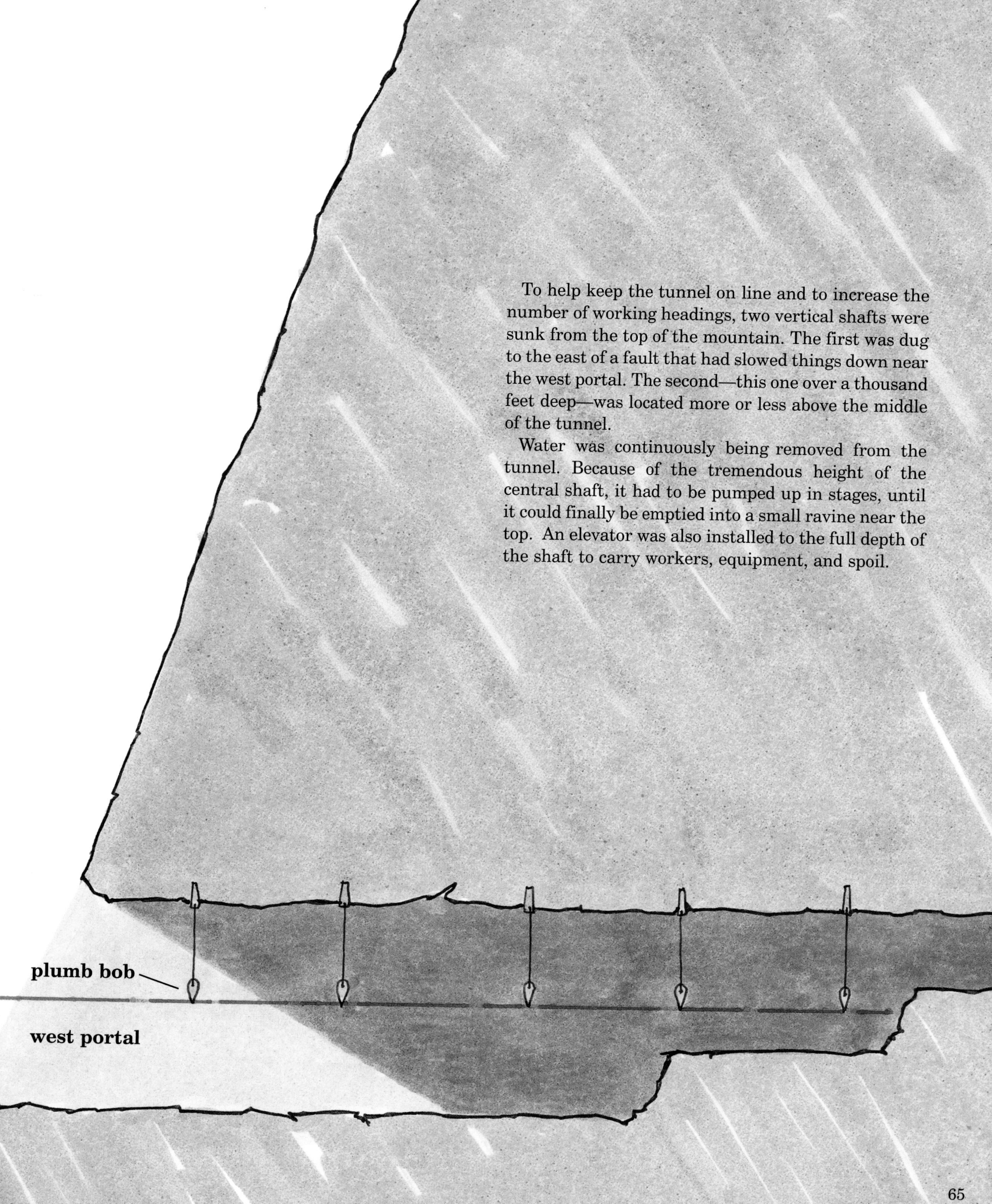

To help keep the tunnel on line and to increase the number of working headings, two vertical shafts were sunk from the top of the mountain. The first was dug to the east of a fault that had slowed things down near the west portal. The second—this one over a thousand feet deep—was located more or less above the middle of the tunnel.

Water was continuously being removed from the tunnel. Because of the tremendous height of the central shaft, it had to be pumped up in stages, until it could finally be emptied into a small ravine near the top. An elevator was also installed to the full depth of the shaft to carry workers, equipment, and spoil.

The finished tunnel required almost 8000 feet of lining, most of it in the western half. This lining varied in thickness from five to eight courses of brick and was built up over a wooden centering. Where the ground was not firm enough to use conventional straight wall foundations, the curved walls of the lining were supported on an invert—basically a continuation of the cylindrical shape. Permanent drains were cut into the rock along both sides of the lining.

The last pieces of the project to be completed were the formal stone arches around each portal. Although moderately impressive, they don't really give much of a clue as to what it took to create the space between them. Building the tunnel was a twenty-one-year struggle, with over fifteen years of actual construction, claiming two hundred lives and costing more than five times the original estimate.

While the tunnelers at Hoosac must often have felt as if they were working under water, when their tunnel finally opened, the first real underwater tunnel had already been in operation for thirty-five years.

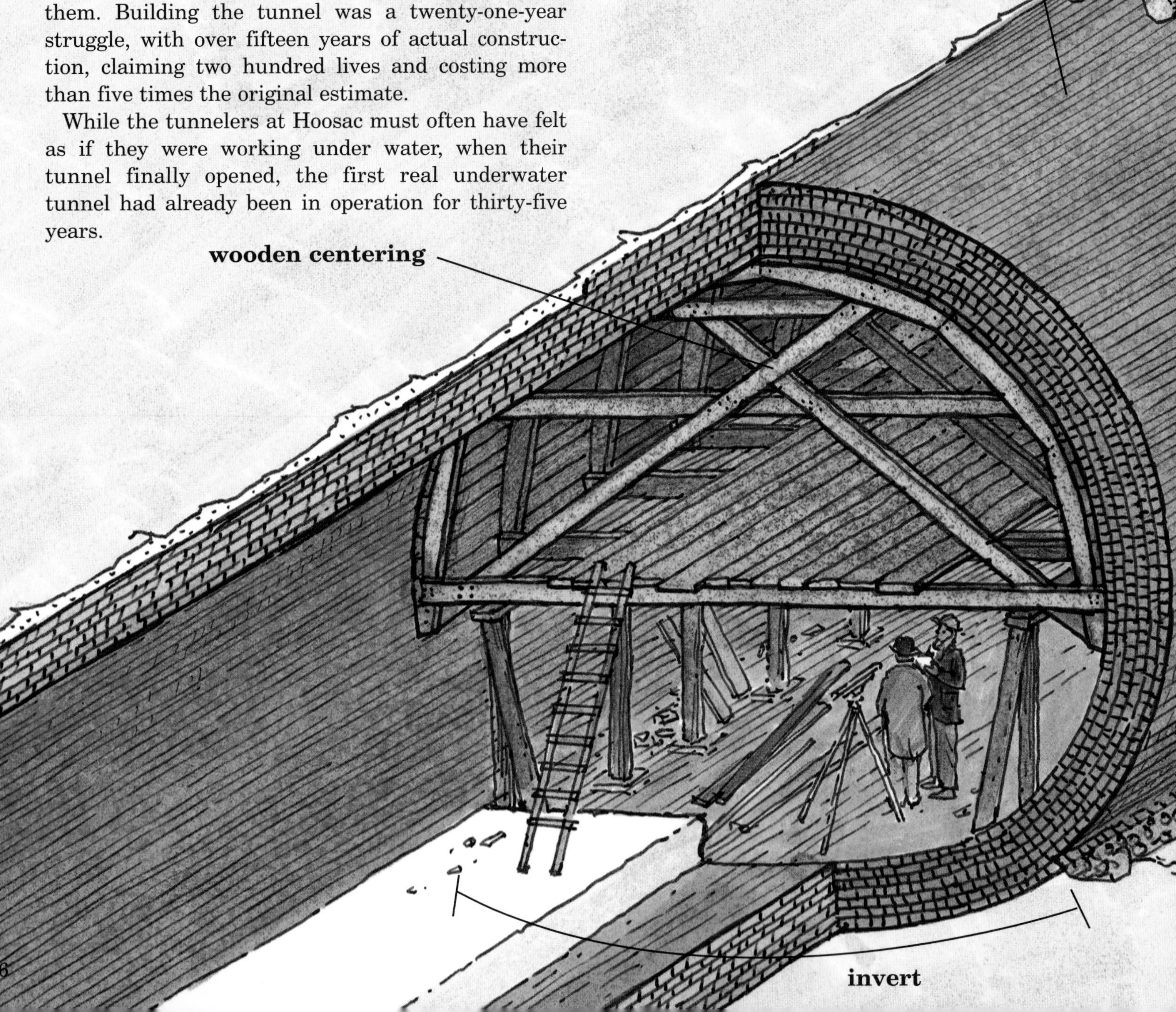

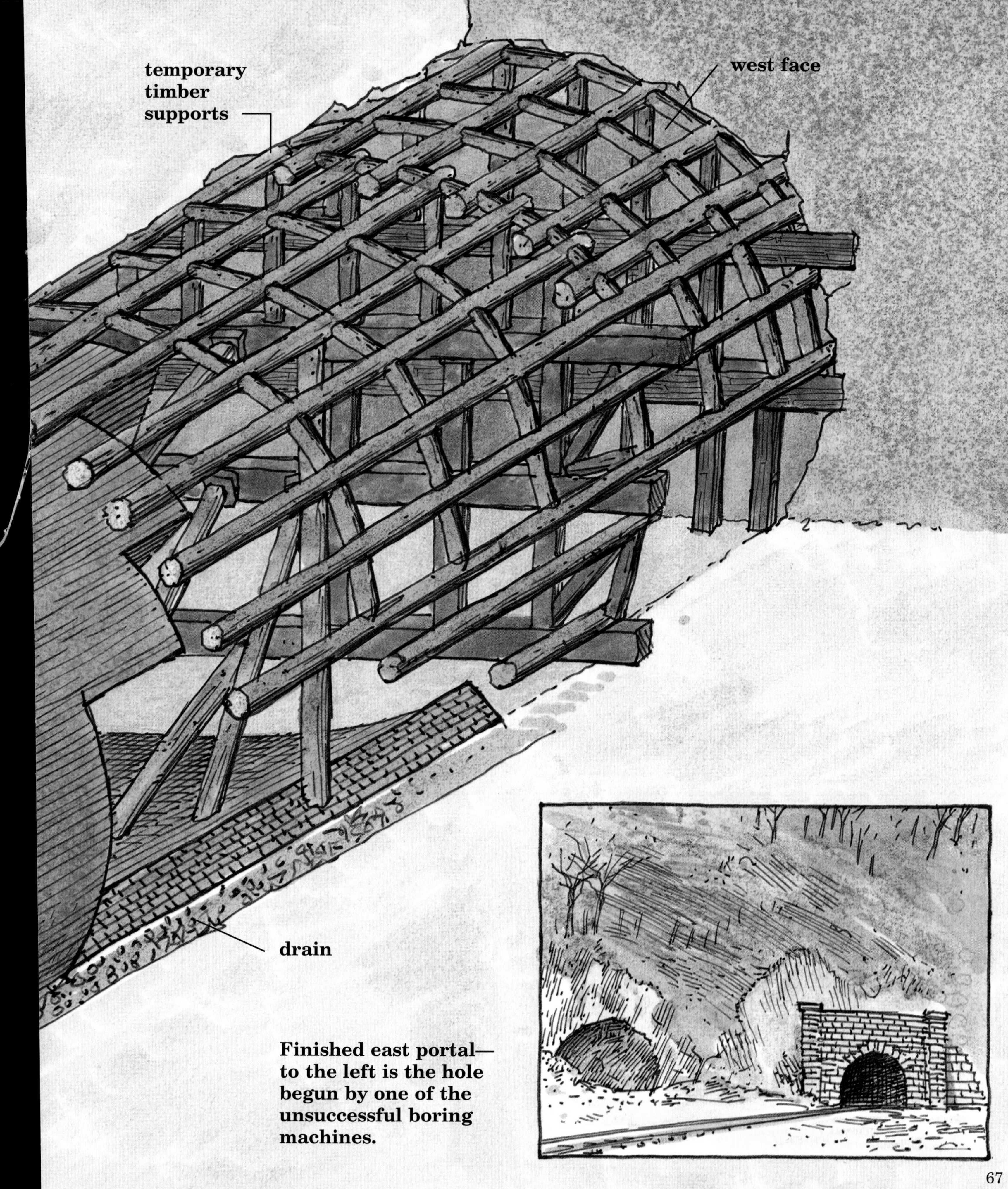

Finished east portal—to the left is the hole begun by one of the unsuccessful boring machines.

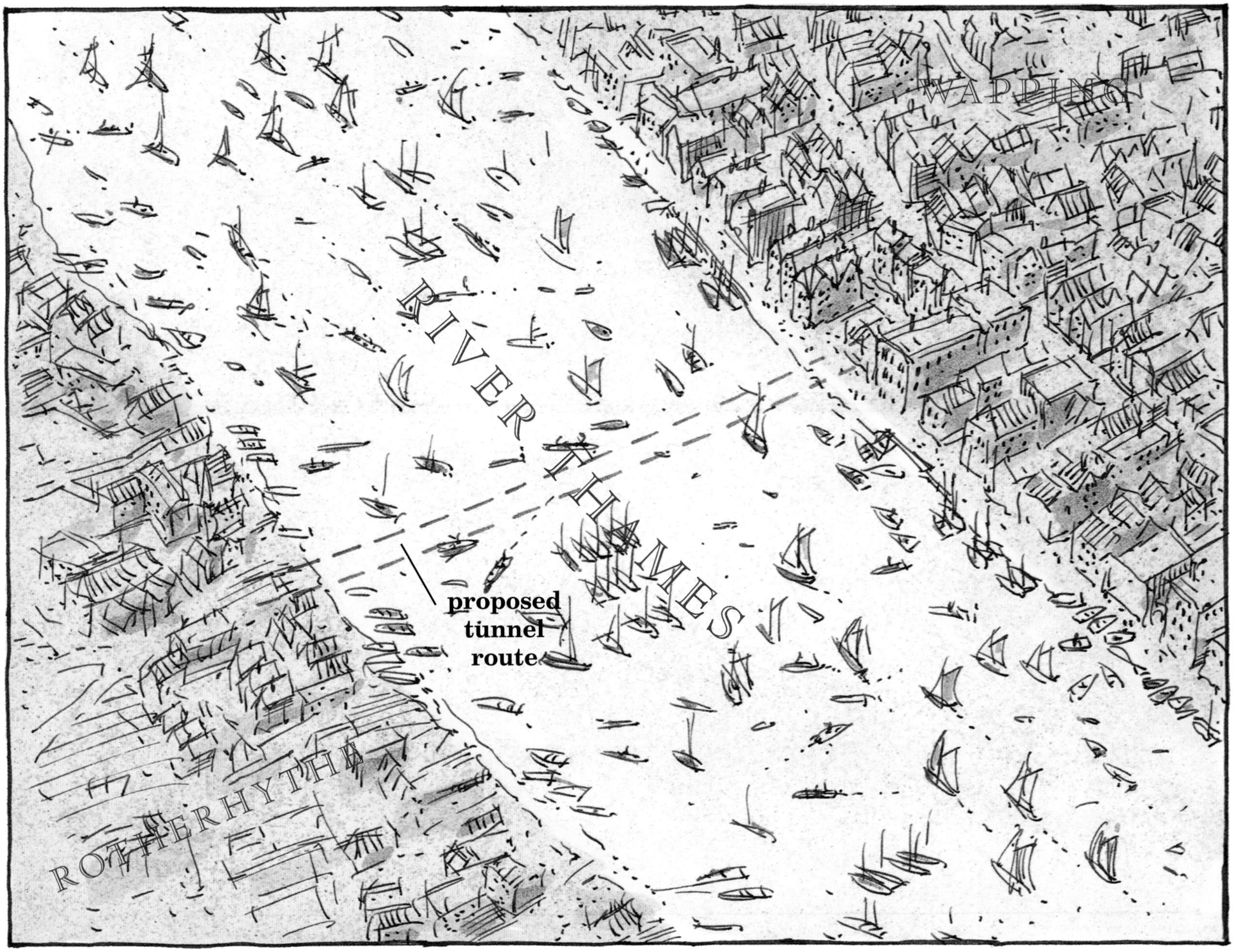

WAPPING
RIVER THAMES
proposed
tunnel
route
ROTHERHYTHE

Rotherhythe
access shaft
high tide
low tide

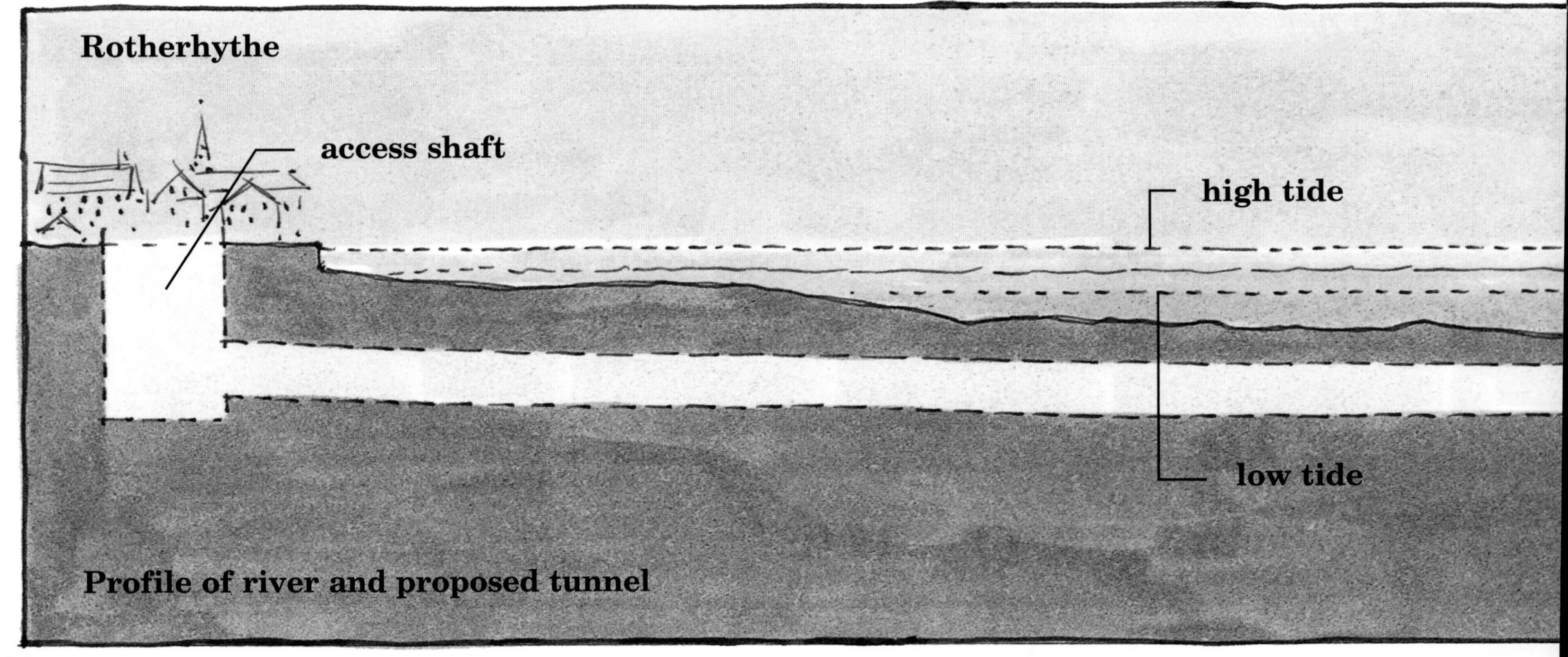

Profile of river and proposed tunnel

THAMES TUNNEL

London, England, 1825: The need for an additional crossing between Rotherhithe and Wapping had been steadily growing, but the idea of building a new bridge must have seemed almost overwhelming. Not only would it have to be able to open in some way so that ships could pass, its construction would further constrict an already congested river.

An engineer named Marc Brunel proposed instead that a tunnel be built. It would contain two roadways, each passing through its own arch-shaped passage, with both passages running through a single masonry block. His suggestion was probably not greeted with wild enthusiasm, since some twenty years earlier, two Cornish miners had almost succeeded in digging a small timber-lined tunnel under the Thames, only to have their efforts abruptly ended by the unpredictable nature of the riverbed. A sudden rush of quicksand and water had sent the workers running for their lives and the tunnel's backers into a different line of business.

But Brunel was convinced that with the proper planning, his efforts could succeed. He would first need to know exactly what was below the river so that he could select the best route for his tunnel as well as the most appropriate method for digging it. A series of borings were taken at regular intervals to retrieve samples of the riverbed. Combining this information with that gained by the earlier tunnelers, Brunel was able to create an accurate cross-section.

cross section of Brunel's tunnel

Between 42 and 76 feet below the riverbed there appeared to be a layer of blue clay—an ideal material for tunneling. It offered good stand-up time yet was soft enough to dig through relatively easily and was more or less impervious to water. If the information was correct and Brunel could keep his tunnel within the clay, things would progress well. Using the cross-section, he determined the depth at which his tunnel should be dug (62 feet) as well as its maximum height (about 20 feet). Accessible from two shafts, one on each shore, the finished tunnel was to be roughly 1200 feet long. Determining the path of the tunnel was one thing, however. Figuring out how to build it was something else.

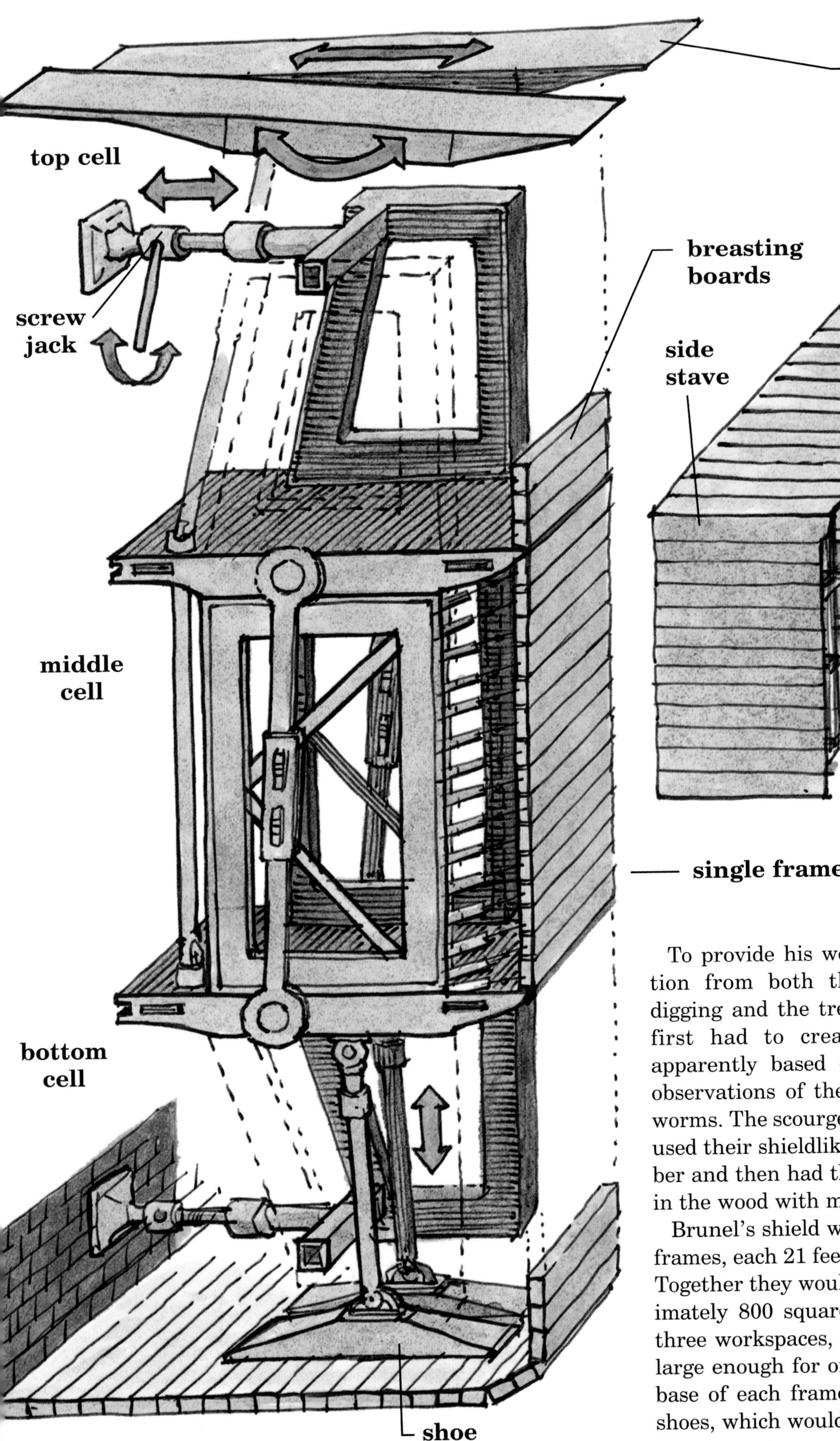

To provide his workers with the necessary protection from both the uncertainties of underwater digging and the tremendous water pressure, Brunel first had to create a shield. The concept was apparently based on (or at least inspired by) his observations of the damage done to wood by shipworms. The scourge of the Royal Navy, these mollusks used their shieldlike shells to bore holes through timber and then had the audacity to create a rigid lining in the wood with material they excreted.

Brunel's shield was made up of twelve independent frames, each 21 feet high, 3 feet wide, and 6 feet deep. Together they would permit work on a face of approximately 800 square feet. Each frame would contain three workspaces, called cells, and each cell was just large enough for one digger and one bricklayer. The base of each frame rested on a pair of plates called shoes, which would distribute the tremendous weight over a greater area to minimize sinking.

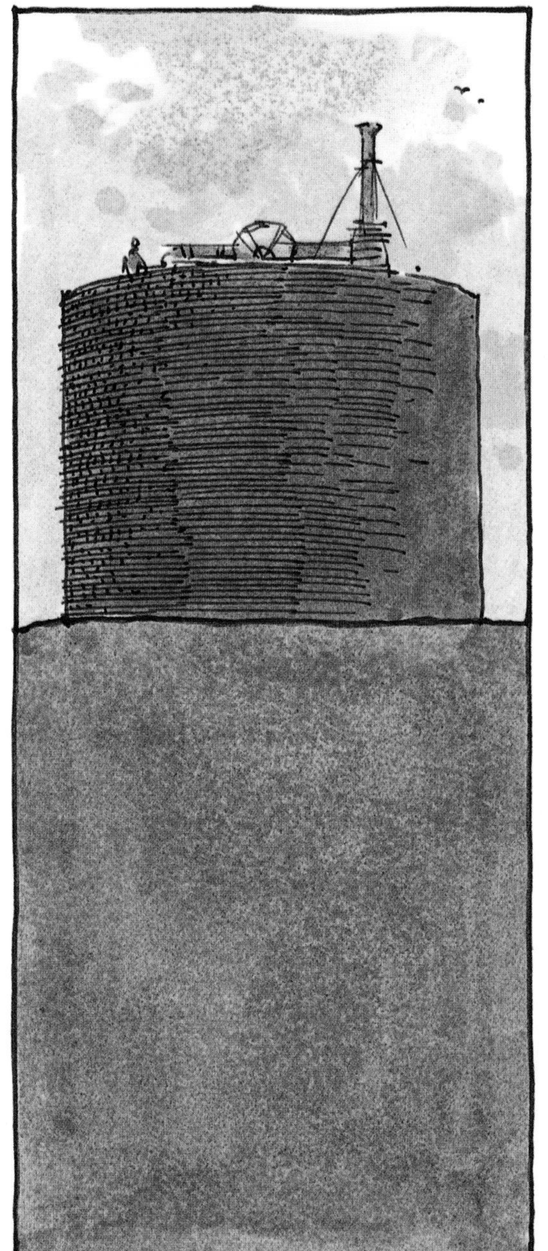

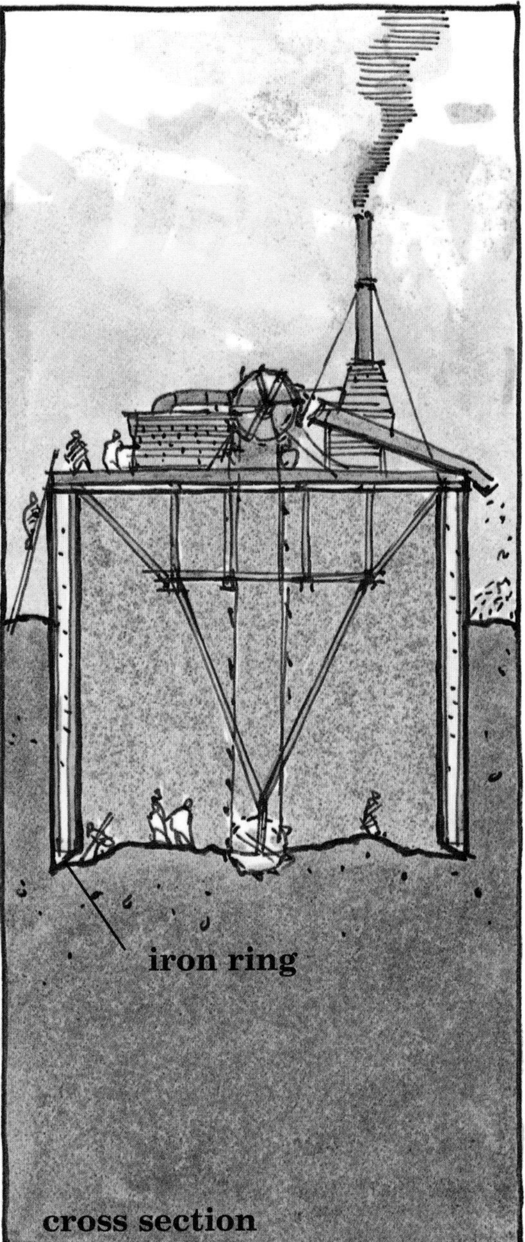

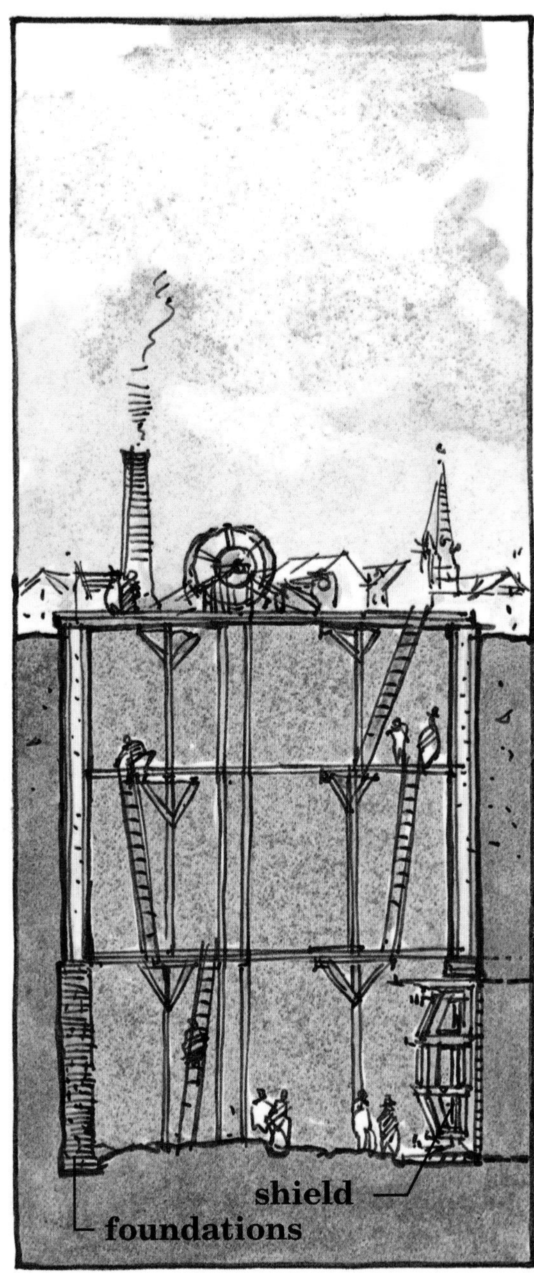

sinking the Rotherhythe shaft

The frames were connected but were not rigidly fixed together, so they could be moved somewhat independently. The top and sides of the shield were protected by heavy plates called staves. Between the shield and the tunnel face was a wall of short timbers known as breasting boards. Each board was held in place by a pair of screw jacks. Except for the breasting boards, the entire thing was made of cast iron.

To get the shield to its starting position, 62 feet below ground, Brunel first built the Rotherhythe shaft from which the tunnel would be dug. Instead of simply excavating a shaft and then lining it, he built the lining aboveground, like a gigantic circular chimney. It was 42 feet high, 50 feet in diameter, and made up of two concentric brick walls resting on top of an iron ring. The 36 inches between the inner and outer walls was reinforced with iron rods and filled with rubble and cement. A second iron ring tied the tops of the walls together, and the whole thing was capped by a wooden superstructure that supported a steam engine.

As workers dug out the earth inside the shaft, the thousand-ton structure began to sink under its own weight. The steam engine busily hoisted buckets of dirt and pumped out water. Within three months, the uppermost iron ring had disappeared below ground. At this point, 20 feet of earth below the bottom iron ring was carefully excavated so that bricklayers could build a permanent foundation. They left an opening 36 feet wide through which the shield would eventually begin its journey.

The tunneling itself was done in the following way. A digger in each cell would loosen one pair of jacks, remove a single breasting board, carve out about four and a half inches of clay, and then immediately replace the board and the jacks that held it in place. The diggers repeated the process until the entire face in front of each cell had been excavated. When all 800 square feet of the face had been carved away, the shield was pushed into it.

But this process was complicated and had to be done one frame at a time. First the protective staves were jacked forward into the clay. The tilt of each stave was adjusted as necessary to make sure the shield was staying on course. Then the ends of all the jacks supporting the breasting boards in front of one frame were slipped off their own frame and onto those immediately adjacent. The feet of that particular frame could now be lifted slightly, transferring much of its weight to the adjacent frames. Finally, powerful jacks pushing against the brick lining inched the frame forward. Once every other frame had been moved forward, the process was repeated for those left behind. It was an incredibly cumbersome undertaking, but on a good day, Brunel hoped to be able to move forward about three feet.

Unfortunately, he was not to be blessed with many good days. Even with the support of a string of capable engineers, including his talented son, Isambard, it took nine years of actual building time to dig a tunnel 1200 feet long. The borings had given the wrong impression about the depth and consistency of the clay. The workers ran into areas of gravel, which has no stand-up time. There were numerous floods. (One occurred half way across the river that was so serious the shield was bricked up and the project abandoned for seven years.) Explosions of methane gas ignited by the candles and lamps created terrifying flames. And there was plenty of foul air from centuries of sewage, which continually made the workers ill.

Yet somehow Marc Brunel beat the odds. With the sinking of the second shaft (which wasn't actually begun until 1840, when it was clear the tunnel would succeed) and its eventual meeting with the shield, he proved that even rivers do not have to be impediments to tunnel building.

Although Brunel's shield now seems a bit like a platoon of creaking Star Wars robots leaning against each other for support as they inch their way nervously through the muck, it did the job; the revised version he built after the resumption of work in 1835 was especially effective. Not only was his thinking farsighted, his tunnel was so well built that it is now part of London's subway system.

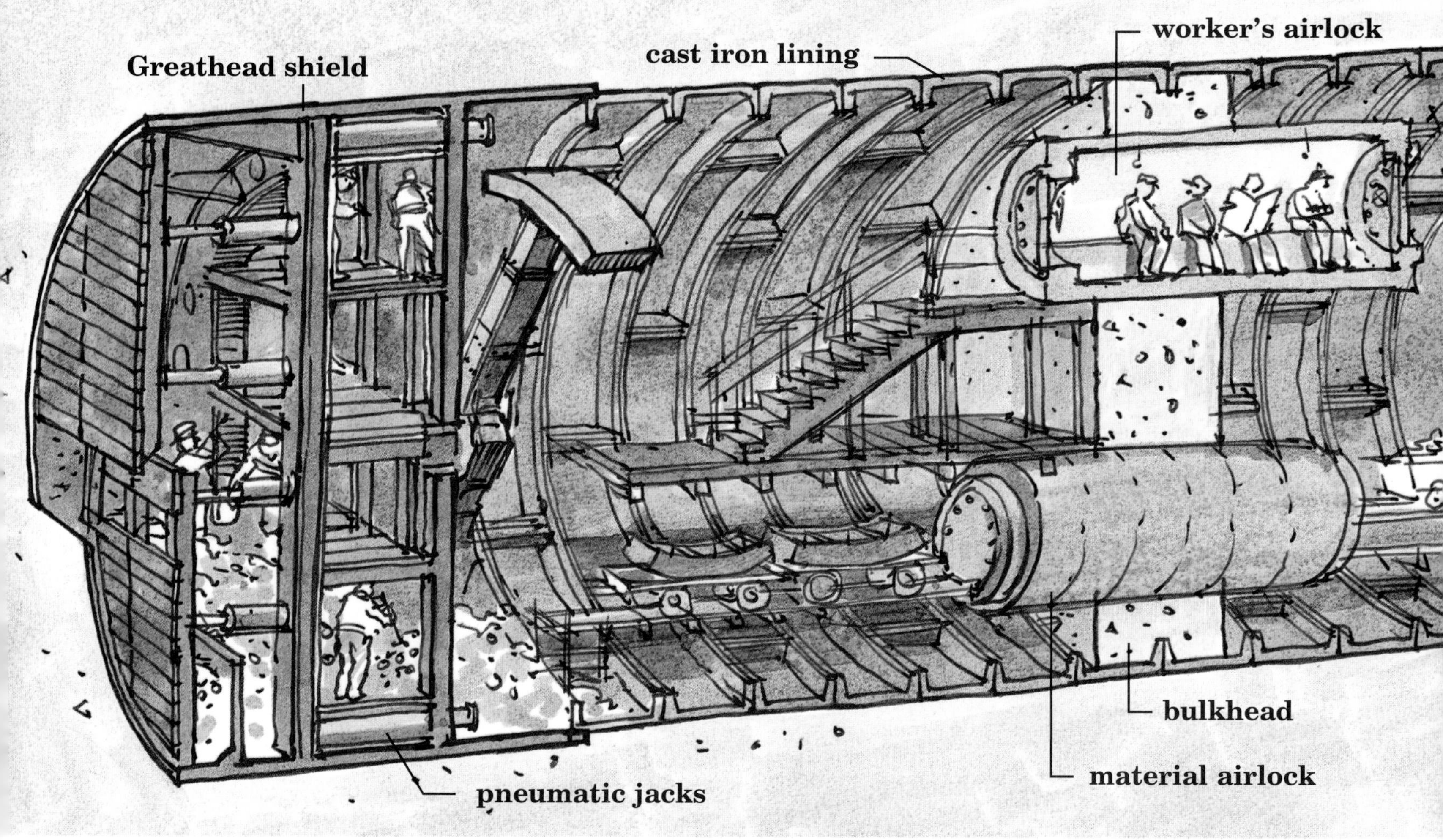

A little less than thirty years after the completion of the first Thames tunnel, the engineers Peter Barlow and James Henry Greathead, used a much more compact version of Brunel's shield to dig a second pedestrian tunnel under the same river. Theirs was basically a tin can instead of a box, and the 8-foot-in-diameter lining it left behind was made of cast iron segments bolted together to form rings. Once again the shield was moved forward by jacks pressing against this lining. The project took less than a year.

As the population of London grew and things on the surface became increasingly crowded, transportation systems, particularly trains, were forced underground. Greathead continued to improve the tunneling shield (which now bore his name), and in fact the whole tunneling operation. His shields were now up to 20 or so feet in diameter and stronger than ever. Increasingly, the work inside them was being mechanized. They were pushed by hydraulic rams instead of screw jacks. A heavy wall or bulkhead was often installed behind the shield, complete with air-locks so that the work area could be pressurized to help keep the water out. He even came up with a way to pump concrete into the narrow space between the outside of the lining and the surrounding earth.

Over the next hundred years, Brunel's vision and Greathead's engineering would unleash an army of manmade ship-worms boring tunnels in every conceivable direction. They worked at previously unheard-of depths and through all kinds of soft and waterlogged material to create the first and still one of the busiest subway systems in the world, the London Underground, appropriately known as "the tube."

Holland Tunnel

New York/New Jersey, 1920—1927: Although popular from the beginning, the steam-and smoke-filled London Underground reached its true potential only with the arrival of much cleaner electric-powered trains. When the engineer Clifford Holland undertook the building of a mile-and-a-half-long automobile tunnel below the Hudson River, his problem was how to eliminate all the exhaust fumes so that drivers wouldn't be passing out at 40 miles an hour.

Once Holland had settled on the basic design of the tunnel—actually two separate tunnels running about 50 feet apart through the silty riverbed—the method of construction was pretty much a given: pressurized Greathead shields. Although these shields were very large (30 feet in diameter) and equipped with mechanized erector arms to fit each of the cast iron lining segments into place, the real breakthrough came in the development of a successful ventilation system—one that set the precedent for tunnels to come.

His solution was to divide each tube into three horizontal layers—one to handle traffic, the other two to move air. Four large ventilation towers, two on each side of the river, would house eighty-four fans. Forty-two of them would blow clean air into the lowest space in each tunnel, forcing it through narrow slots along the curb and into the traffic area. The other forty- two would extract all the dirty air from the roadway through roof vents into the upper space and eventually out to the towers, where it would be discharged. When traffic was at its peak, the air in each tunnel could be completely changed every ninety seconds.

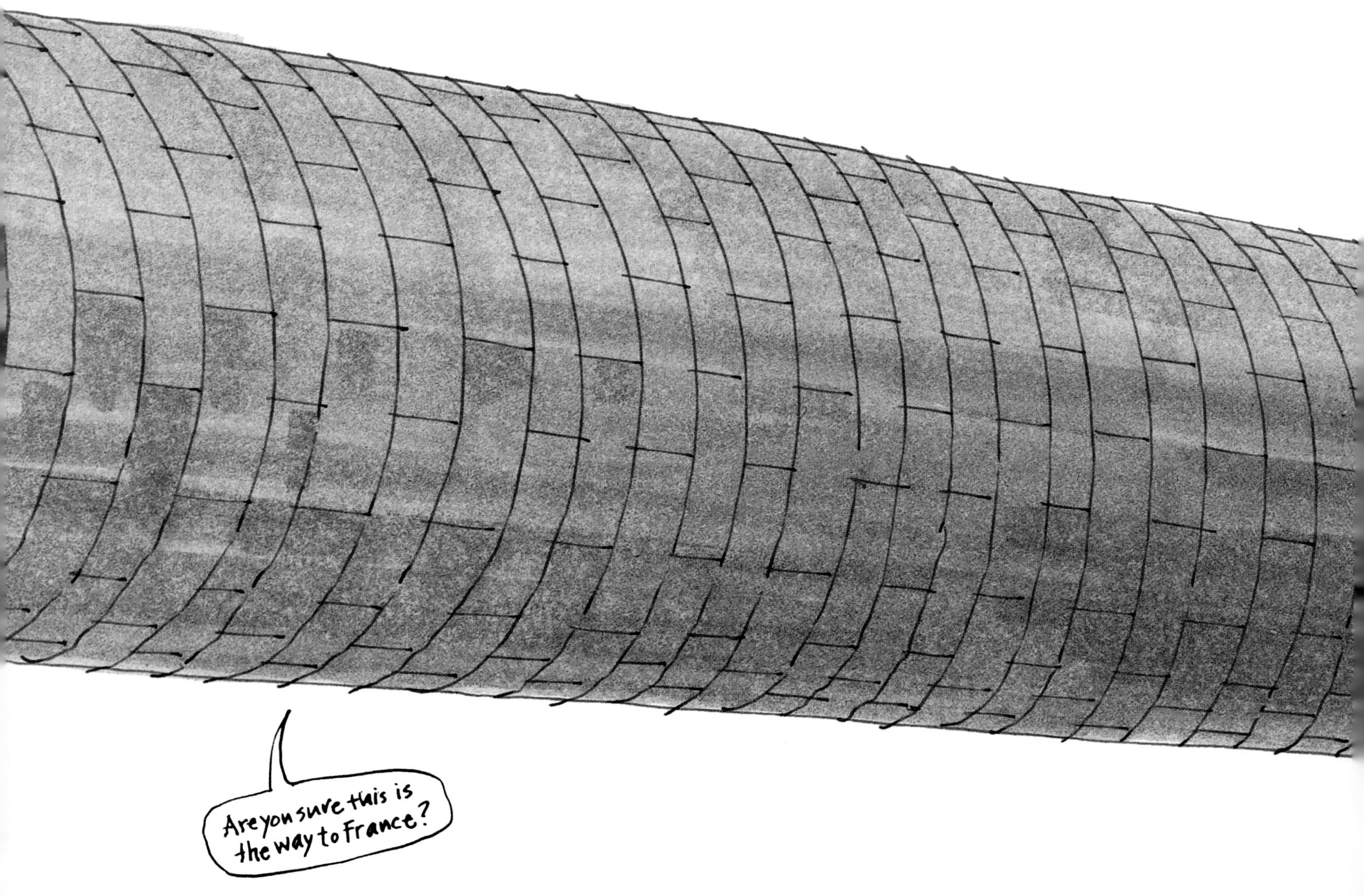

Jersey City
exhaust
intake
Manhattan
Hudson River
silt
bedrock

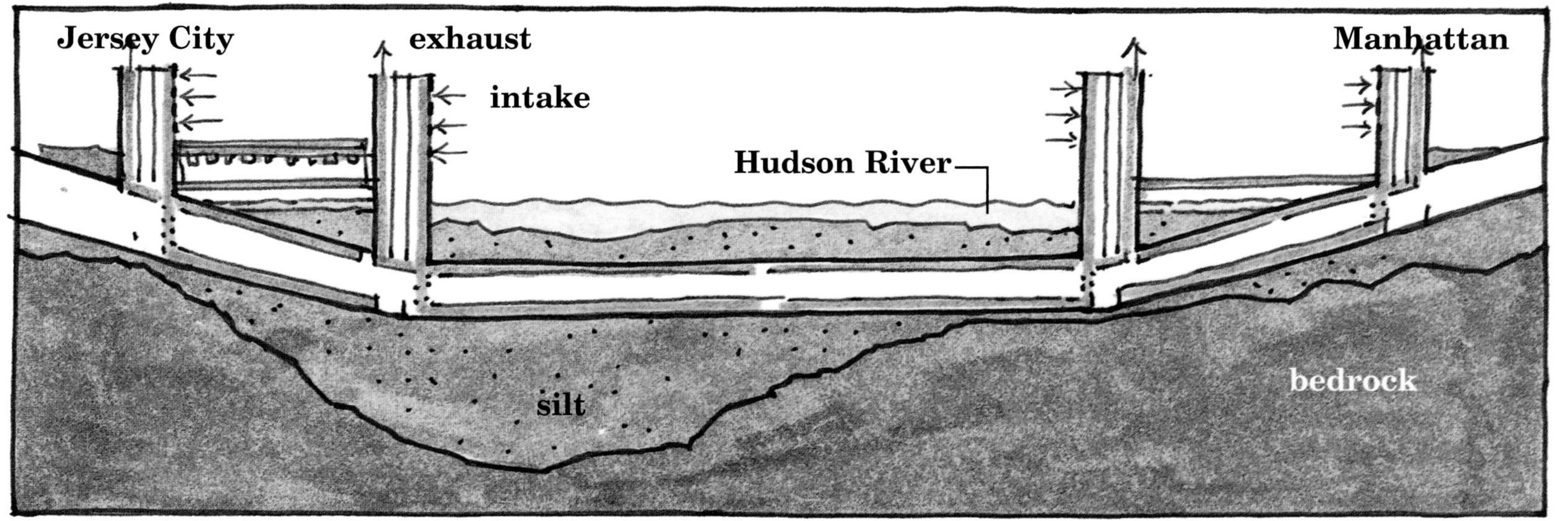

Arrangement of ventilation towers

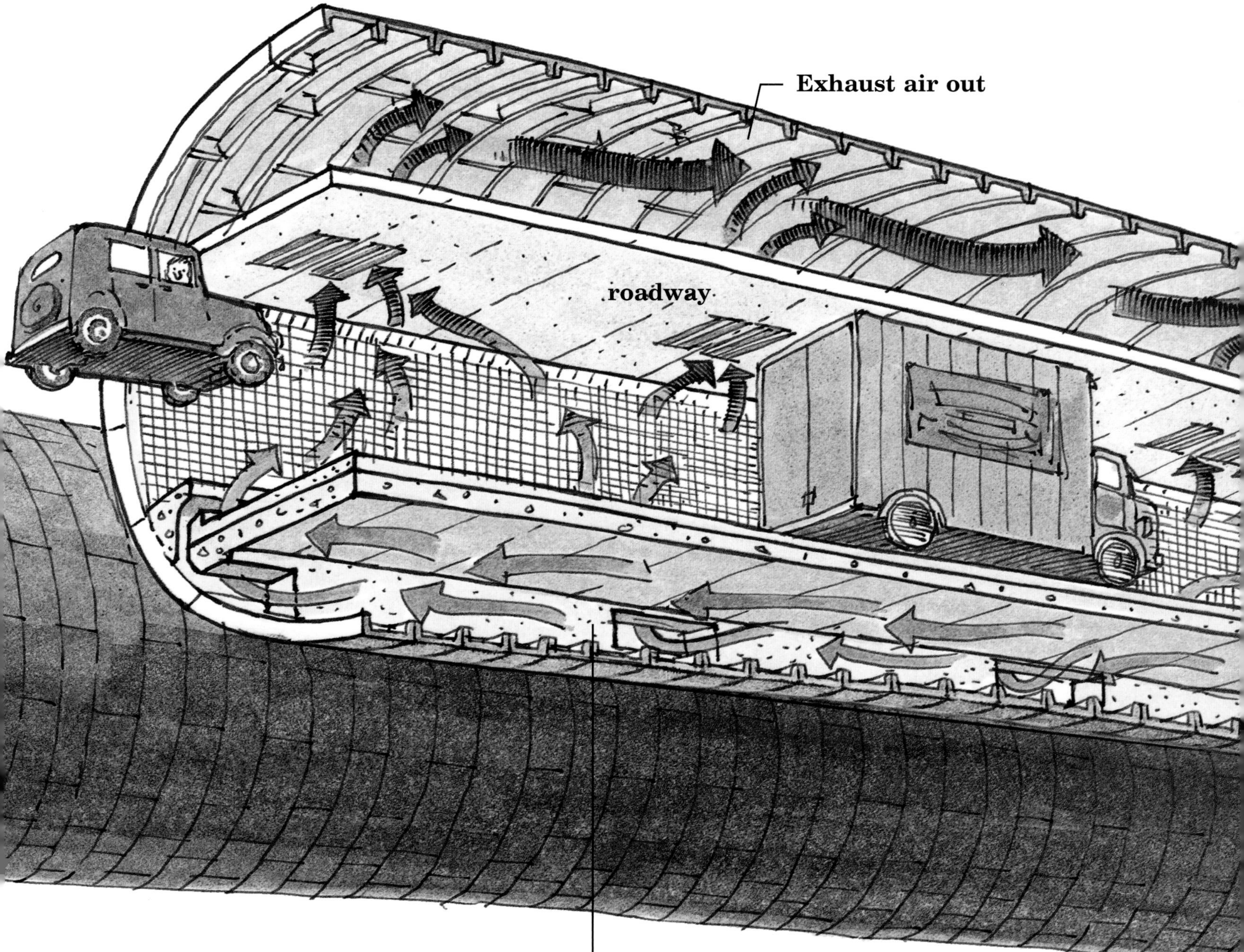

Exhaust air out
roadway
clean air in

THE CHANNEL TUNNEL

The English Channel/La Manche, 1987–1994: After centuries of distrust punctuated by prolonged military confrontations, the French and the British were finally united by a mutual dislike of seasickness. The body of water that has separated the United Kingdom and France for the past 8000 years can be very rough, making ferry crossings sometimes unforgettable. But Britain's unshakable belief in the importance of retaining what amounts to a moat for security reasons forced travelers into the air or kept them hanging over the rails as they crossed one of the world's busier shipping lanes. With the political and monetary unification of the European Community, the time was right for the creation of some kind of fixed physical link between the two old rivals. A variety of proposals were submitted, including tunnels, bridges, and combinations of the two. In the end, a tunnel proposal was selected.

One of the reasons for this decision was evidence from earlier tunneling attempts. Below the water, the two countries are linked by a layer of soft rock called chalk marl—a combination of chalk and clay, ideal for tunneling. Not only is this material fairly easy to dig through, it has a good stand-up time and is more or less waterproof. Extensive borings and sophisticated sound reconnaissance allowed geologists to create what they hoped would be an accurate picture of the various layers of material below the channel, which the engineers could then use to select the best route.

To control travel through the tunnel and to avoid the enormous ventilation problems that a 24-mile-long automobile tunnel would present, the engineers decided to build only a rail tunnel. Now, instead of driving your car or truck onto a ferry, you would drive it onto one of two specially designed trains. Rain or shine, the crossing would take a painless thirty-five minutes from terminal to terminal, only twenty-six minutes of which would actually be spent in the tunnel. A third kind of train, called the Eurostar, would carry passengers from the center of London to the center of either Paris or Brussels in roughly three hours.

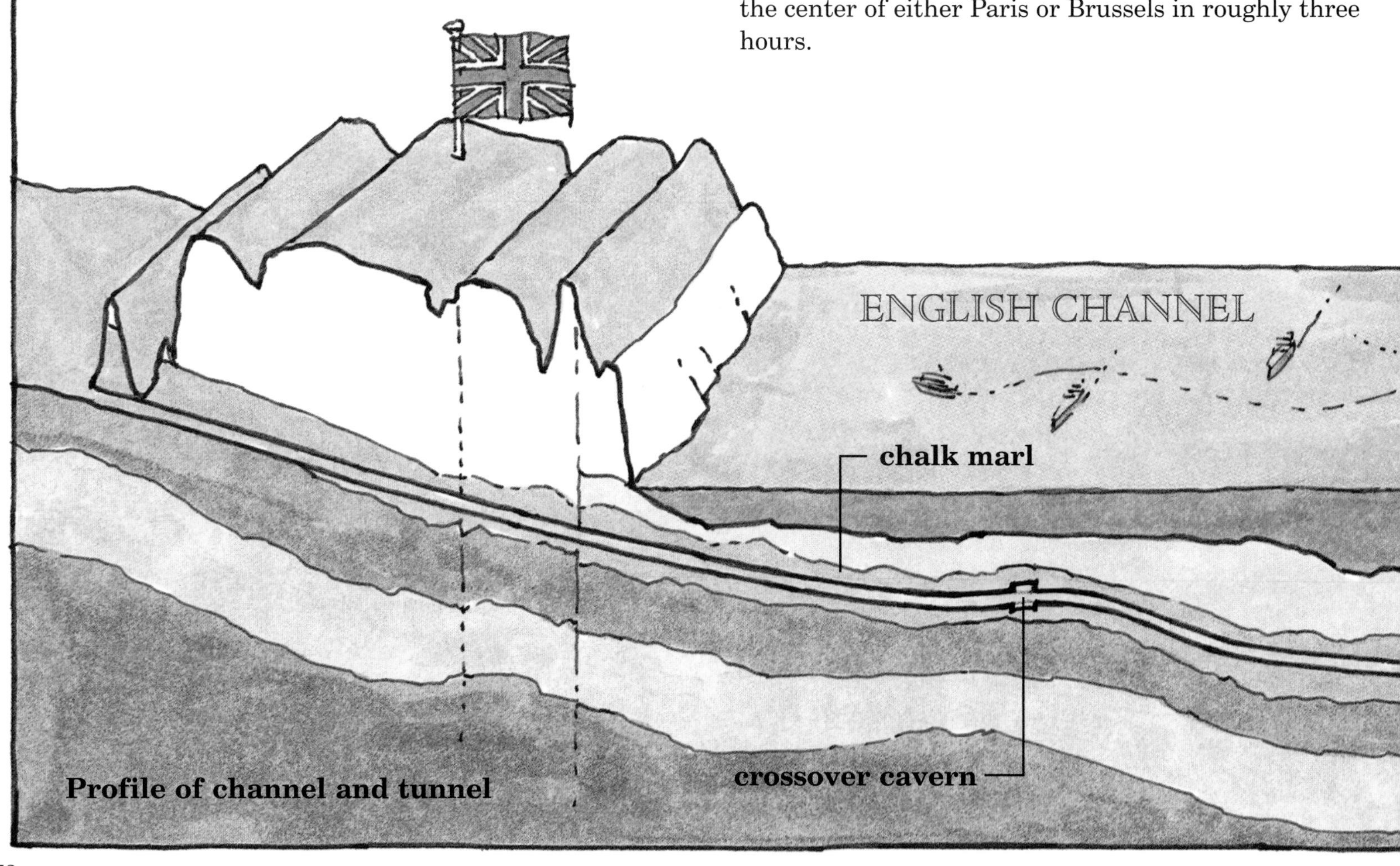

Profile of channel and tunnel

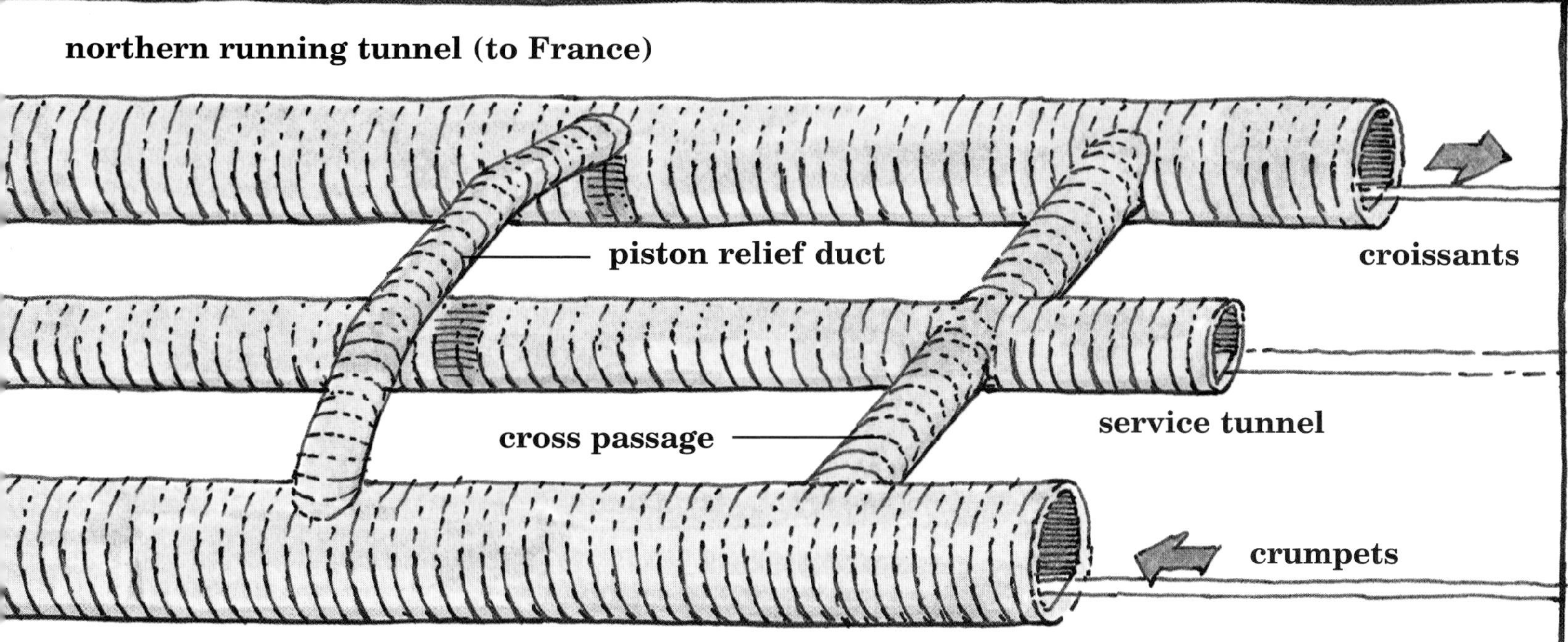

The Channel Tunnel is really three tunnels that run parallel to one another for most of the journey. The northernmost tunnel carries trains from Britain to France, the southern one from France to Britain, and a smaller service tunnel travels between them. Its primary function is to provide access to the main "running" tunnels for periodic maintenance and to serve as an escape tunnel if some kind of problem arises. Higher air pressure is maintained in the service tunnel to keep out any smoke or fumes that might result from a fire in one of the main tunnels. All three tunnels are linked by cross-passages approximately every 1200 feet. The two running tunnels are also linked at 800-foot intervals by smaller tunnels called piston relief ducts, which permit the air that builds up ahead of a fast-moving train in one tunnel to pass harmlessly to the other.

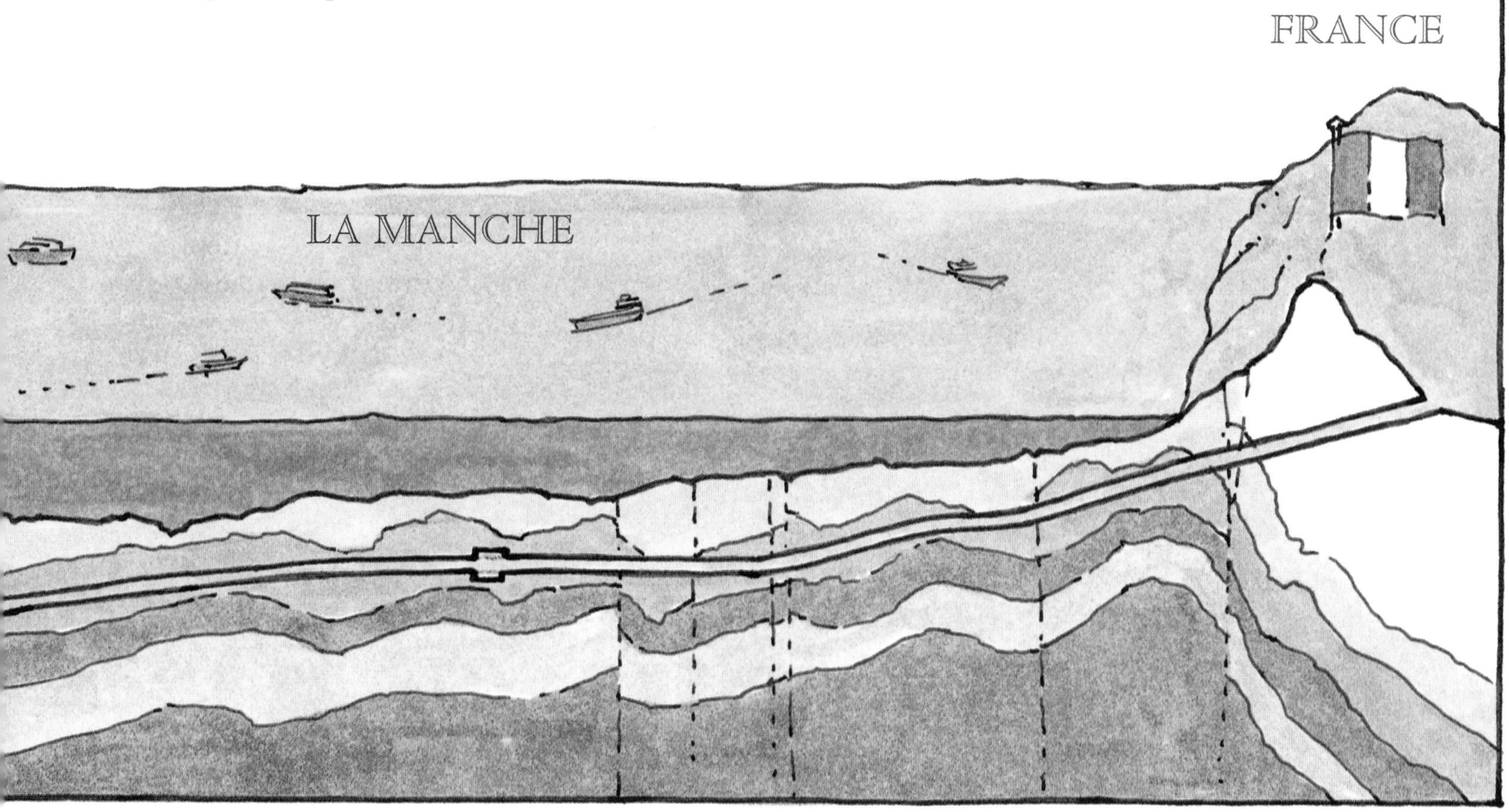

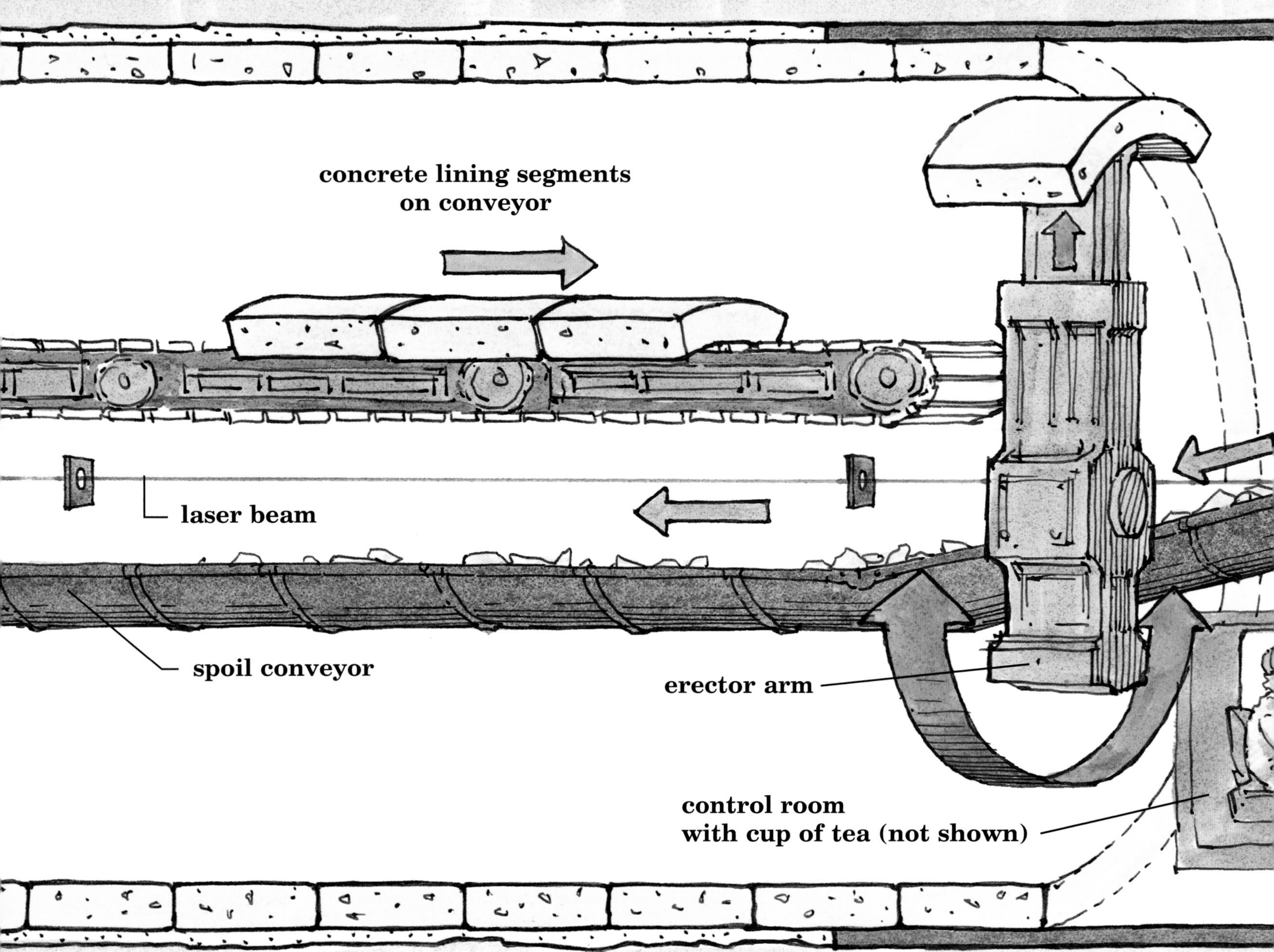

The tunnels were to be dug by specially designed tunnel boring machines, or TBMs. These are space-age versions of the Greathead shield and also leave behind them a completely lined cylindrical passage. They are highly sophisticated and almost completely automated. At the front end of each TBM is a rotating cutting head, which is thrust against the rockface by a ring of hydraulic rams immediately behind it. These rams also steer the cutting head. A second set of rams forces large gripper pads against the wall of the tunnel to provide a firm surface for the thrust and steering rams to push against. Behind the gripper pads is the control room, from which the driver of the TBM can monitor the machine's movement. A laser guidance system keeps it absolutely on course. The last piece of the TBM is the erector arm, which installs the segments of tunnel lining. Extending another 800 feet behind the TBM is the service train. It delivers the lining segments, carries away spoil and supplies clean air, compressed air, water, and electrical power as well as sanitation, first aid, and dining facilities– in short, whatever might be necessary to keep things moving.

The tunnels were begun from access shafts near each coast, down which the TBMs and all the other equipment could be lowered. After undergoing final assembly, six of the eleven TBMs to be used began their journeys towards each other, three from Britain, three from France. The other five began moving inland toward the future portals. The service tunnel was to be finished first and would serve as a kind of advance party for the running tunnels.

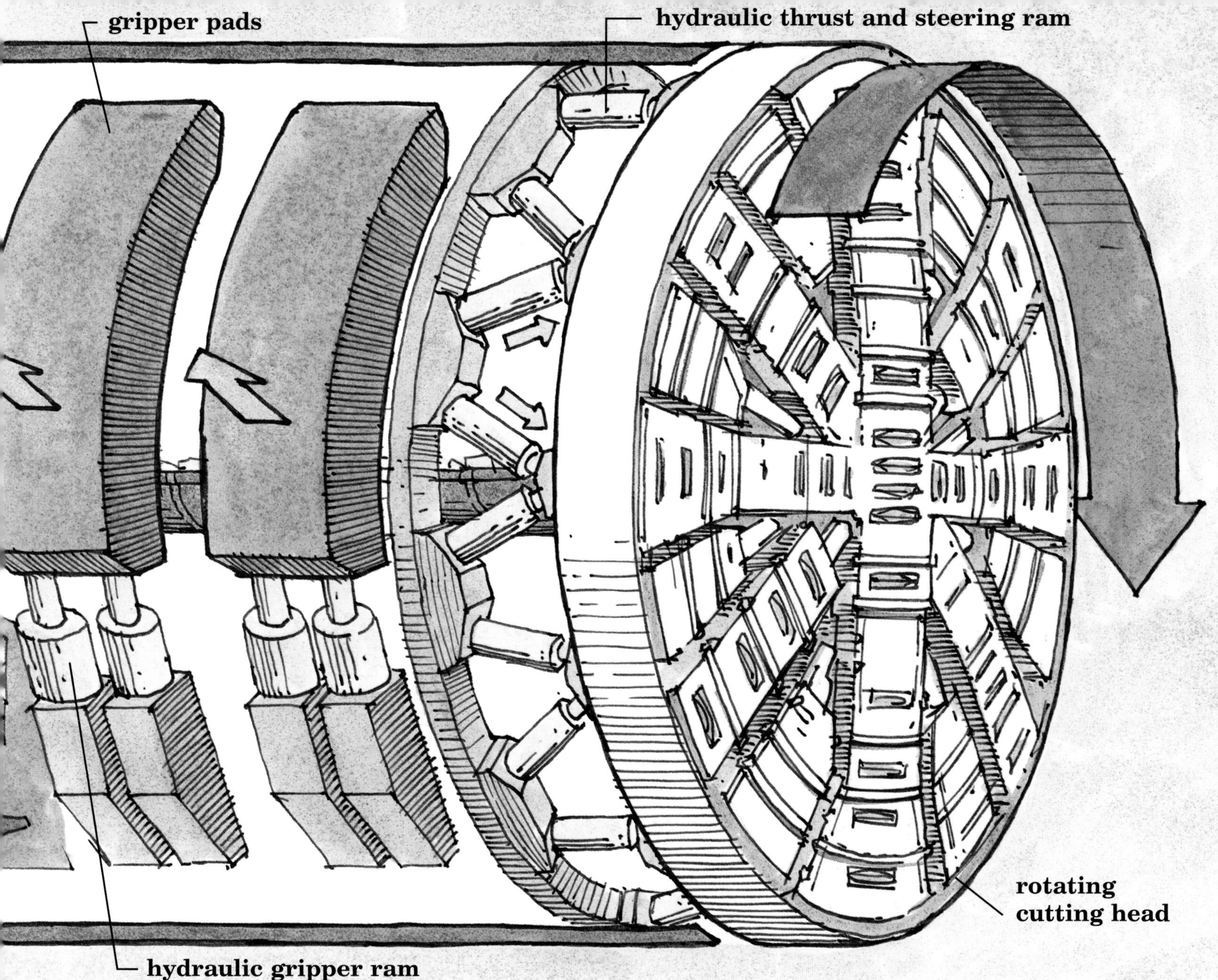

The largest of the rotating cutting heads, all of which revolve two or three times a minute, was almost 30 feet in diameter. Each head was studded with chisel-shaped cutting teeth or inset with steel disks, or had a combination of the two. As it slowly rotated, the cutting head carved a series of concentric rings of hills and valleys in the chalk marl. The natural stresses in the rock caused the hills to split off as the valleys between them reached a certain depth. The pieces of stone fell through spaces in the cutting head and onto the first part of the conveyor system that carried it all back to waiting spoil cars at the rear of the service train.

But even in the state-of-the-art Channel Tunnel, things did not go exactly as planned. All the preliminary exploration had suggested that the British TBMs would have to contend only with dry conditions, and it was with this in mind that they were designed. Needless to say, it wasn't long before a large amount of water began pouring in through fissures in the chalk marl forcing the TBM at the British end of the service tunnel to a complete standstill. Months were lost while a liquid cement called grout was pumped into the cracks, then a space above the TBM was dug out and lined with steel plates and sprayed-on concrete called shotcrete. Only when this oversized umbrella was in place and the flood stemmed could work resume.

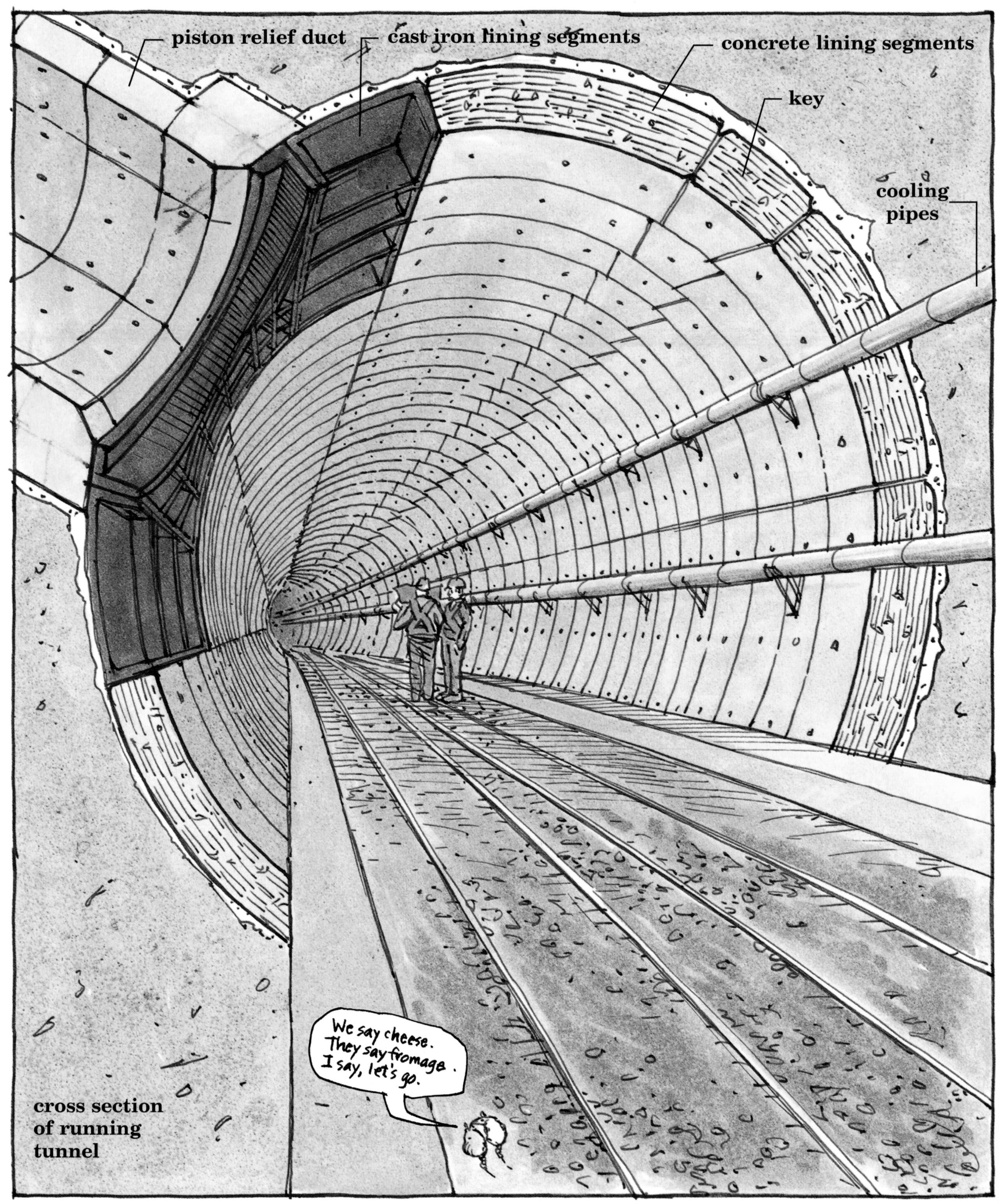
piston relief duct
cast iron lining segments
concrete lining segments
key
cooling pipes
We say cheese. They say fromage. I say, let's go.
cross section of running tunnel

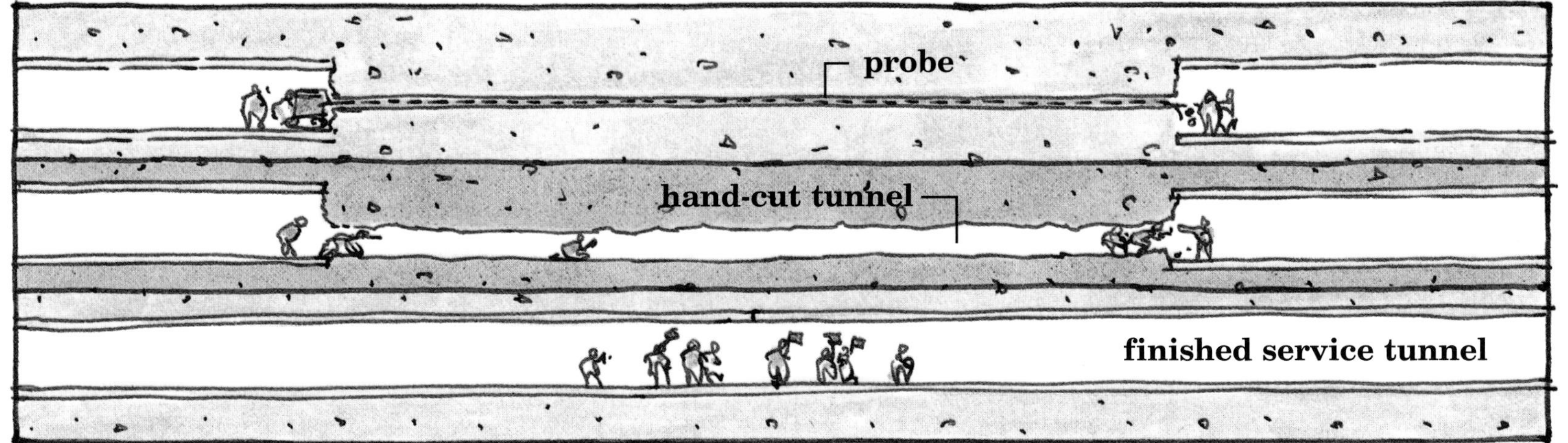

All three tunnels are lined with rings, and the rings are built up of segments. The last piece to be inserted into each ring, a wedge shape piece smaller than all the others, is called the key, and serves as a little reminder that these structures all members of the arch family. Most of the segments are made of reinforced concrete. Those around the cross-passage and piston relief duct connections are made of cast iron.

In October 1990, when the service tunnels were a little over 300 feet apart, the TBMs were stopped. To make sure that the halves of the tunnel were in proper alignment, a two-inch-in- diameter probe was drilled through from the British side. Once it had burrowed into the French excavation, an access passage was cut by hand. Then the entire section was enlarged to its final diameter, using smaller excavation machines called road headers.

Six months later, the running tunnels also broke through. This followed what appeared to be a rather chivalrous gesture but was in fact simply a matter of economics. Rather than going to the trouble and expense of dismantling and removing the cutting heads of the British TBM's, the engineers simply aimed them downward to dig their own graves. Once all the ancillary equipment had been removed, the holes were filled with concrete, and the French TBMs passed over them and into the British tunnels.

Getting the spoil out of any tunnel requires careful planning from the beginning, as does finding a new home for it. When the tunnel is thirty-two miles long, the amount of spoil generated makes this planning critical. The British built an enormous sea wall enclosing a couple of artificial lagoons near the entrances to their access shafts. As the spoil came up through the shafts, it was dumped into the lagoons, forcing out the water. Eventually the spoil dried out, making England slightly larger. The French, having more wet spoil to deal with, mixed it with water and pumped it into a specially created lake over half a mile from the coast. Once their spoil had dried out, it was planted with grass. Though this approach may not have increased the size of France, it has added to its oxygen supply.

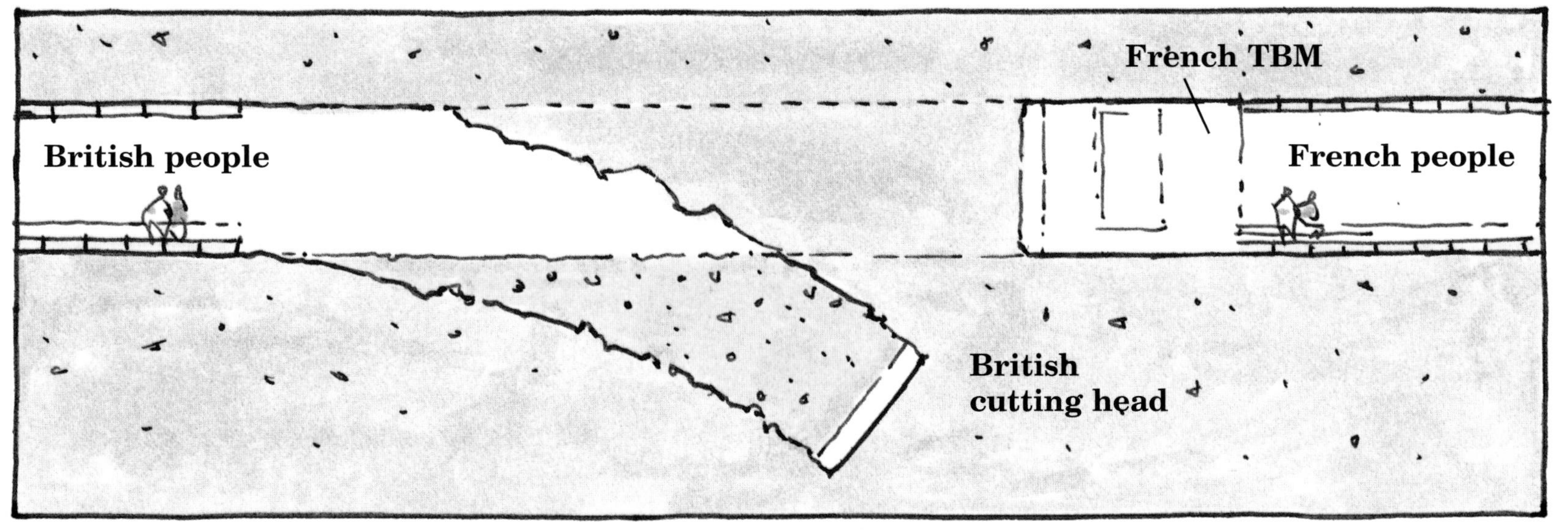

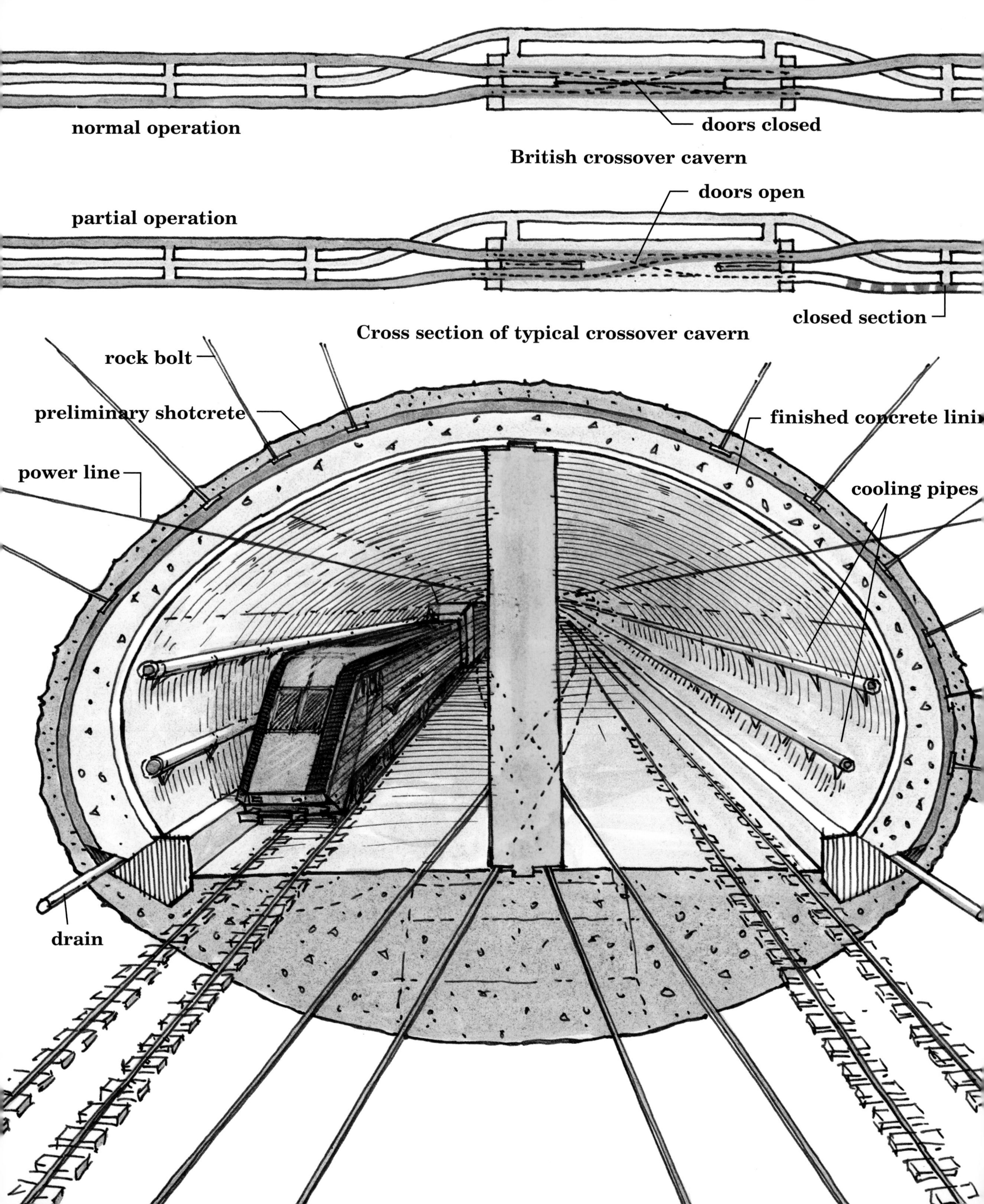
normal operation
doors closed
British crossover cavern
partial operation
doors open
closed section
Cross section of typical crossover cavern
rock bolt
preliminary shotcrete
finished concrete lini
power line
cooling pipes
drain

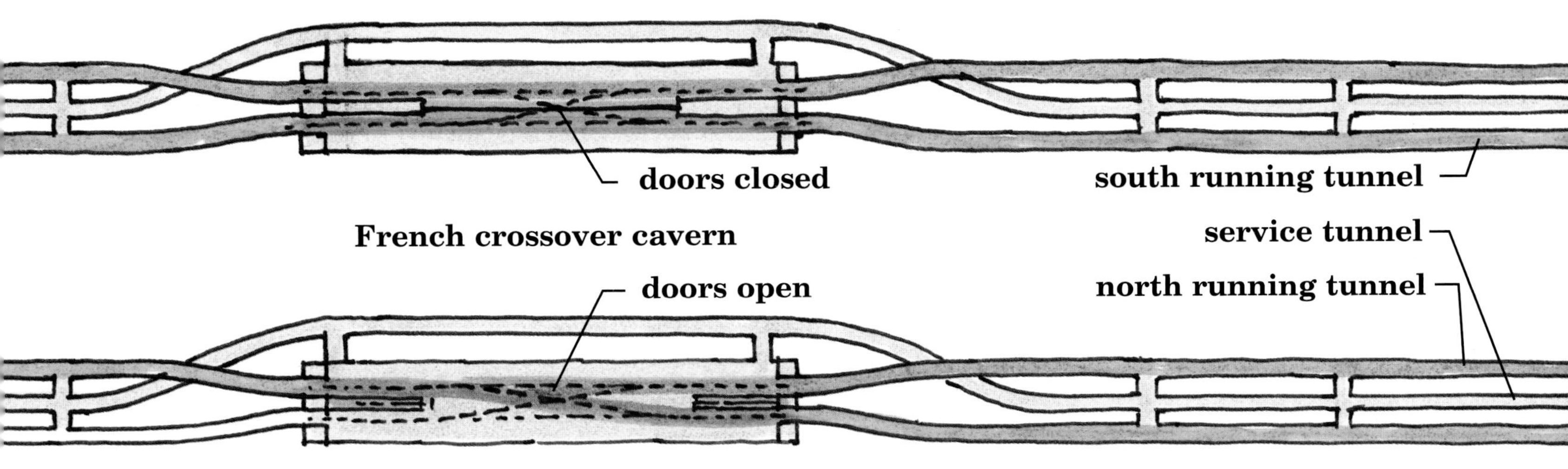

To keep the trains running twenty-four hours a day, even when part of the tunnel might be temporarily blocked, the engineers built two huge rooms called crossover caverns about a third of the way in from each coast. In these spaces, the tracks were linked so that a train could cross from one running tunnel to the other in order to bypass the closed section. At the next crossing it would move back to its original track, at which time the train that had been waiting could safely continue its journey. While this would certainly slow things down considerably, it also meant that under all but the most extreme circumstances, the Channel Tunnel need never close completely.

During the excavation, the service tunnel was the only link to the caverns, bringing in supplies and carrying away spoil. Before it was lined, each space was approximately 500 feet long, 70 feet wide, and 50 feet high. When necessary, the chalk marl around the openings was reinforced with shotcrete and 12- to 18-foot-long steel dowels called rock bolts. As the caverns were being built, workers installed measuring devices deep in the surrounding chalk that would allow them to monitor ground conditions. If they detected a problem, they could increase the thickness of the lining or the length of the bolts.

Massive doors were installed inside the finished caverns to prevent the spread of fire and to keep the air in each running tunnel separate. They would be opened only when the crossover system was required.

Work continued for two more years after all the tunnels had broken through. Miles of wiring were run for the security systems, signaling, lighting, and pumping equipment. Also installed were two large pipes through which chilled water would be continually fed, to help reduce the heat created by the high-speed trains. Everything was then tested and retested, including the trains. By the end of 1993, the Channel Tunnel was finished, and in May 1994 the most expensive civil engineering project in history was officially opened for business. But as everyone knows, records are made to be broken.

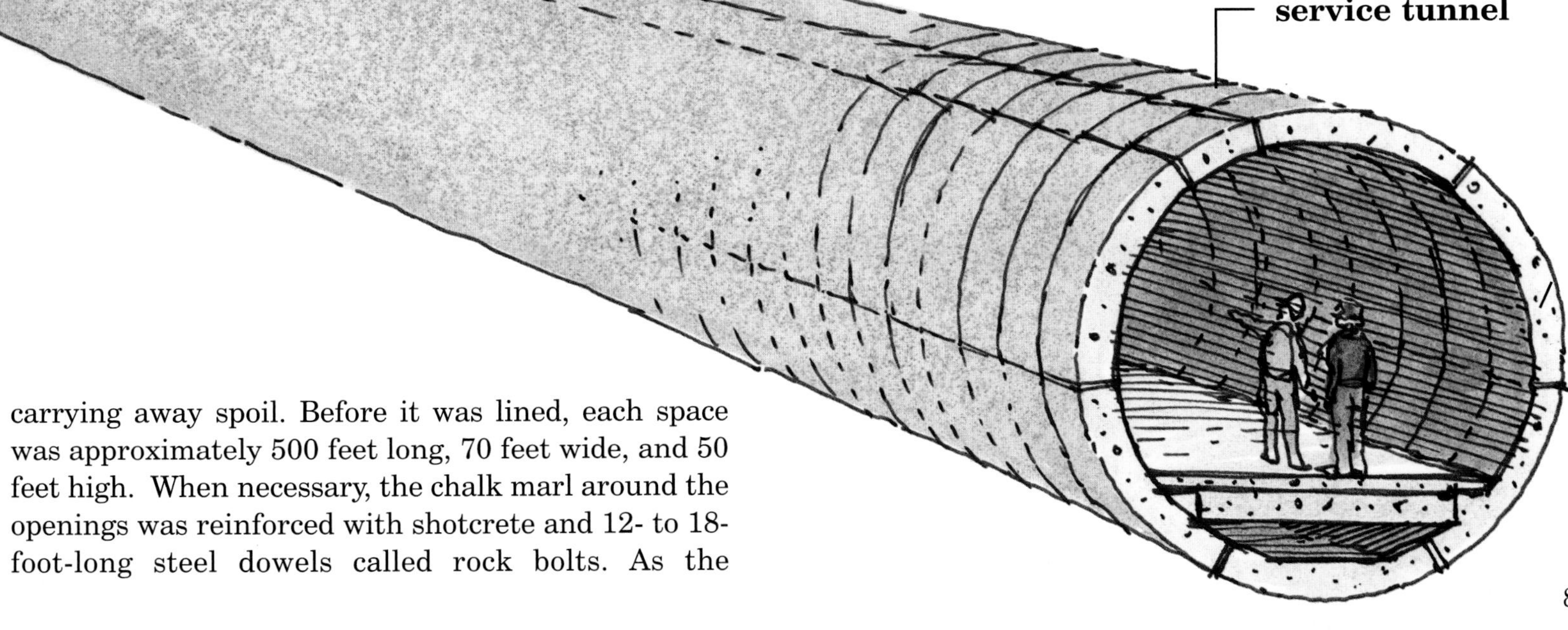

Prefabricated steel section of the Ted Williams Tunnel

The Big Dig

Boston, Massachusetts, 1985–: Like so many cities these days, Boston is being strangled by its own success. Traffic is often so congested that nothing moves. In an attempt to improve the situation, work began on the Central Artery/Tunnel project, better known as the Big Dig. While much of it is directed at replacing the old elevated expressway with a new and wider highway directly below it, a number of connections that have to be made in this extremely complicated and busy site have required the building of several interesting tunnels.

The Ted Williams Tunnel runs under Boston Harbor and connects a couple of major highways with the airport. With plenty of clearance between the floor of the harbor and the ships above, engineers were able to avoid the more expensive deep tunneling approach, using instead something called sunken tube design. The underwater portion of this tunnel is made up of twelve prefabricated steel sections, each a pair of 40-feet-in-diameter tubes roughly 300 feet long. They were made in Baltimore and towed up to Boston where all the rough concrete work was done inside them. This included building supports for the road, enclosures for the air-handling passages and utilities, and a complete lining. One by one, the finished sections were then towed out into the harbor, filled with water, and lowered into a specially prepared 50-foot-deep trench. Once anchored, each section was pumped dry and opened up to the adjoining section.

Not far away, three other tunnels are under construction. They are also prefabricated, although this time not in Baltimore and not of steel. And instead of running below the harbor, these must pass under busy railroad lines. The problem is to get them built without causing any major disruptions to train service or damage to the track beds.

The solution the engineers have chosen, called jacking, has been around for a while, although it is generally used to install underground pipes. Powerful jacks push the pipes through the ground as the soil inside them is removed. This ensures that the surrounding soil pressure remains unchanged, minimizing uneven settling. The process has been used recently to jack tunnels, but not on this scale. The tunnel fondly known as Ramp D is made up of two hollow concrete boxes 80 feet wide, 30 feet high, with a combined length of 150 feet.

A work pit slightly larger than the tunnel must be excavated on one side of the tracks. It will be enclosed by a high concrete retaining wall, which is built first. As the trench in which the wall will be formed is excavated, it is filled with a soupy substance called slurry to prevent collapse. This keeps the pressure in the trench the same as in the surrounding soil. Once the trench reaches the required depth, concrete is pumped in from the bottom up as the slurry is pumped out. When the concrete has cured, the soil enclosed by the wall is excavated.

Two tunnels, both ten feet in diameter, are bored through the ground below the tracks and then filled to about half their height with concrete. These will serve as guides to prevent the main tunnel from dipping as it slides over them. A thick concrete slab is poured at

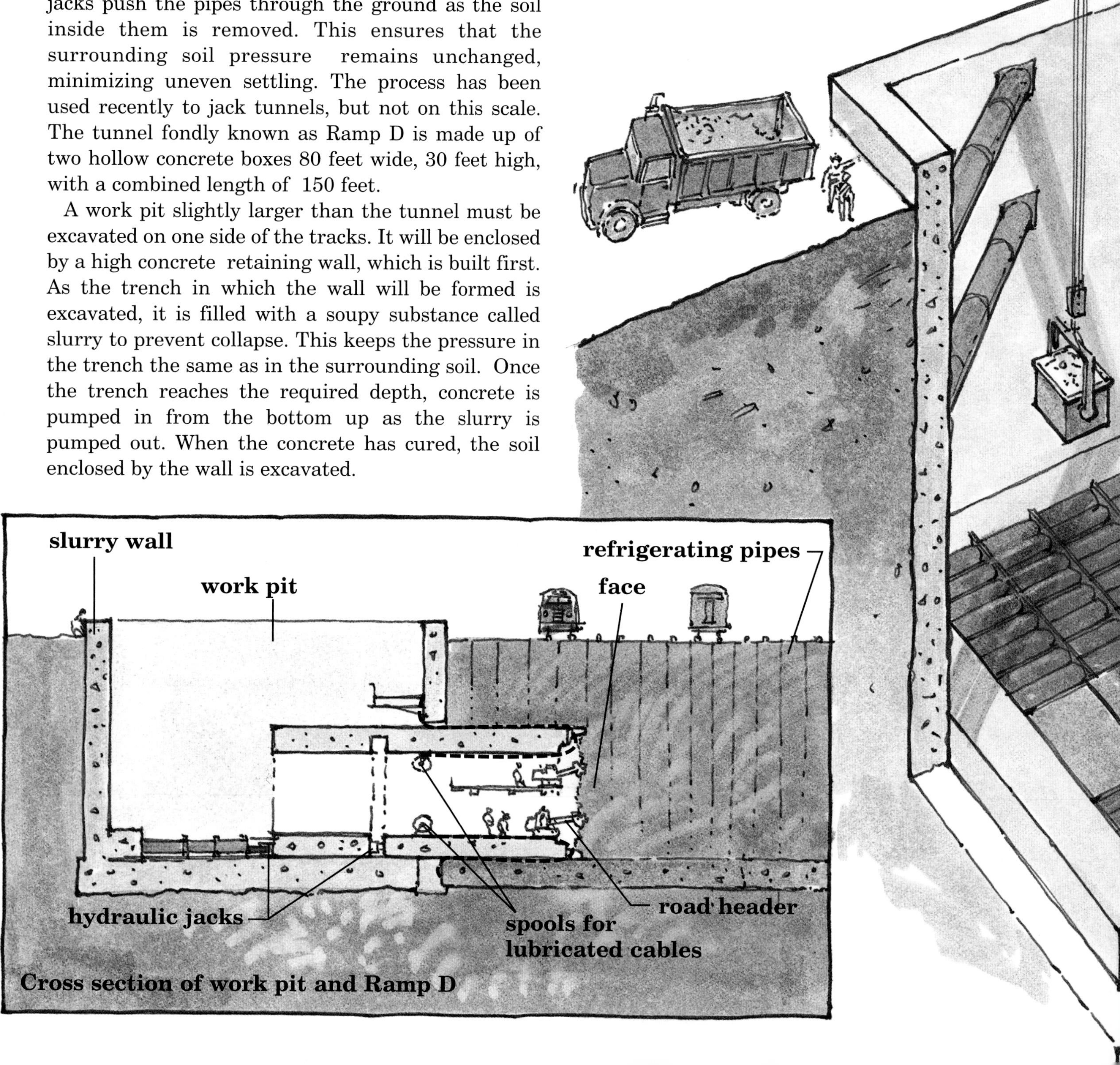

Cross section of work pit and Ramp D

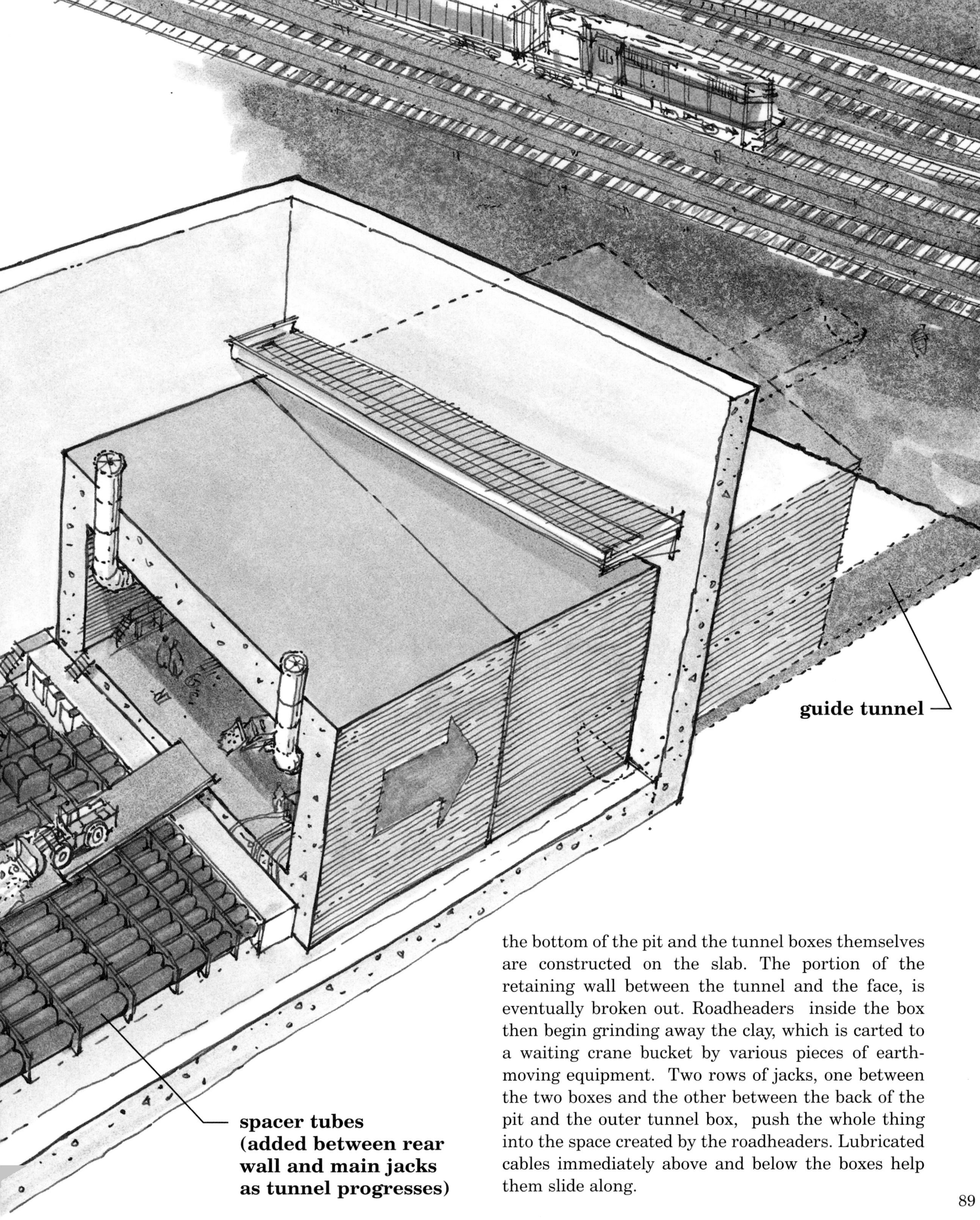

the bottom of the pit and the tunnel boxes themselves are constructed on the slab. The portion of the retaining wall between the tunnel and the face, is eventually broken out. Roadheaders inside the box then begin grinding away the clay, which is carted to a waiting crane bucket by various pieces of earth-moving equipment. Two rows of jacks, one between the two boxes and the other between the back of the pit and the outer tunnel box, push the whole thing into the space created by the roadheaders. Lubricated cables immediately above and below the boxes help them slide along.

As we've already seen, one of the biggest headaches for tunnel engineers is caused by changing soil conditions along the route. However, it is now possible in many situations to make the soil behave in a more uniform and therefore predictable way. The clay into which Ramp D was jacked was actually frozen first by pumping refrigerant through pipes sunk between the tracks.

When the time came to build a highway under the South Station subway line, things were more complicated. Engineers had to deal with four different soil conditions and a lot of ground water. Two parallel tunnels were first bored below the subway. A precise pattern of angled holes was then drilled through the floor of these tunnels into which short pipes called sleeves were placed. These would serve as guides for the main pipes through which workers injected a special chemical into the unstable soil below to improve stand-up time and help control the water. Once the soil had been stabilized, more tunnels were bored below each grouting gallery, one directly below the other. As each was finished it was filled with concrete. A third row of tunnels, this one horizontal, was then bored between the grouting galleries. These would house huge concrete beams. When all the pieces of this enormous subterranean log cabin were in place, the soil inside could be safely excavated and the four-lane highway tunnel built.

Because of both the unpredictable nature of tunneling and the changes incorporated since the project began, the Big Dig, like Hoosac, has suffered cost overruns and numerous slips in schedule. But also like Hoosac, the Big Dig is an ambitious and far-sighted undertaking.

The surfaces of our cities have become so clogged with traffic trying to navigate worn-out roads which are constantly being dug up for repair or to replace overburdened utility systems, that just getting through is almost as challenging as finding a place to park. Subway systems built over a hundred years ago to help address this very problem are now running at capacity. Yet the importance and appeal of cities doesn't seem to be lessening. The increase in population that comes with each new office and apartment building, shopping arcade and sports arena, simply adds to the burden. But that's the price of success.

There is little doubt that more and more tunnels will have to be built just to keep our cities livable. And they will have to be dug through or below the maze of foundations, subways, and utility systems on which we already depend. Complex projects like the Channel Tunnel and the Big Dig remind us that engineering technology and ingenuity are up to the challenge. It's just a matter of cost. How much are we willing to pay to help insure the health and success of our cities for generations to come?

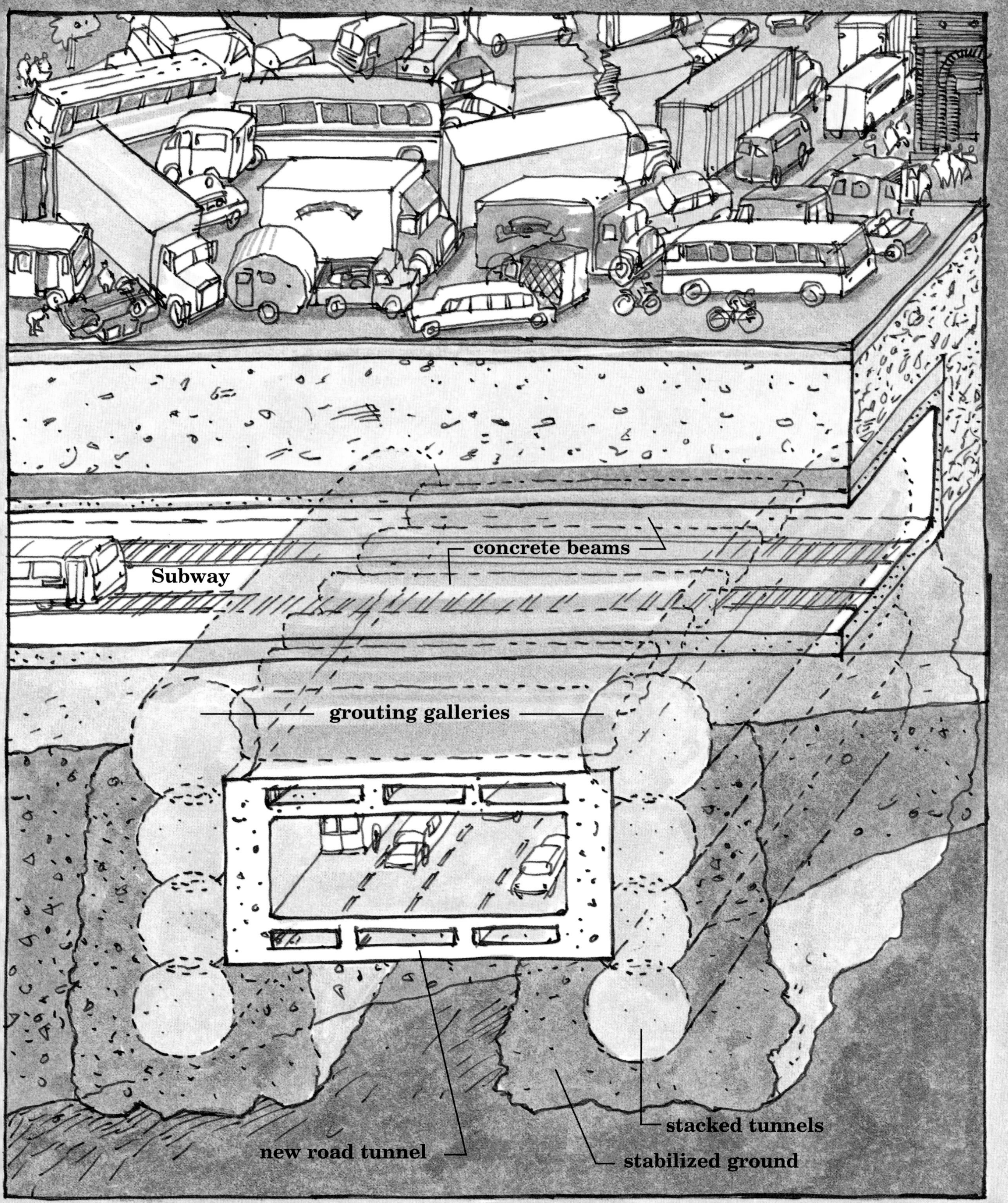
concrete beams
Subway
grouting galleries
stacked tunnels
new road tunnel
stabilized ground

Dams

Of all the big things in this book, dams feel to me like the biggest. The highest ones would barely reach halfway up the tallest skyscrapers, and with only rare exceptions do dams stretch as far as the longest bridges. Yet they seem bigger than both. Perhaps it's because we find them off the beaten path, where there is little to compare them to. Or maybe it's their simplicity. There aren't a lot of small pieces to dams that might reduce their visual scale. Then again, it might not be the way they look at all but, rather, what they do. With a single bold gesture, dams affect everything immediately around them and can have an impact on life hundreds of miles away.

Regardless of their size, all dams have two fundamental components, an impervious barrier to prevent the flow of water and some kind of structure to keep that barrier in place. When designing a dam, engineers work with two primary elements. The first is the shape and configuration of the structure. The second is the material with which it is built. While the four examples that follow present aspects of design and construction common to all dam projects, they also illustrate how the specific requirements of each dam combine with the uniqueness of a particular site to help engineers arrive at the most appropriate design.

When all is said and done, dams have one job—controlling water. By raising a river's level or diverting it, they help produce electricity, reduce flooding, improve irrigation and navigation, and even promote recreation. Controlling water, however, is not as easy as it might sound, especially when you're talking about millions of gallons. As every dam engineer knows, water also has one job, and that is to get past anything in its way.

ITÁ DAM

Uruguai River, between Santa Catarina and Rio Grande do Sul, Brazil, 1996-2000: In 1987, after several years of study, the government of Brazil formally approved an ambitious dam-building project intended to meet the country's electricity needs well into the twenty-first century. Of the twelve dams planned, the largest was to be built on the Uruguai River. The site was chosen because of the large amount of rainfall in the region, the expected height of the water at the dam and the potential capacity of the reservoir behind it, and the solid rock layer below the soil.

Masonry dams are those built of concrete, cut stone, or brick, whereas embankment dams are made primarily of rock, sand, earth, and clay. Because of the high cost of working entirely in concrete and the almost unlimited availability of sound rock in the area, Itá was to be an embankment dam.

A straight wall across any river will soon be pushed over if it isn't heavy enough to resist the horizontal force of the water behind it. The builders can either make it thicker or pile up material in front of it with enough weight to counteract the push of the water. If the wall is supported at an angle, some of the water's force will push downward and actually help keep the dam in place.

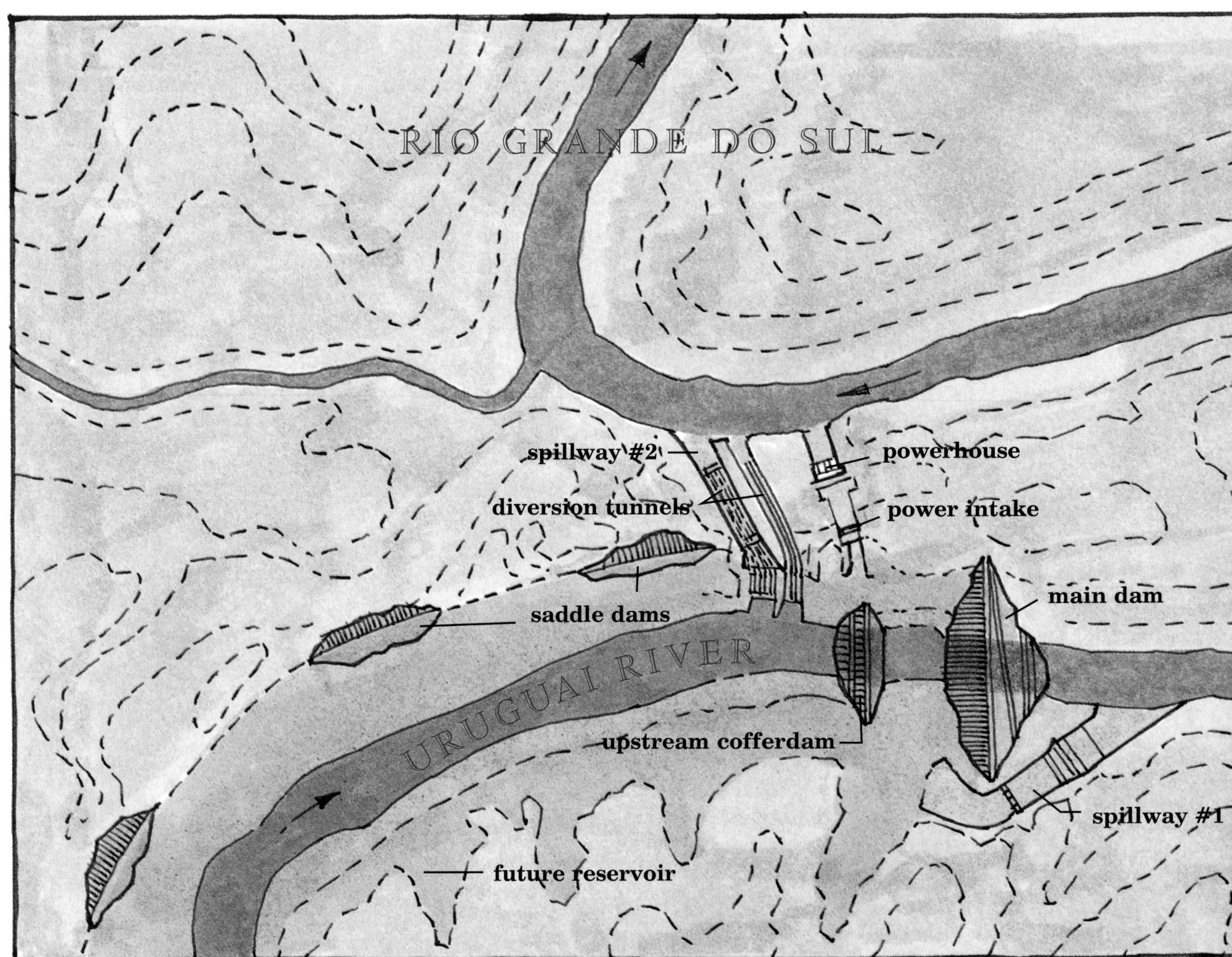

This is the principle behind all embankment dams. The impervious barrier at Itá would be a layer of concrete. The structure supporting it would be a man-made mountain of quarried rock about 400 feet high and half a mile long.

As is generally the case, Itá dam was to be just one part—albeit a very big part—of a complex of structures. It would also require two cofferdams, three saddle dams (to seal off depressions in the landscape that fall below the expected height of the reservoir), two spillways, ten tunnels, and a powerhouse containing five electrical generators.

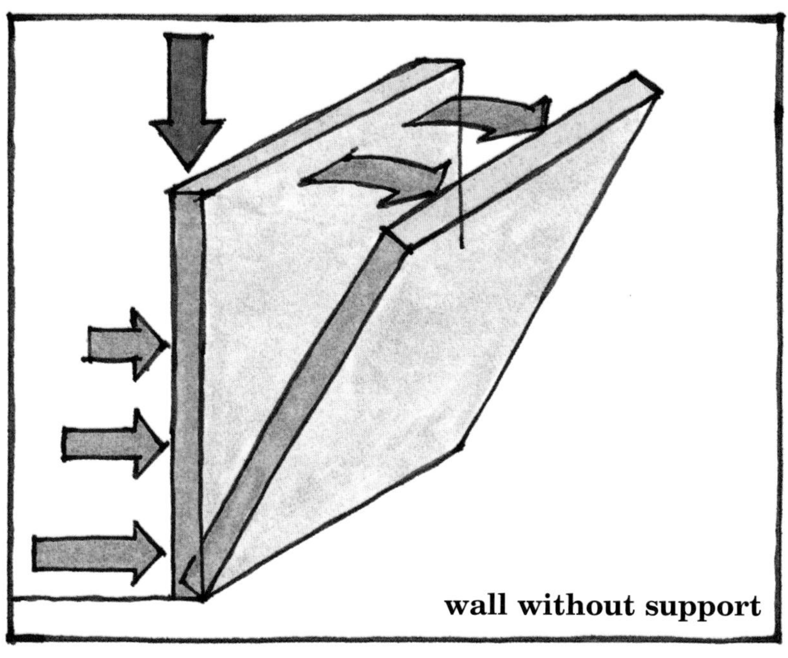

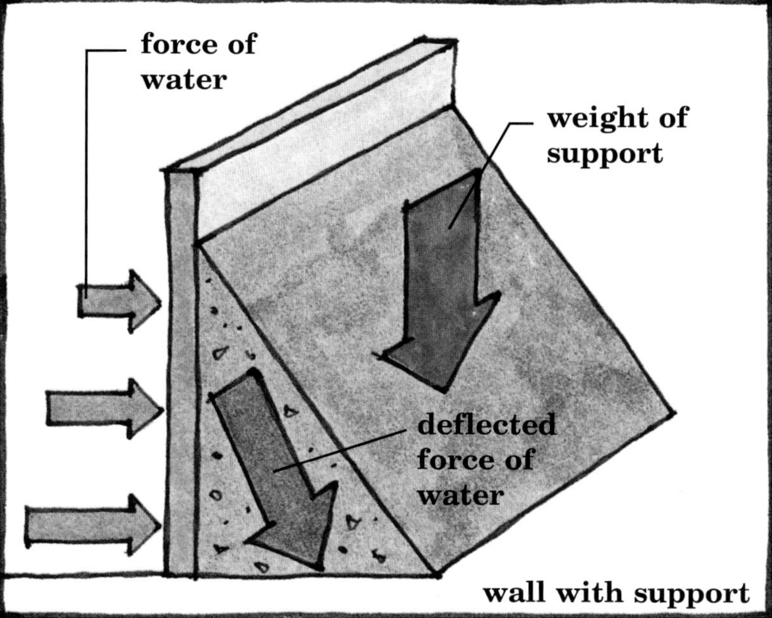

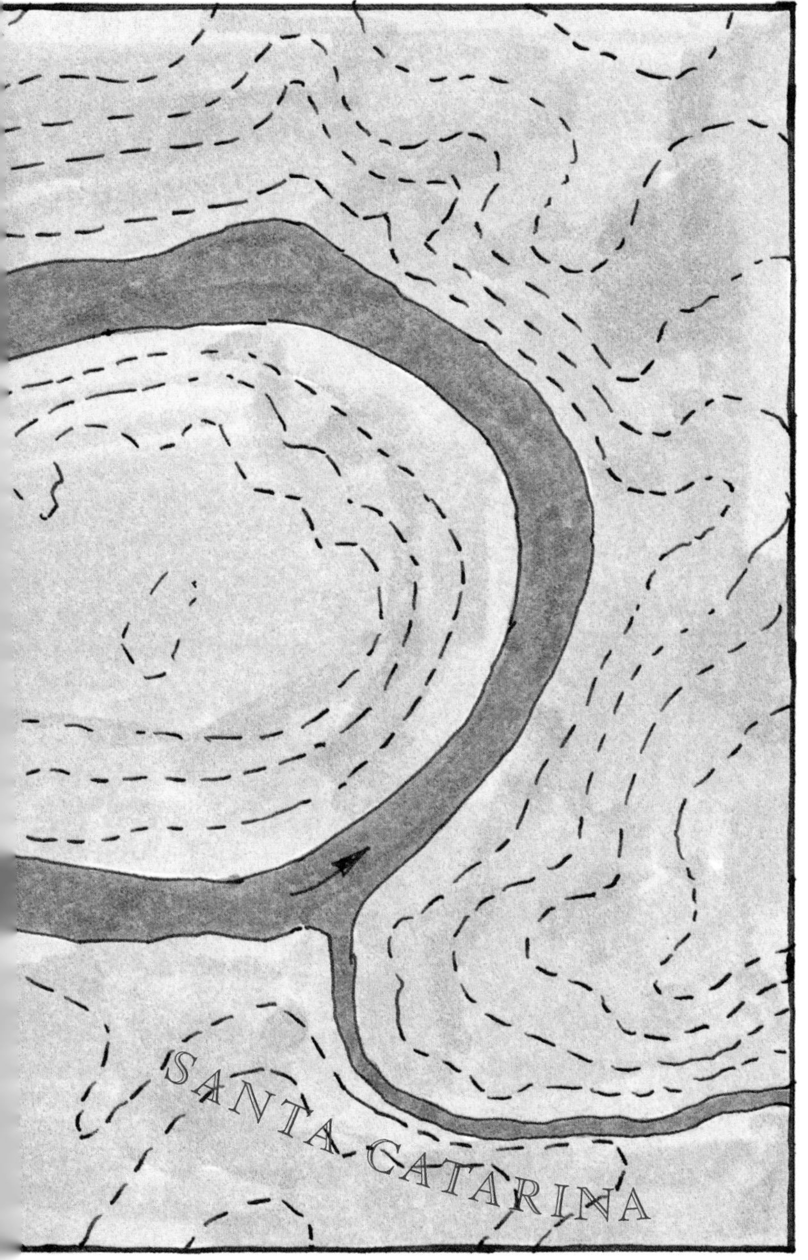

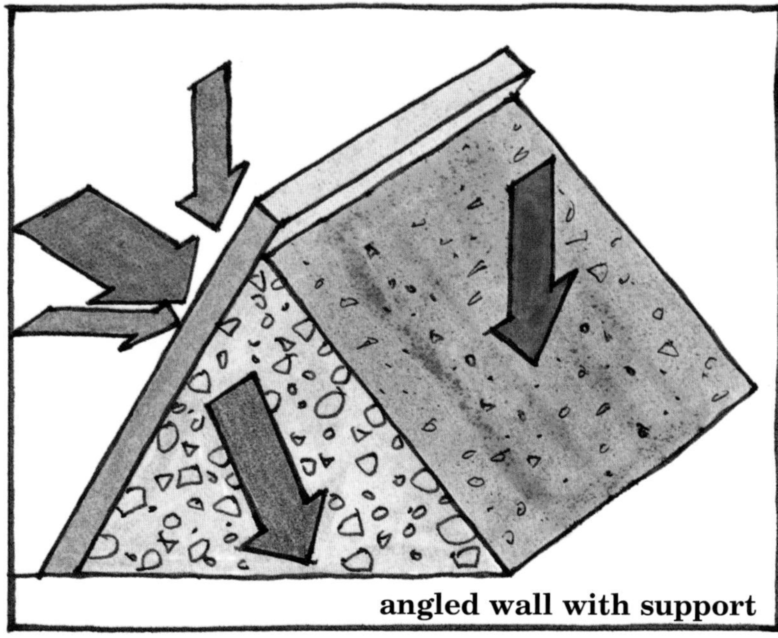

setting up the wooden templates

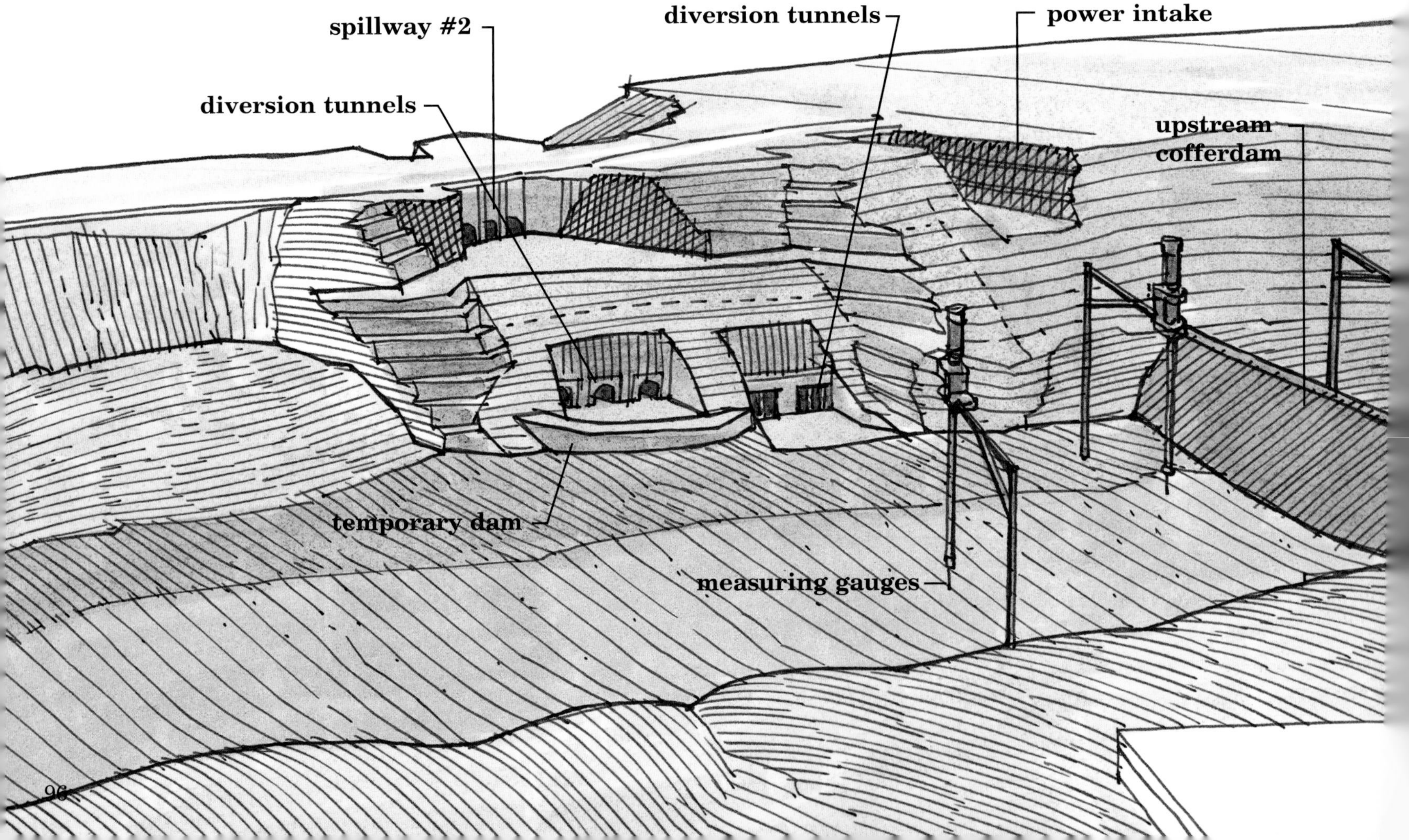

spillway #2
diversion tunnels
diversion tunnels
power intake
upstream cofferdam
temporary dam
measuring gauges

To help establish the layout and dimensions of each structure and to get some idea of how the water would behave, engineers built a huge scale model. Working from detailed maps, they drew the path of the river on the concrete floor of a large, open building. Using a transit for accuracy, they then set up precisely measured and cut wooden templates along the outlines of the river. By filling the space between the templates with crushed stone and cement, they were able to replicate the topography of the area.

Once all the hills and valleys were in place, the pieces of the dam complex were added. By flooding the model, the engineers could now begin to see how the design was working. Readings taken from various gauges were interpreted and analyzed, and the necessary adjustments were made. Eventually things learned from this process were added to the data—geological reports, technical calculations, and so on—required before a final plan could be developed.

Even as the model was being constructed and studied, preparations for the project were underway. Many people operated small farms along the riverbanks upstream from the dam site. Still others lived and worked in the town of Itá. All of them would have to be relocated, because by 2001, the only residents of this valley would be fish. By 1990, many of these people were settling into brand-new homes along the brand-new streets of Nova Itá (paved with cobblestones from Old Itá). They had a new community center, a small museum in which pictures and souvenirs of the old town were displayed, and a new church. Near it was the new cemetery, to which the remains of Itá's deceased had been carefully transported. Three hundred and fifty miles of new roads and ten new bridges were also created to carry workers, equipment, and materials to the dam site. But just when everything appeared to be ready, public funds ran out and the whole project ground to a halt. Six years passed before a consortium of public and private partners was finally able to begin construction in 1996.

Building anything in a strong current is difficult and dangerous, so before construction of the dam began, engineers diverted the river around the site. Since the Uruguai River doubles back on itself, making a large loop, they decided to connect the waters above and below the dam site with five tunnels driven straight through the rock. A large cofferdam was built which forced the river into the tunnels. A second cofferdam, built downstream from the site, prevented the river from flowing back into the work area. Stone removed during the excavation of the tunnels—in this case a hard basalt—was used to build both cofferdams and part of the main dam. All three dams were built up in layers, a process that was begun during the dry season. Although the ends of the main dam were already being built up against the banks, they would not be extended across the river until both cofferdams were finished, the area between them had been pumped dry, and the riverbed had been cleared to provide a strong rock foundation.

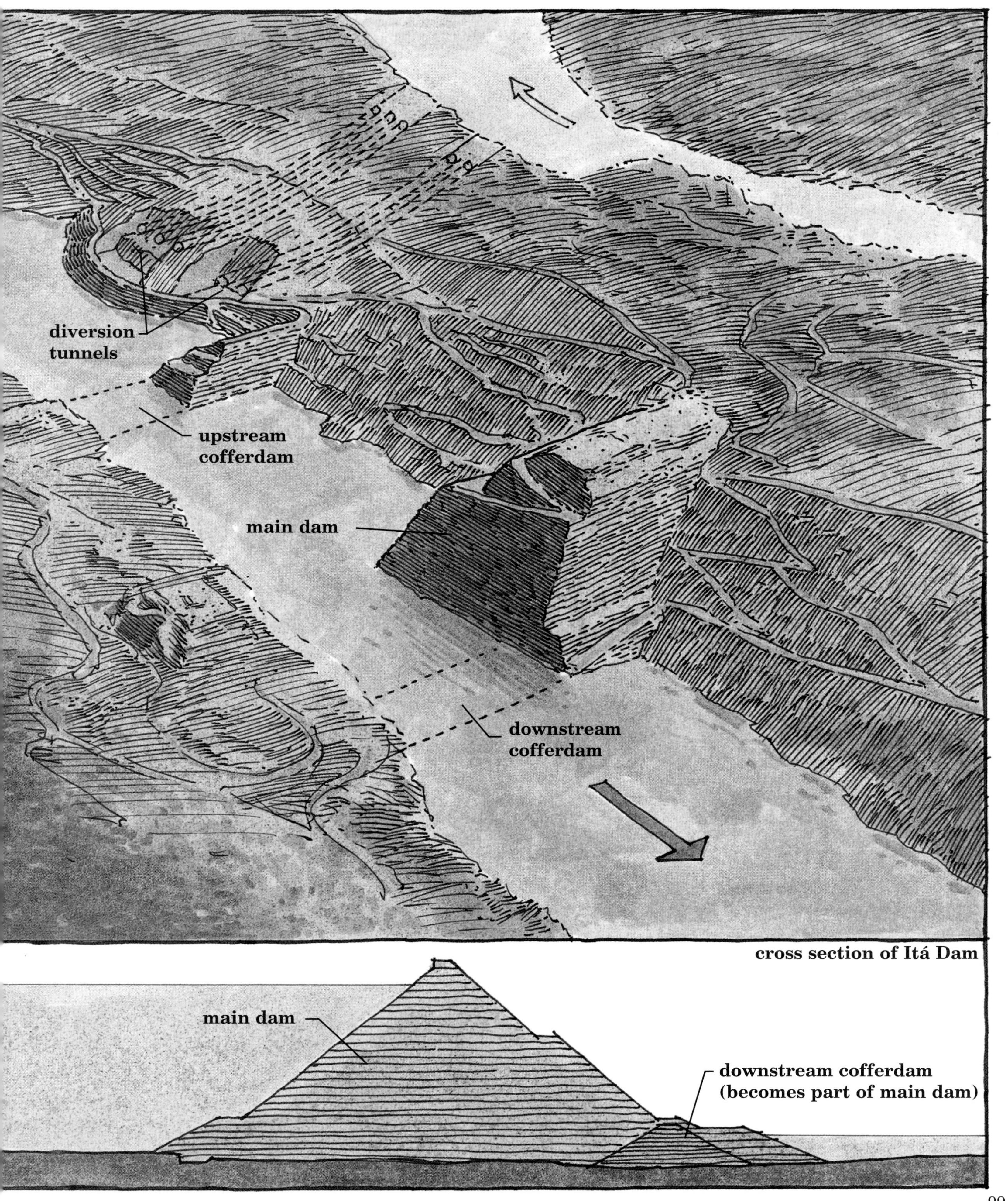
diversion tunnels
upstream cofferdam
main dam
downstream cofferdam
cross section of Itá Dam
main dam
downstream cofferdam (becomes part of main dam)

If water can't get through a dam, it will try to go around or under it. For this reason a reliable watertight seal between the concrete face and both the rock foundation and abutments is essential. A trench is cut into the stone along this entire line and a thick concrete pad called a plinth is built into it. Holes are drilled at regular intervals through the plinth and into the rock, and grout is then pumped down into them to fill any cracks. Long steel rods are also inserted to tie the plinth and surrounding rock together.

While the plinth was under construction, the dam itself was being built up one horizontal layer of rockfill at a time. These layers varied from three to six feet thick and were compacted using heavy vibrating rollers. When the plinth was completed, layers of crushed stone only a foot and a half thick were built up behind it. Known as the transitional area, this part of the dam must be built very carefully, since its job is to evenly distribute the tremendous force of the water pressing against the thin concrete face (18" thick at the bottom and only 12" at the top). As each layer of transitional material was placed, a cement curb was precisely extruded along the entire length of the face so that the finished surface would be as uniform as possible.

Only when the transitional material and the plinth were in place (this took about two years) could the face itself be constructed. It was built in a series of vertical sections each about 40 feet wide and extending the full height of the dam. Each section was enclosed between temporary wooden forms, and workers then inserted a grid of reinforcing steel. The first concrete was poured at the base, creating the all-important watertight connection between the face and the plinth. A flexible joint between the two would permit the face to move slightly as the reservoir eventually rose against it.

cross section of dam base on upstream side

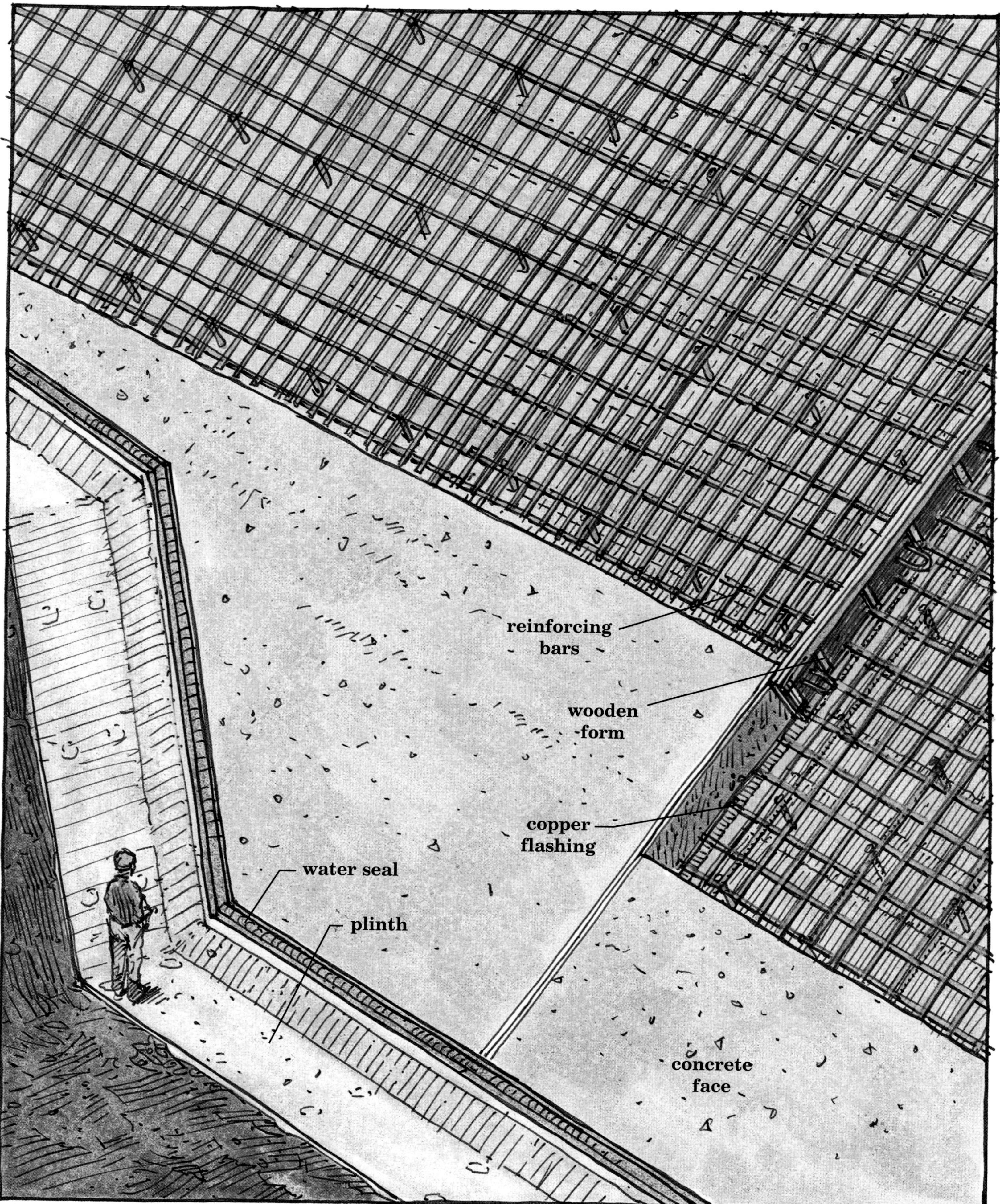
reinforcing bars
wooden form
copper flashing
water seal
plinth
concrete face

The concrete was delivered down long chutes that extended all the way from the crest. After each pour, a steel platform the width of the section was slowly winched up over the wet concrete. From the platform, some of the workers vibrated the concrete to ensure even distribution while others troweled it smooth. A perforated pipe, dragged along behind the platform, provided a continuous trickle of water to keep the concrete from drying too quickly and cracking.

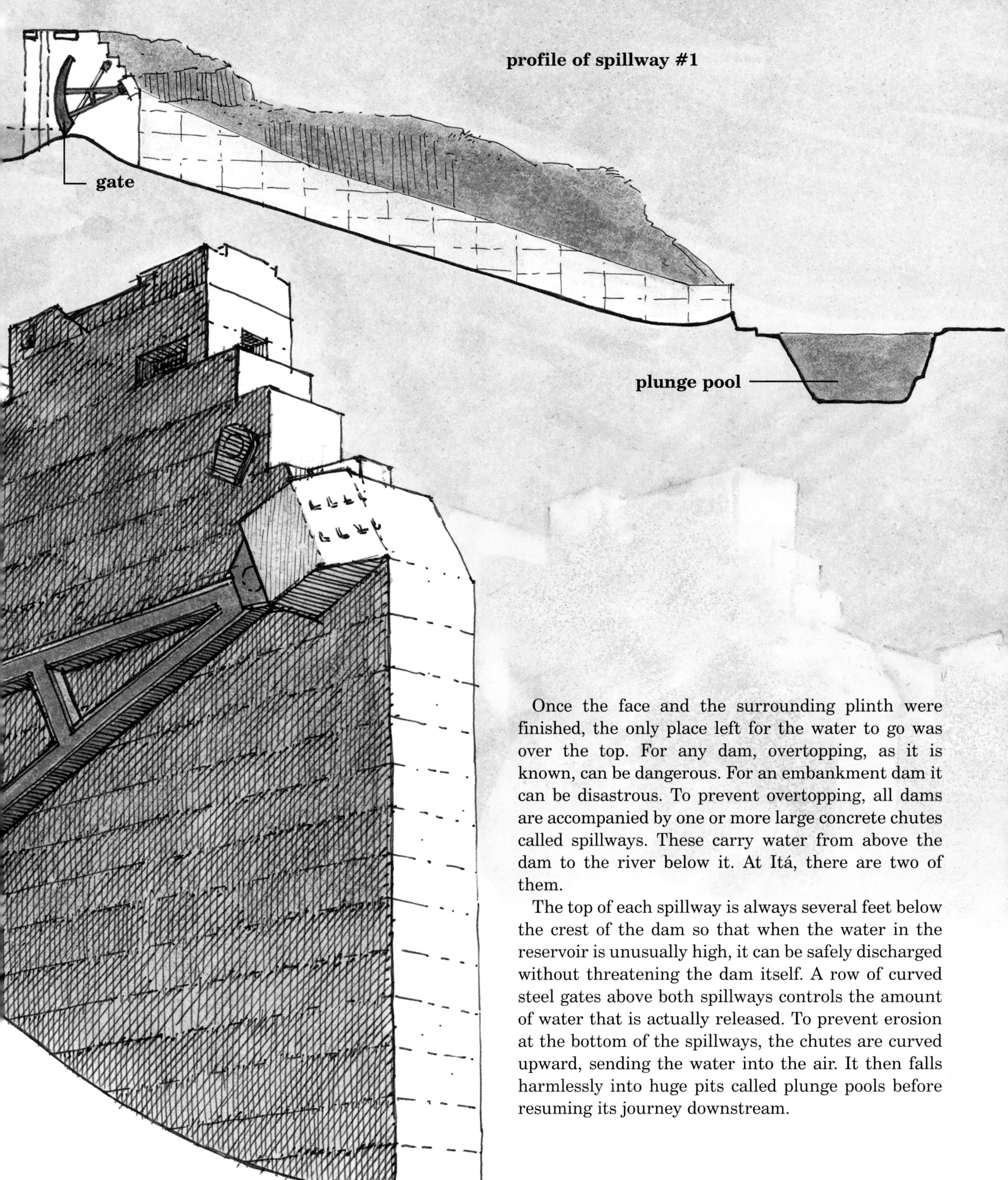

Once the face and the surrounding plinth were finished, the only place left for the water to go was over the top. For any dam, overtopping, as it is known, can be dangerous. For an embankment dam it can be disastrous. To prevent overtopping, all dams are accompanied by one or more large concrete chutes called spillways. These carry water from above the dam to the river below it. At Itá, there are two of them.

The top of each spillway is always several feet below the crest of the dam so that when the water in the reservoir is unusually high, it can be safely discharged without threatening the dam itself. A row of curved steel gates above both spillways controls the amount of water that is actually released. To prevent erosion at the bottom of the spillways, the chutes are curved upward, sending the water into the air. It then falls harmlessly into huge pits called plunge pools before resuming its journey downstream.

The last major piece of the complex, and the primary reason for the dam in the first place, is the powerhouse. This is the building that houses the generating equipment, and it is always built as far below the level of the reservoir as possible to insure that the water has as much force as possible when it arrives.

At Itá, the water begins its journey to the powerhouse by passing through another set of enormous gates. Unlike the gates above the spillways, these slide up and down like the portcullises of medieval castles. The water enters one of five separate tunnels, called penstocks, each over 20 feet in diameter. Screens called either trashracks or stoplogs, depending on the sizes of their openings, prevent debris from passing through the gates that might either block the penstocks or damage the turbines below. Because of the tremendous water pressure that builds up inside them, the penstocks are lined with either concrete or steel.

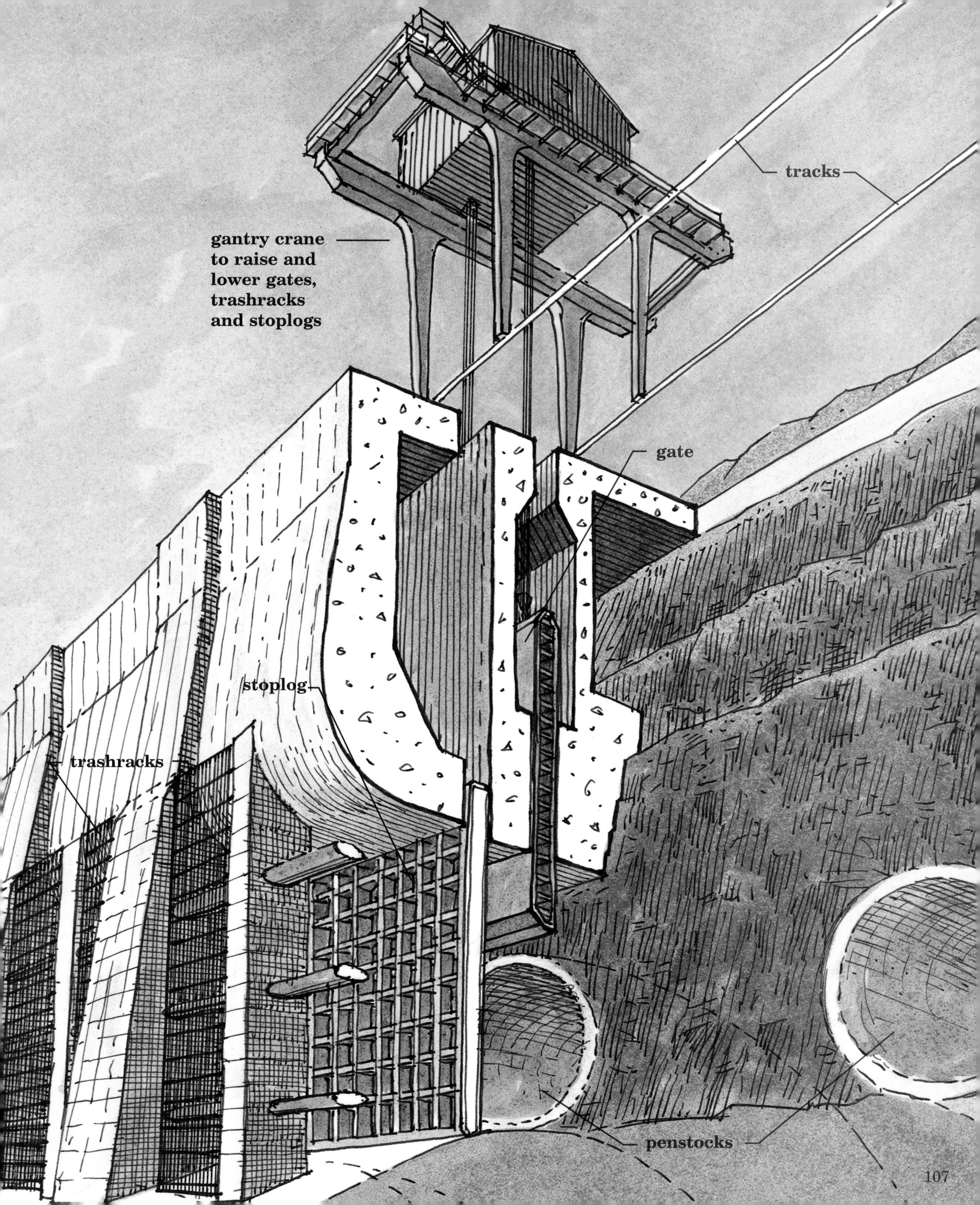
gantry crane
to raise and
lower gates,
trashracks
and stoplogs
tracks
gate
stoplog
trashracks
penstocks

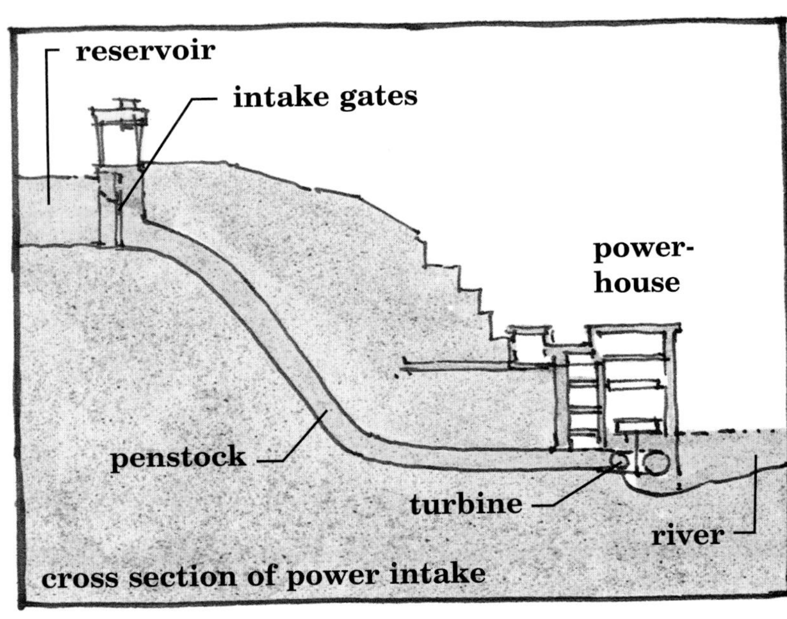

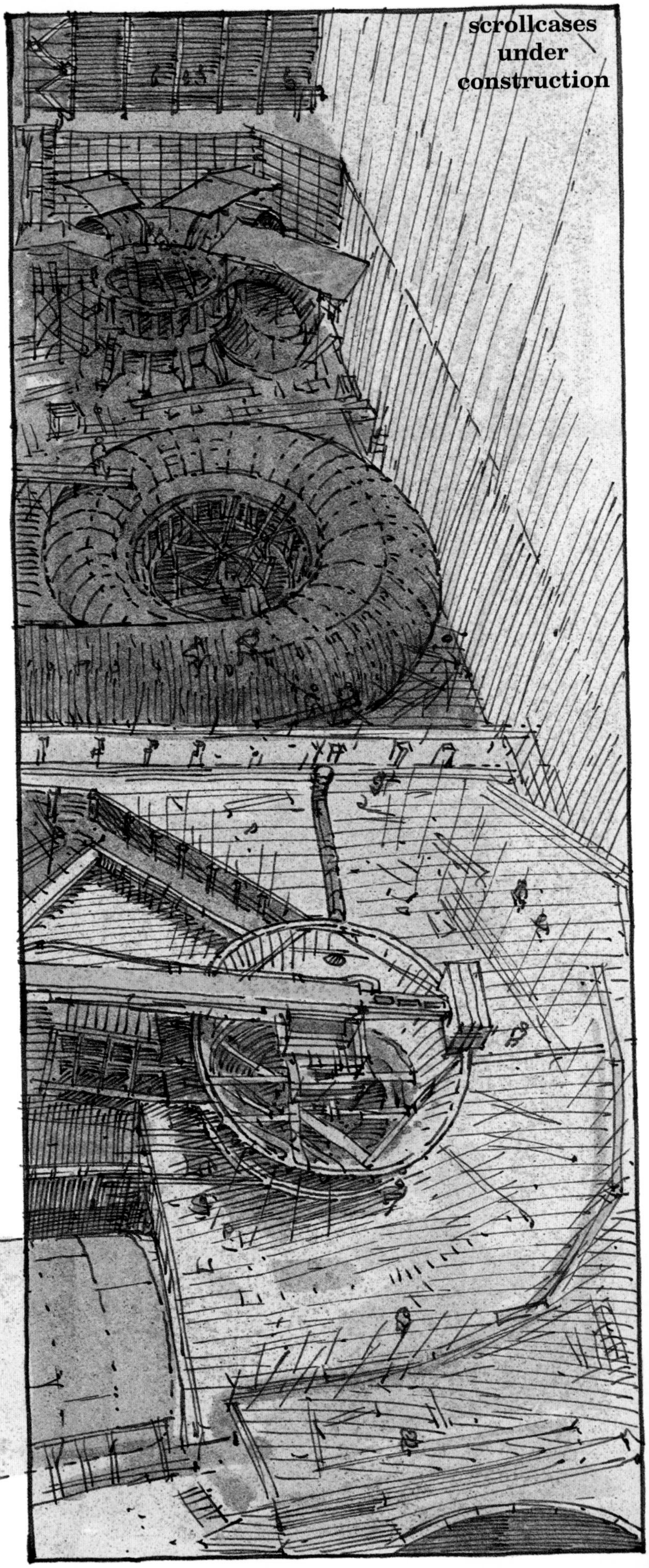

scrollcases under construction

Once it reaches the powerhouse, the water flows from the penstocks into a spiraling steel pipe called a scrollcase. This in turn is wrapped around a bladed wheel called a turbine. As the water leaves the scrollcase, it pushes against the blades and spins the turbine. The axle or shaft of the turbine connects directly to the shaft of a second wheel called a rotor, which is lined with magnets. The rotor turns inside a large fixed rim called a stator. The movement of the magnets transforms a small current in the stator into a much more powerful current, which is then drawn off and readied for distribution.

Because of the tremendous expense of such projects, it is essential that they be completed and producing electricity as quickly as possible. For this reason, the various parts of the Itá complex were built simultaneously. In June of 2000, the first electrical power from the Itá dam reached its Brazilian customers.

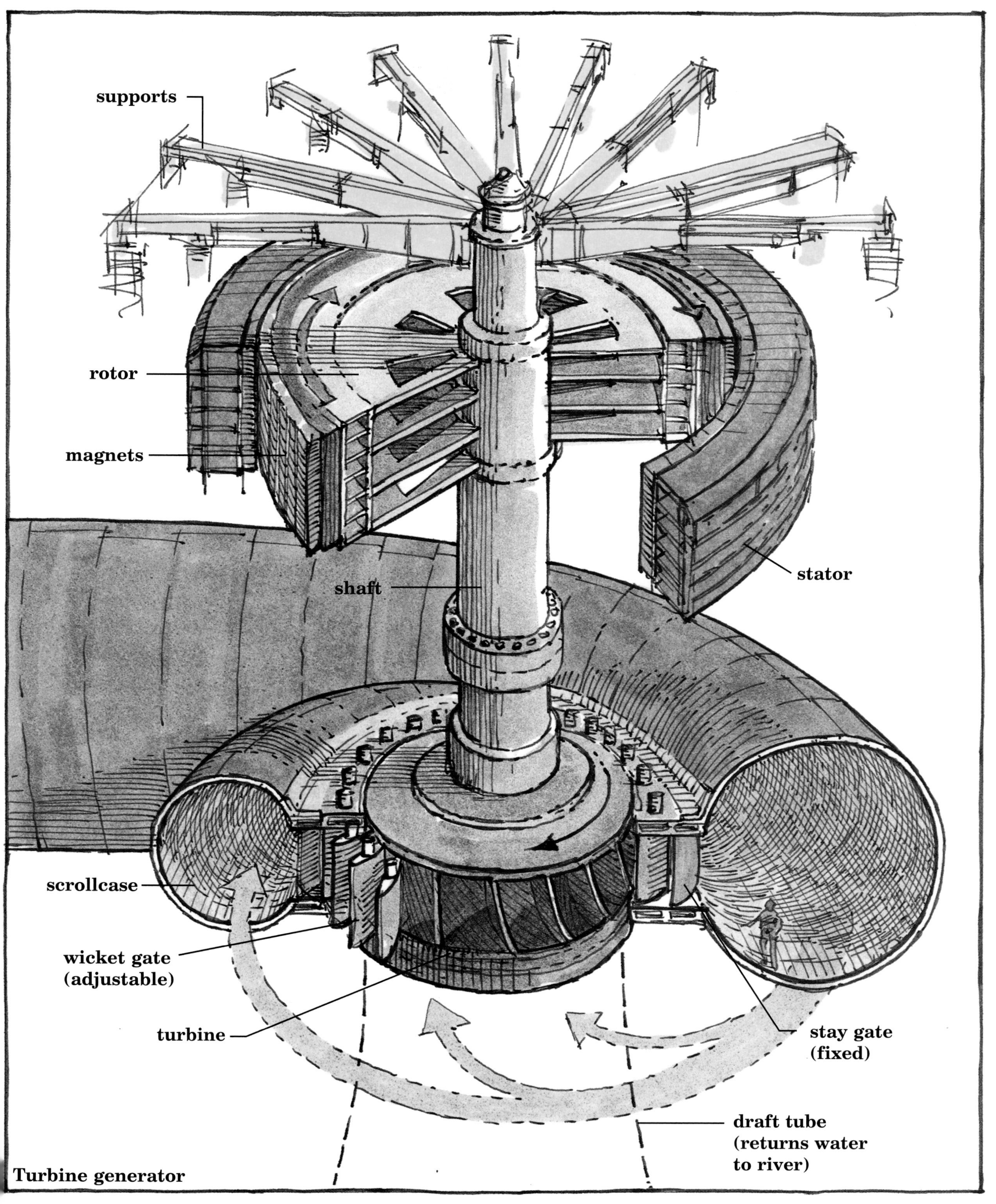

Turbine generator

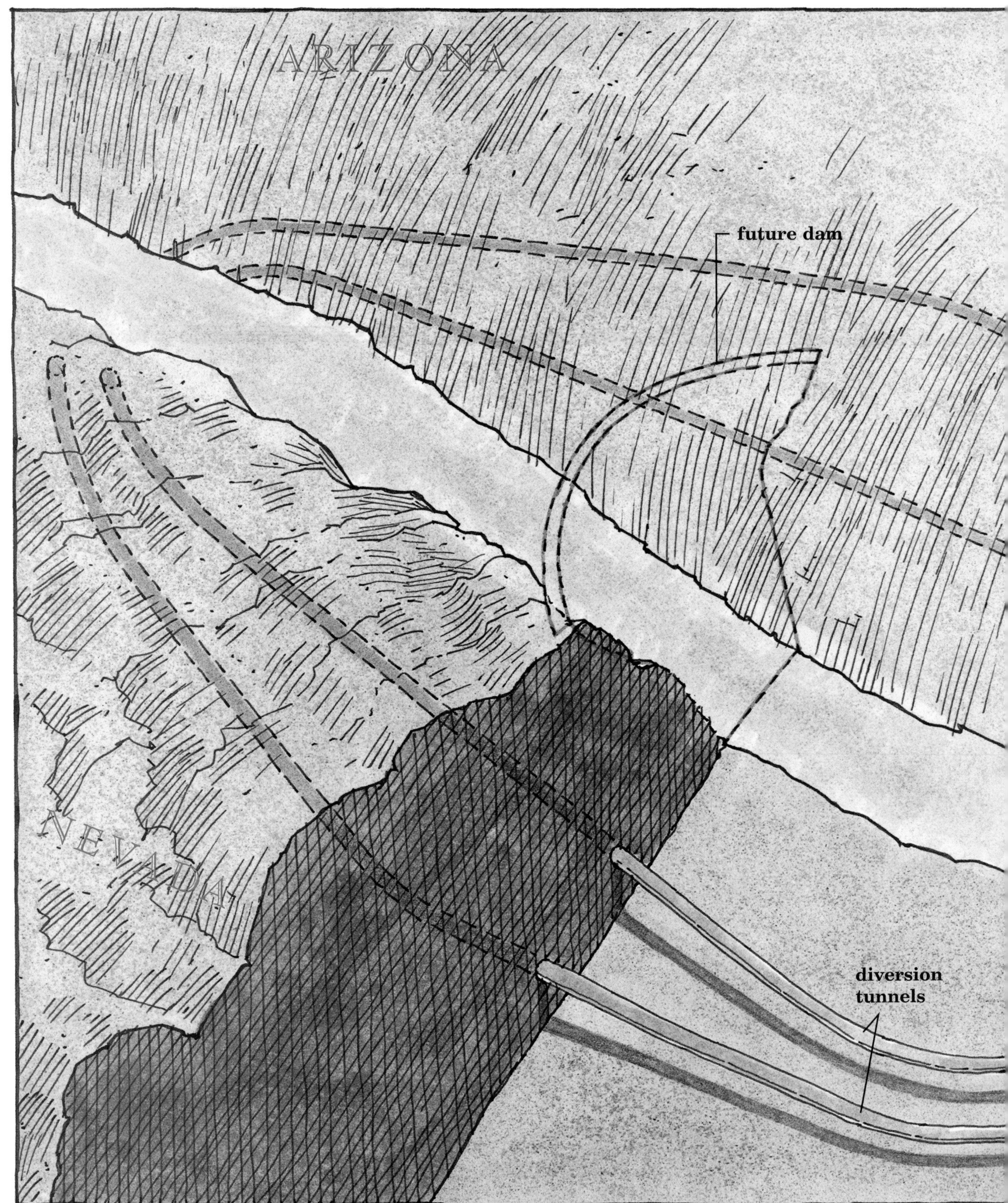
ARIZONA
future dam
NEVADA
diversion
tunnels

Hoover Dam

The Colorado River, between Nevada and Arizona, 1931-1936: A dam across the Colorado was proposed for four reasons. The first was to irrigate the arid Southwest. The second was to control the often unpredictable river and minimize flooding. The third was to collect silt carried by the river, and the fourth was to generate electricity. It wasn't until the growing cities of southern California agreed to buy much of that electricity that the Hoover Dam project finally got under way.

The Bureau of Reclamation had been looking at various dam sites along the Colorado almost since the turn of the century. By 1928 it had whittled the number of possibilities down to two—Boulder Canyon and Black Canyon. Both sites had the capacity for very large reservoirs, but in the end, Black Canyon was chosen. Its walls were higher and the river was narrower there which meant that a smaller dam could do the job. (It is hard to imagine that a solid concrete structure 700 feet high, 1200 feet wide at its crest, and 660 feet thick at its base could be considered smaller than anything, but that's the dam business.)

The river was first diverted around the site through four tunnels. Each was about three quarters of a mile long, 56 feet in diameter, and lined with a three-foot-thick layer of concrete. By the end of 1932, the two tunnels on the Arizona side were ready, and the barriers blocking their portals were blasted away allowing the water to enter.

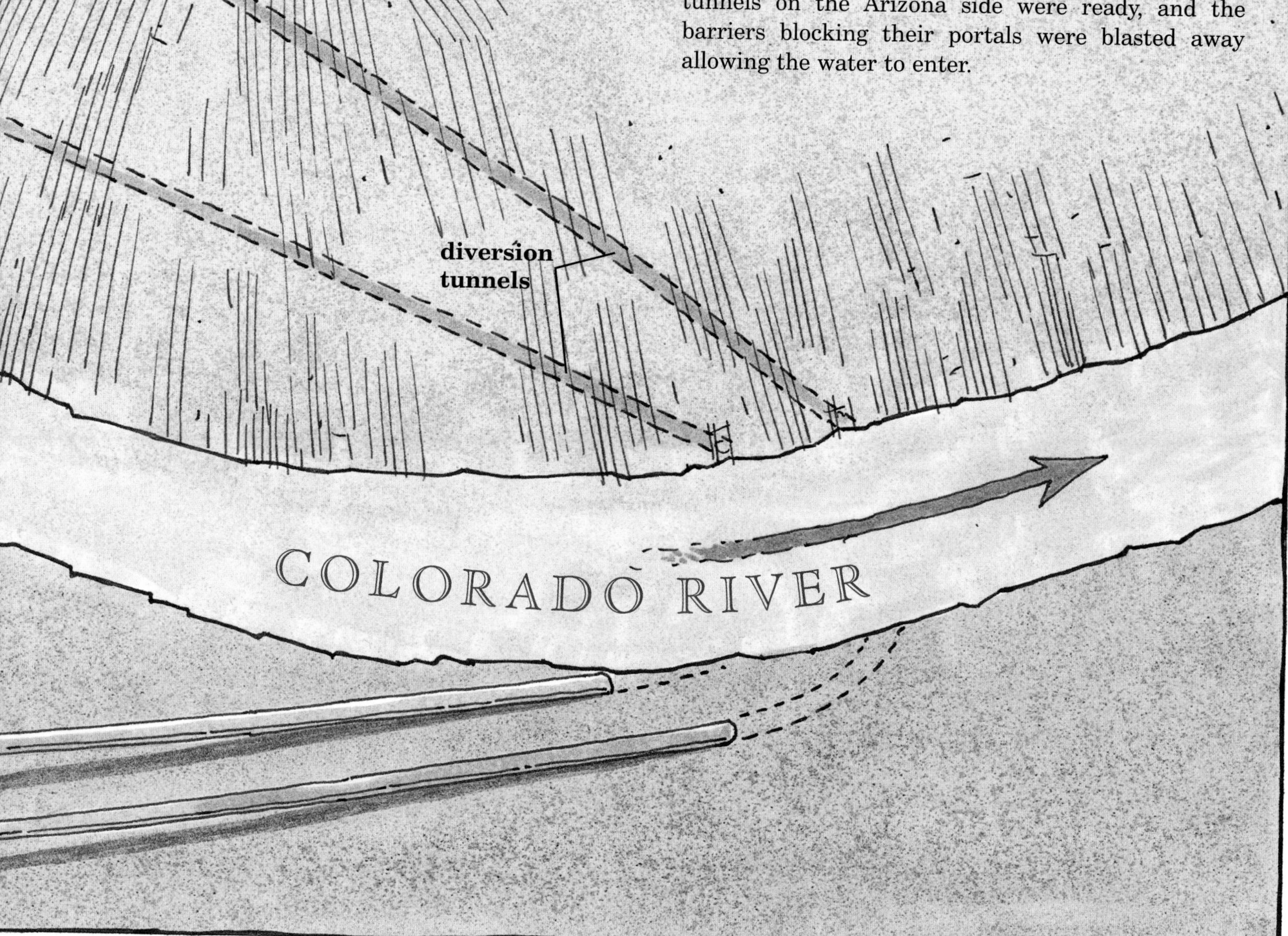

Immediately, workers began building the upstream cofferdam, which would eventually reach a height of 98 feet and be faced with concrete. Within five months, both the upstream and downstream cofferdams were finished and the space between them was pumped dry.

Forty feet of accumulated silt and mud were then excavated to expose and prepare the bedrock. Much of the muck was hoisted from the riverbed by a specially designed cable system that linked both walls of the canyon. The cables were suspended from towers which could be rolled along tracks in order to pick up and deposit their loads wherever needed. At the same time that the riverbed was being prepared, the walls of the canyon were being cleared of all loose and unstable rock. This was one of the most dangerous jobs on the project and was performed by men known as high scalers. Like performers in some kind of demented circus, they hung from the tops of the canyon walls on long cables and operated powerful jackhammers—all without a net.

The Hoover Dam, like the Itá Dam, is basically a gravity dam, but because of its shape and height it had to be built entirely of concrete, making the impervious surface and its supporting structure one and the same. In cross section, Hoover is basically a right triangle with most of its mass near the base, where the water pressure behind it is greatest. The upper half of the dam curves in the upstream direction. This portion also works like an arch, directing some of the force pushing against it into the sturdy canyon walls on either side. A channel was cut into each abutment to support the ends of the arch. Although Hoover is an arched gravity dam, it is highly unlikely, given its enormous weight, that the arch was really necessary. But people seem instinctively to trust arches, and just seeing that curved crest pushing back against the water makes anyone standing on the dam feel secure.

By the middle of 1933, construction of the dam itself began. Because of the enormous amount of concrete that would be needed and to guarantee an uninterrupted supply, two concrete mixing plants were built right at the site. A small railway line was also built along the Nevada canyon wall to transport the concrete from the downstream plant to the hoists of the cable system.

cable system towers and temporary railway line on the Nevada side

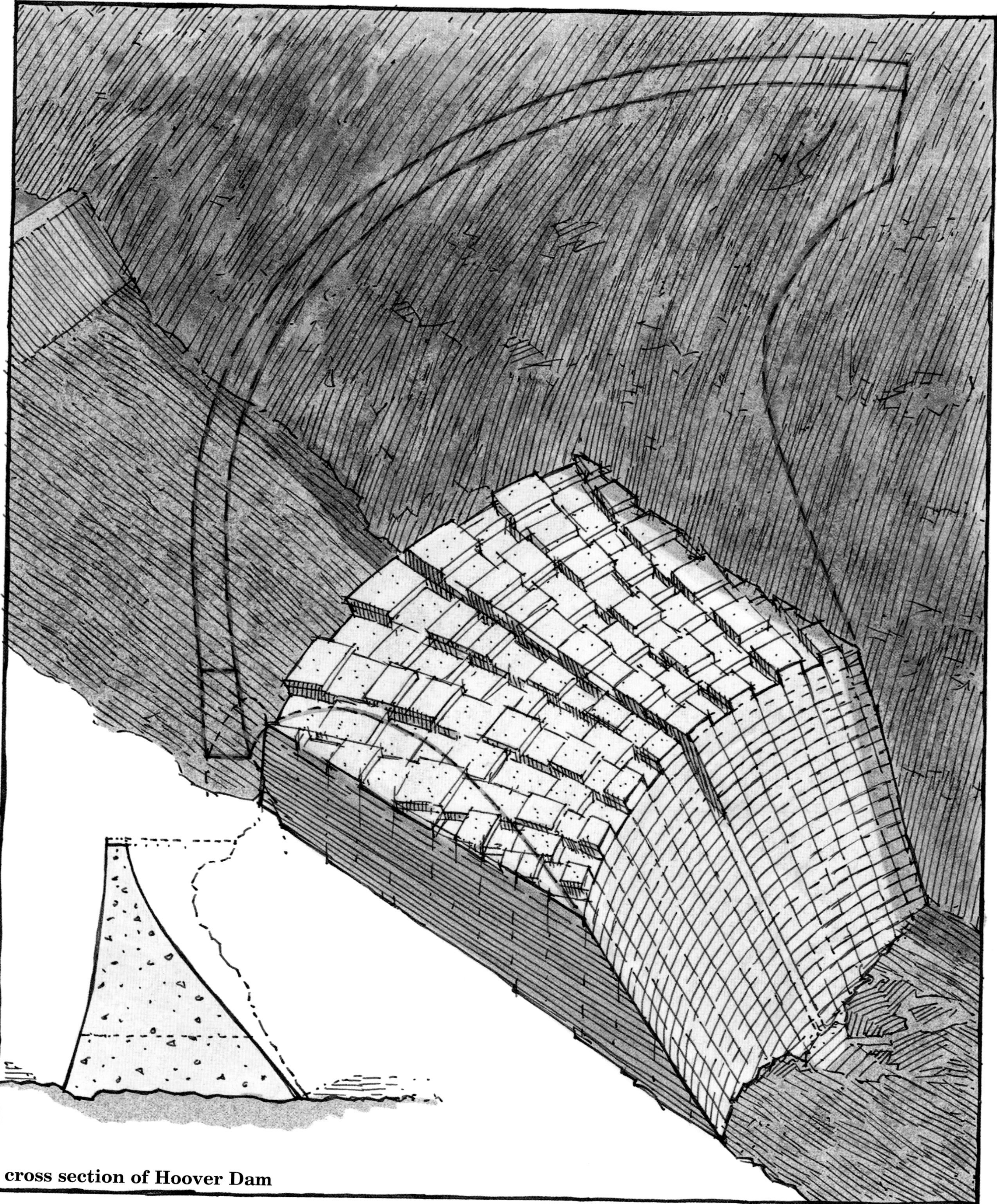
cross section of Hoover Dam

pipes of
cooling system
wooden
forms

The dam is composed of 230 vertical columns, each approximately 25 by 60 feet in area. Each column was built up 5 feet at a time, and all were staggered so that the wooden formwork that held the wet concrete in place could be maneuvered more easily. The sides of the columns were ribbed, either horizontally or vertically, so they would interlock. This ensured that the finished dam would act as a monolithic mass. By limiting the size of each pour or lift, workers could make sure that the concrete spread evenly and completely within the form. A number of vertical shafts and horizontal galleries were built into the dam as it rose. These would be used for inspection and drainage, and also for grouting as the concrete dried.

Concrete is a mixture of crushed stone, sand, and cement. When water is added, the cement undergoes a chemical reaction called hydration. This results in the formation of crystals that tie themselves and the rest of the ingredients together. But hydration also produces considerable heat. If this heat dissipates too quickly or unevenly, cracks can form. Cracks in a dam are not a particularly welcome addition, and the builders make every effort to eliminate them.

The amount of heat that would be generated by and then trapped inside the enormous amount of concrete created two problems for the Hoover Dam engineers. The first was the danger of cracking because of uneven cooling as the heat slowly worked its way out. The second was the fact that the joints between the columns could not be grouted until the entire structure had cooled down. Without help, the Hoover Dam still wouldn't be cool enough for another 50 years.

To accelerate and control the cooling process, the engineers embedded pipes in each lift and pumped ice-cold water through them. The rate of cooling was constantly monitored and if necessary adjusted by changing the temperature of the water. An 8-foot-wide slot was left open at the center line of the dam to house the large pipes that carried water between the structure and the refrigeration plant. The slot was filled in a series of 50-foot lifts as the dam grew around it. The entire structure was successfully cooled within twenty months of the last pouring early in 1935.

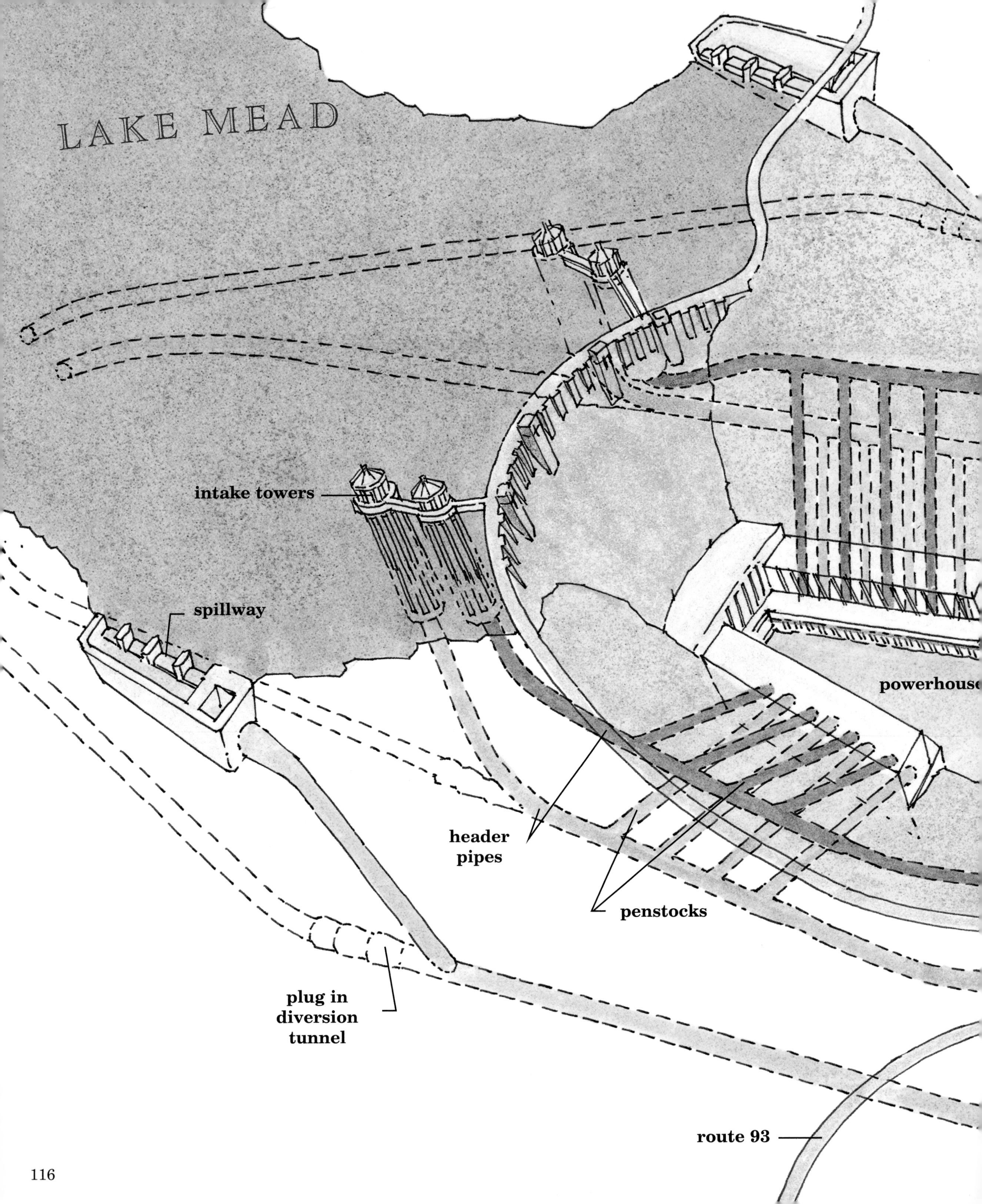
LAKE MEAD
intake towers
spillway
powerhouse
header pipes
penstocks
plug in diversion tunnel
route 93

Immediately upstream of the dam are four thirty-four-story-high intake towers. Water from the reservoir passes through them into the steel header pipes and penstocks, which lead either to the twin powerhouses at the foot of the dam or to two outlet buildings. The intake towers stand on ledges cut into the canyon walls over 300 feet above the riverbed and can be closed by enormous cylindrical gates. The space between the base of the towers and the riverbed provides the pocket needed to collect the silt. The primary function of the outlet buildings is to discharge the water needed for irrigation downstream.

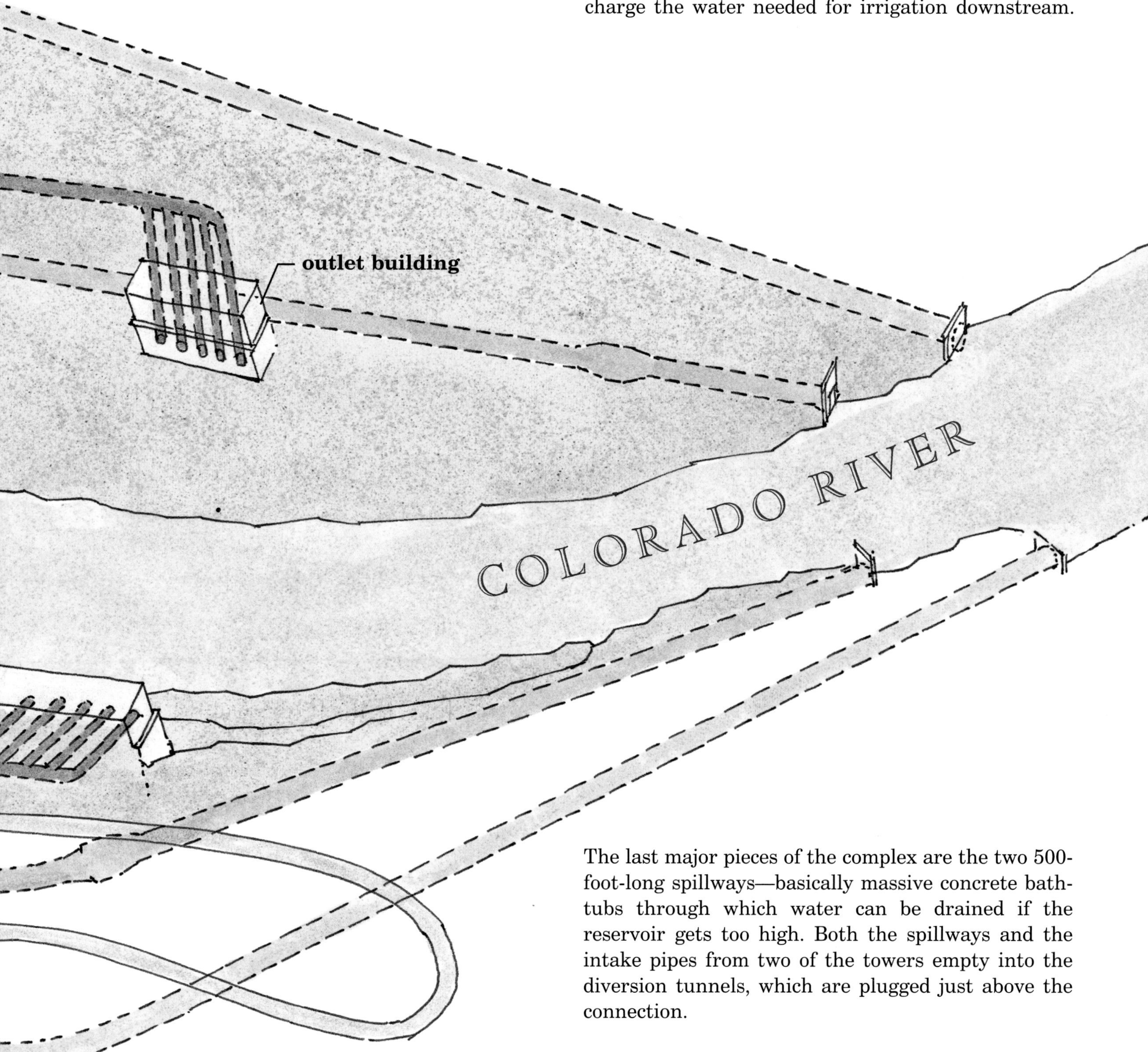

The last major pieces of the complex are the two 500-foot-long spillways—basically massive concrete bathtubs through which water can be drained if the reservoir gets too high. Both the spillways and the intake pipes from two of the towers empty into the diversion tunnels, which are plugged just above the connection.

Aswan High Dam

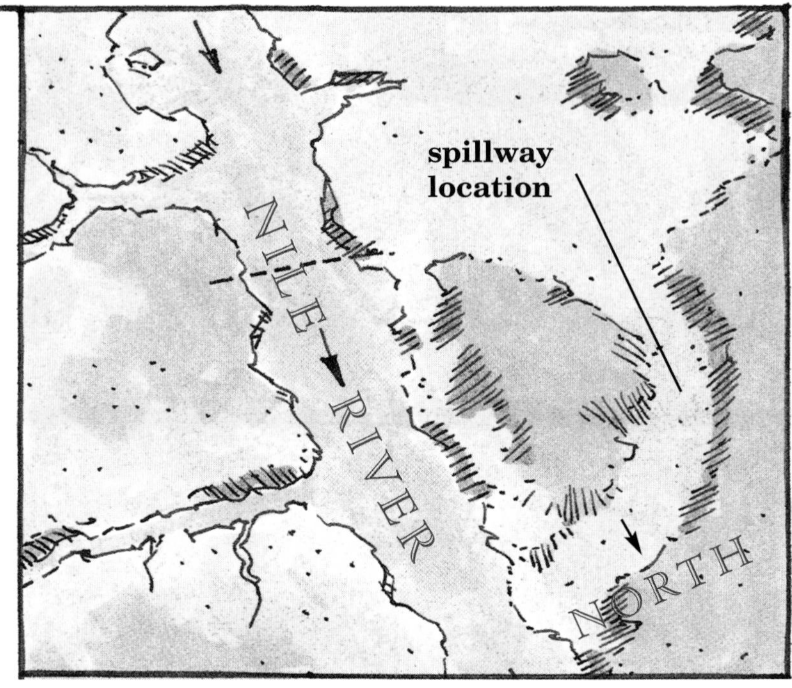

The Nile River, Egypt, 1960-1971: Twenty-four years after the completion of the Hoover Dam, dam engineers were once again eyeing a river for retraining—this one a lot wider and a lot more famous than the Colorado. For more than four thousand years, the Nile had provided the farmers along its banks with rich, nutrient-filled silt to replenish the fields and water to irrigate them, and in so doing had helped create one of the world's great civilizations. But the Nile, like the Colorado, could also be unpredictable. Some years it was too generous, flooding villages and destroying crops. Other years it could be incredibly stingy, causing widespread famine.

By the end of the nineteenth century, when Egypt's population was steadily growing, particularly in and around Cairo, the country's almost complete dependence on the whims of the Nile had become intolerable. In an attempt to address the situation, British engineers designed and oversaw the construction of the first dam across the river, an impressive masonry structure at a place called Aswan. In the years that followed, its height was increased a couple of times, but the dam still wasn't big enough to satisfy demands.

Starting in the 1950s, engineers made studies and eventually drew up plans for a much larger structure, which, to distinguish it from its predecessor, was to be called the Aswan High Dam. It would provide much more electrical power than the old dam both for industry and to improve Egypt's standard of living. By impounding a huge reservoir, it would also greatly reduce flooding and guarantee a constant water supply, making farming a year-round rather than seasonal operation. Egypt, although still dependent on the Nile, would at last be the master of its own fate.

Once again cofferdams were built above and below the site and the river was diverted around them. This time, however, while the current between the cofferdams was eliminated, the water was not. Because the Nile is wide and its abutments are low, the engineers settled on an embankment dam. Its impervious barrier would be a solid clay core held in place by layers of rockfill and sand.

cross section of Aswan High Dam

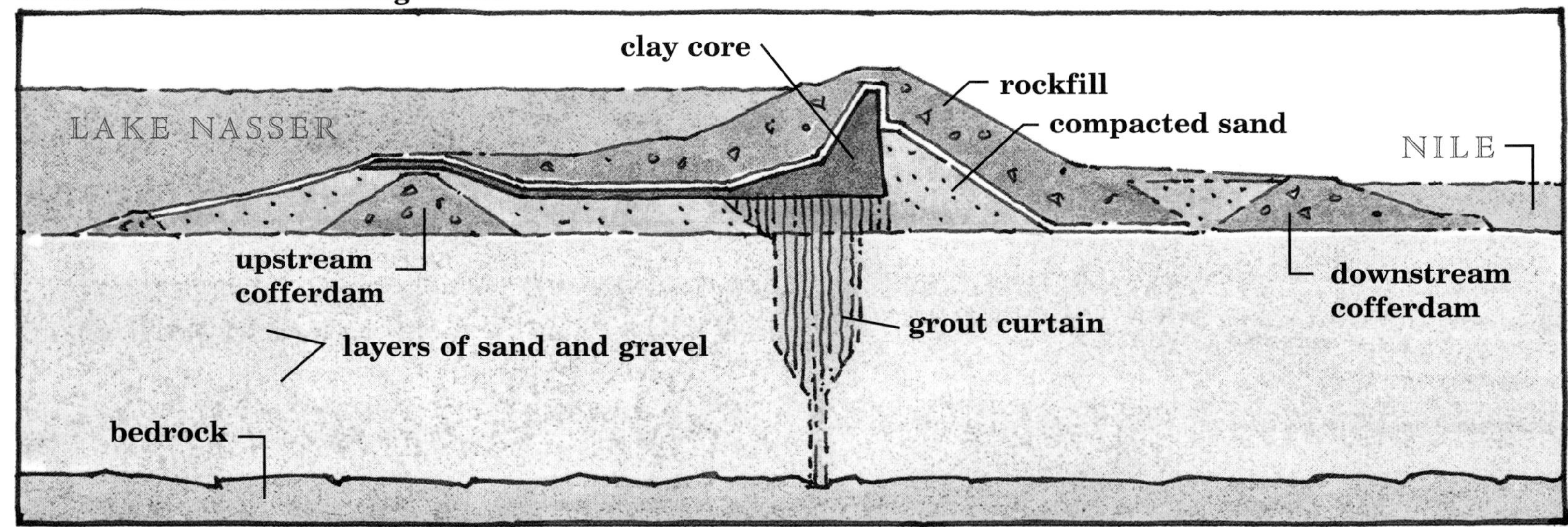

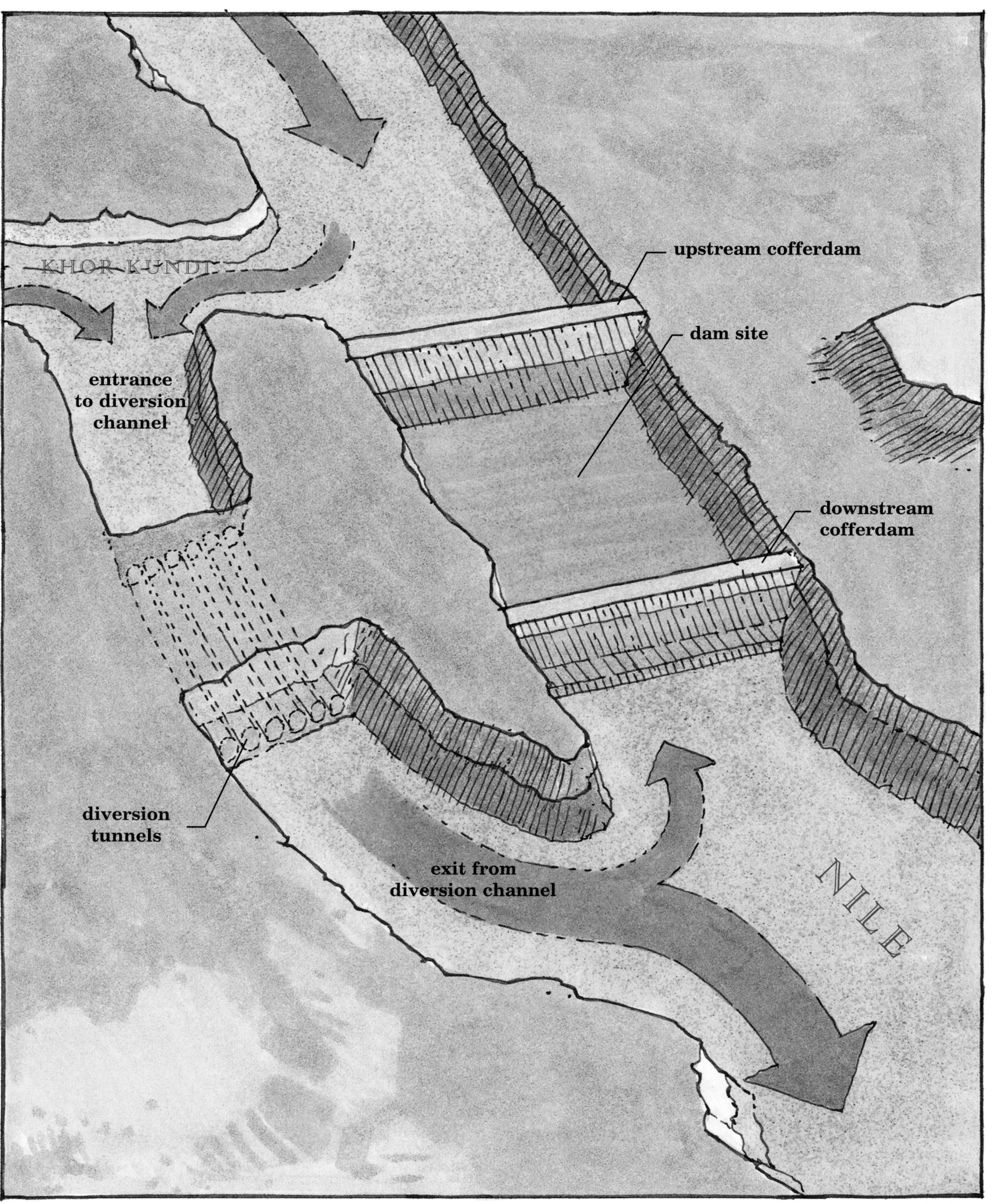

KHOR KUNDI
upstream cofferdam
dam site
entrance
to diversion
channel
downstream
cofferdam
diversion
tunnels
exit from
diversion channel
NILE

creating the grout curtain
rockfill
clay core

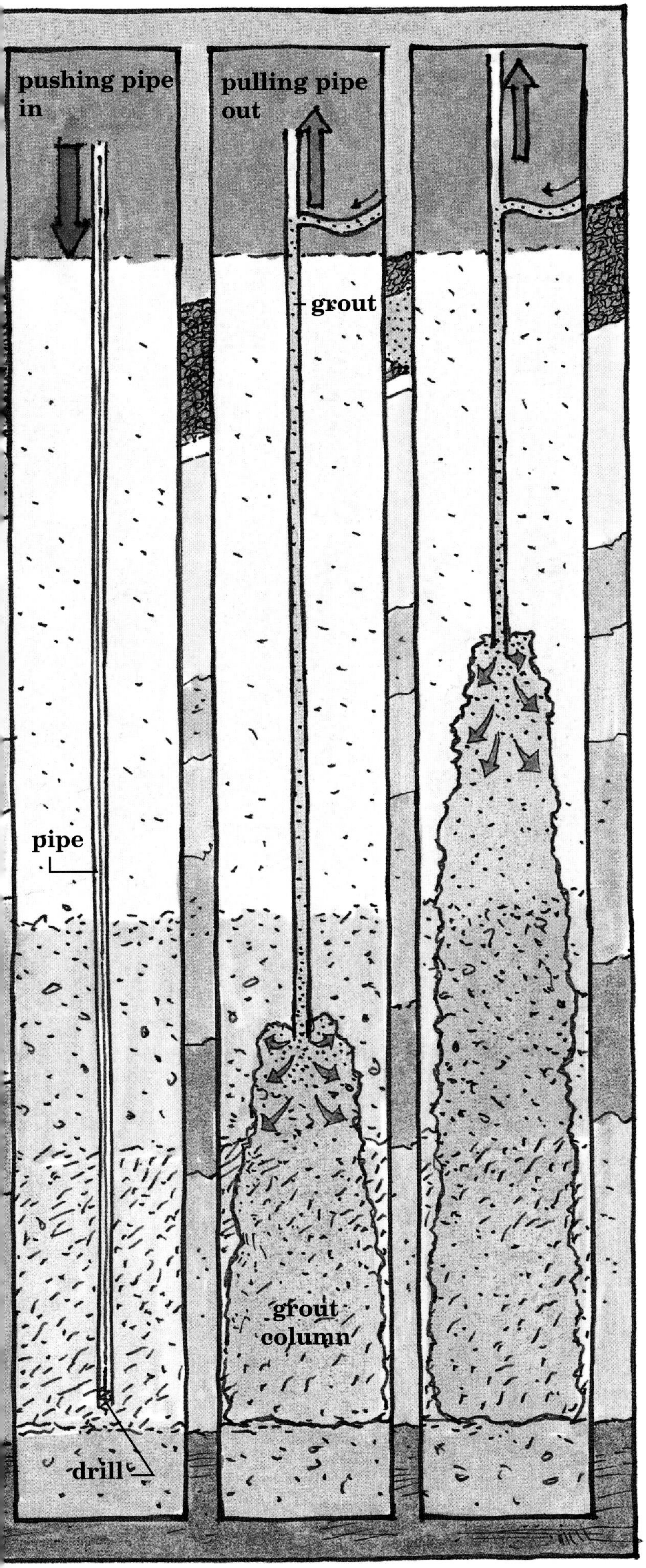

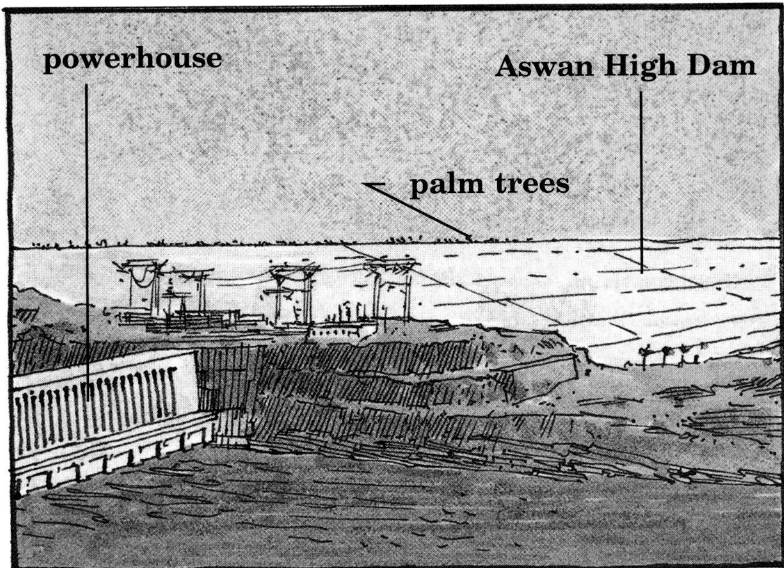

Although the Nile does not have the high abutments of the Colorado, it does have a canyon. Unfortunately, though, this one goes down rather than up, descending roughly 600 feet below the river, and is filled with sand and gravel. While the clay core would keep water from passing through and around the dam and an emergency spillway would prevent overtopping, the engineers needed to provide some way to keep the water from escaping under the dam, threatening it from below.

They solved the problem by building an underwater barrier called a grout curtain—basically, a continuous wall of interconnected columns. A predetermined pattern of holes was drilled across the river. The deepest ones went down the full 600 feet to bedrock. As each hole was drilled, a three-inch-in-diameter pipe was inserted into it. Once a hole reached the desired depth, the pipe was pulled out as grout was forced in. As soon as the grout passed through the end of the pipe, it quickly expanded into the surrounding material. When this dense mixture of grouted sand and gravel set, it created a permanent column almost five feet in diameter. As rows of columns were drilled and grouted, the workers eventually built a continuous waterproof barrier.

By the time the various layers of compacted material were in place above the grout curtain, both cofferdams had been incorporated into a structure that now stretched more than half a mile up and down the riverbed at a height of 400 feet. The Aswan High Dam took 30,000 workers almost ten years to complete and claimed 500 lives in the process.

ITAIPU DAM

The Paraná River between Brazil and Paraguay, 1975-1991: In April of 1974, the governments of Brazil and Paraguay signed a treaty that set in motion the building of the world's largest hydroelectric dam. The agreement followed a four-year study during which various locations and combinations of dams were considered. In the end, the countries decided to build a single large dam at a place called Itaipu. With its eighteen enormous turbines, the finished dam would provide Paraguay with more electricity than it could use and satisfy about 30 percent of Brazil's current needs.

The structure, almost five miles long, is a combination of both masonry and embankment dams. The first piece of the dam to be built is a solid gravity concrete structure through which the entire river was initially diverted. Next to it, extending across the river, is a hollow gravity concrete dam. Since the hollow part doesn't have to be as heavy, the sloping faces are supported by a row of parallel walls separated by enormous cavities. Extending from both ends of this structure are two concrete buttress dams. These have only one face, and it is supported by a row of exposed sloping walls. Embankment dams with clay cores and outer shells of rockfill or earth complete the structure. In fact, the only significant dam type not represented at Itaipu is the arched dam, but two of them were used originally to block the diversion channel while the solid gravity structure was being built. As soon as it was finished, these dams were blown up, and the course of the river was diverted over the rubble.

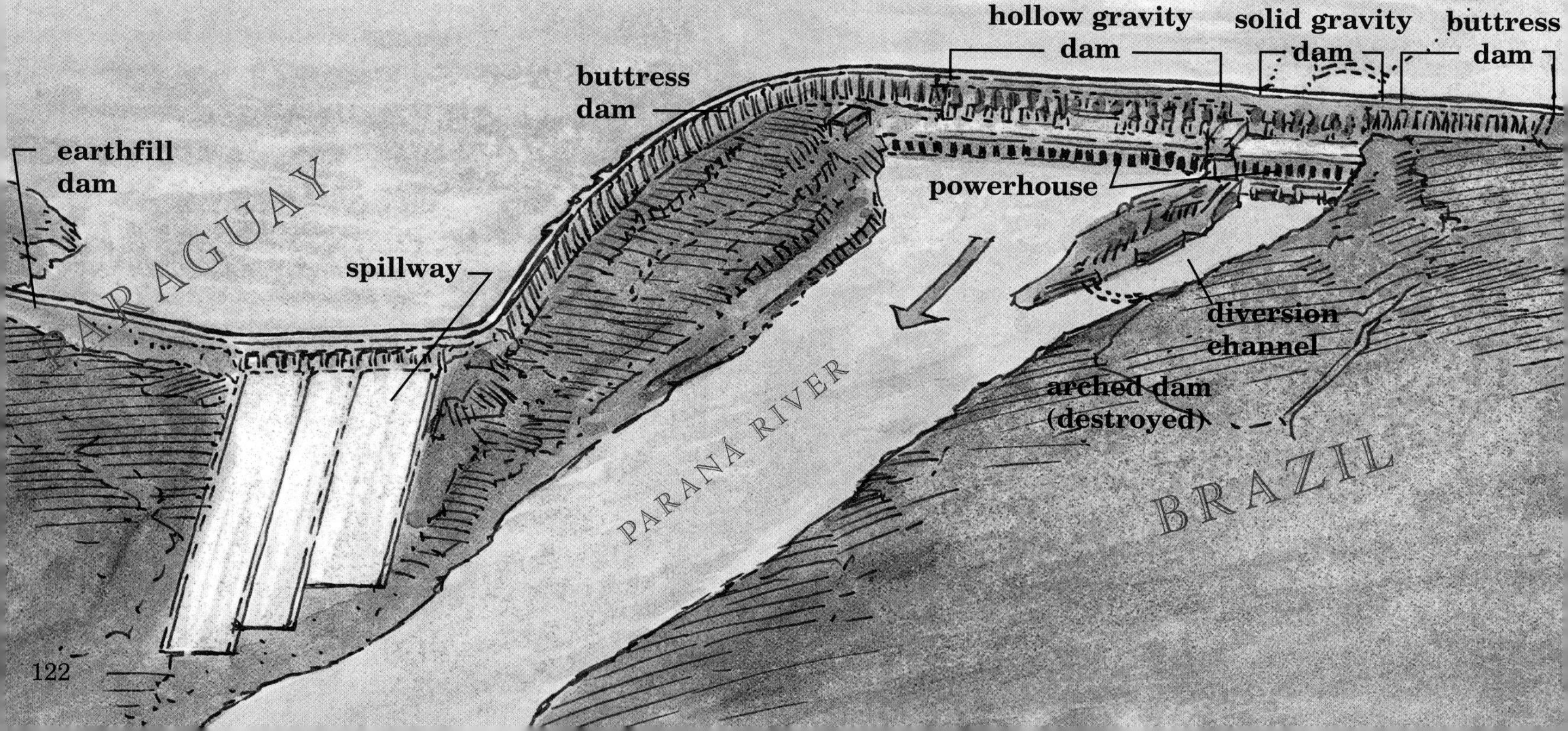

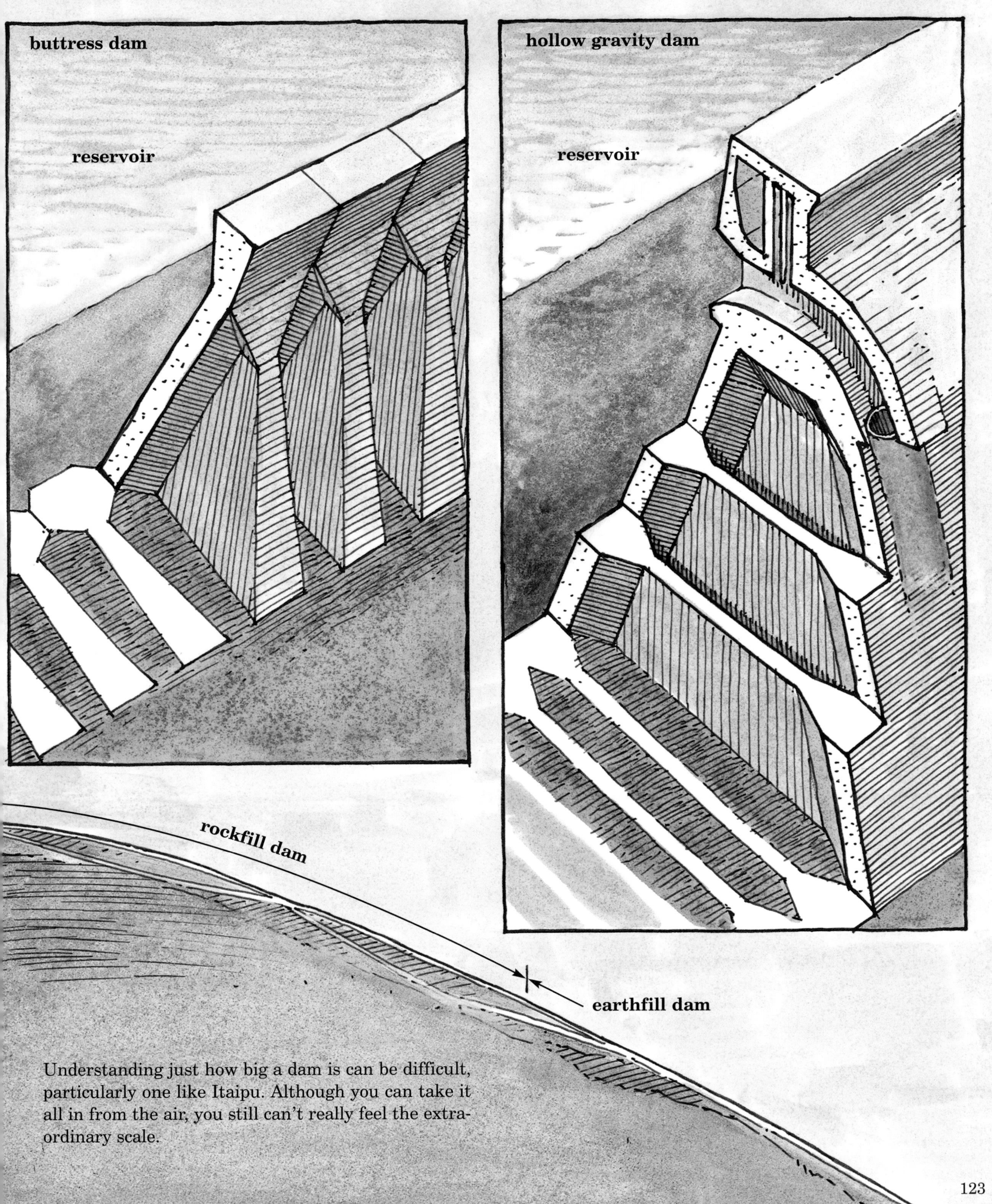

Understanding just how big a dam is can be difficult, particularly one like Itaipu. Although you can take it all in from the air, you still can't really feel the extraordinary scale.

So here is the view from what is called the upstream road of some of the 34-foot-in-diameter penstocks as they emerge below the crest of the dam and begin their descent to the turbines. That's an average-sized compact car parked up against the second penstock.

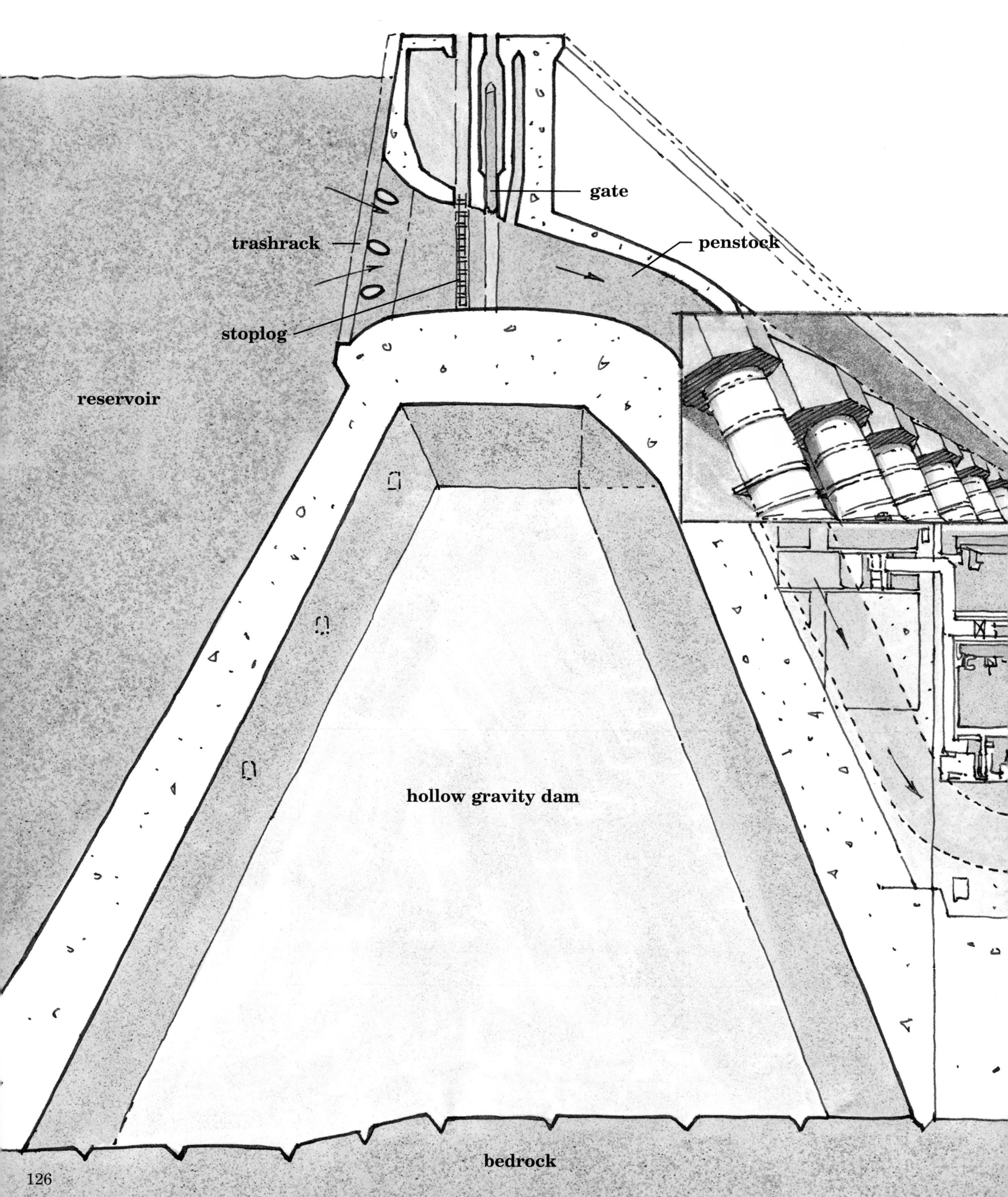
gate
trashrack
penstock
stoplog
reservoir
hollow gravity dam
bedrock

Now, when we take the previous image and insert it into its rightful place in a cross-section of the main dam and powerhouse, perhaps it is a little easier to comprehend the reality of building big.

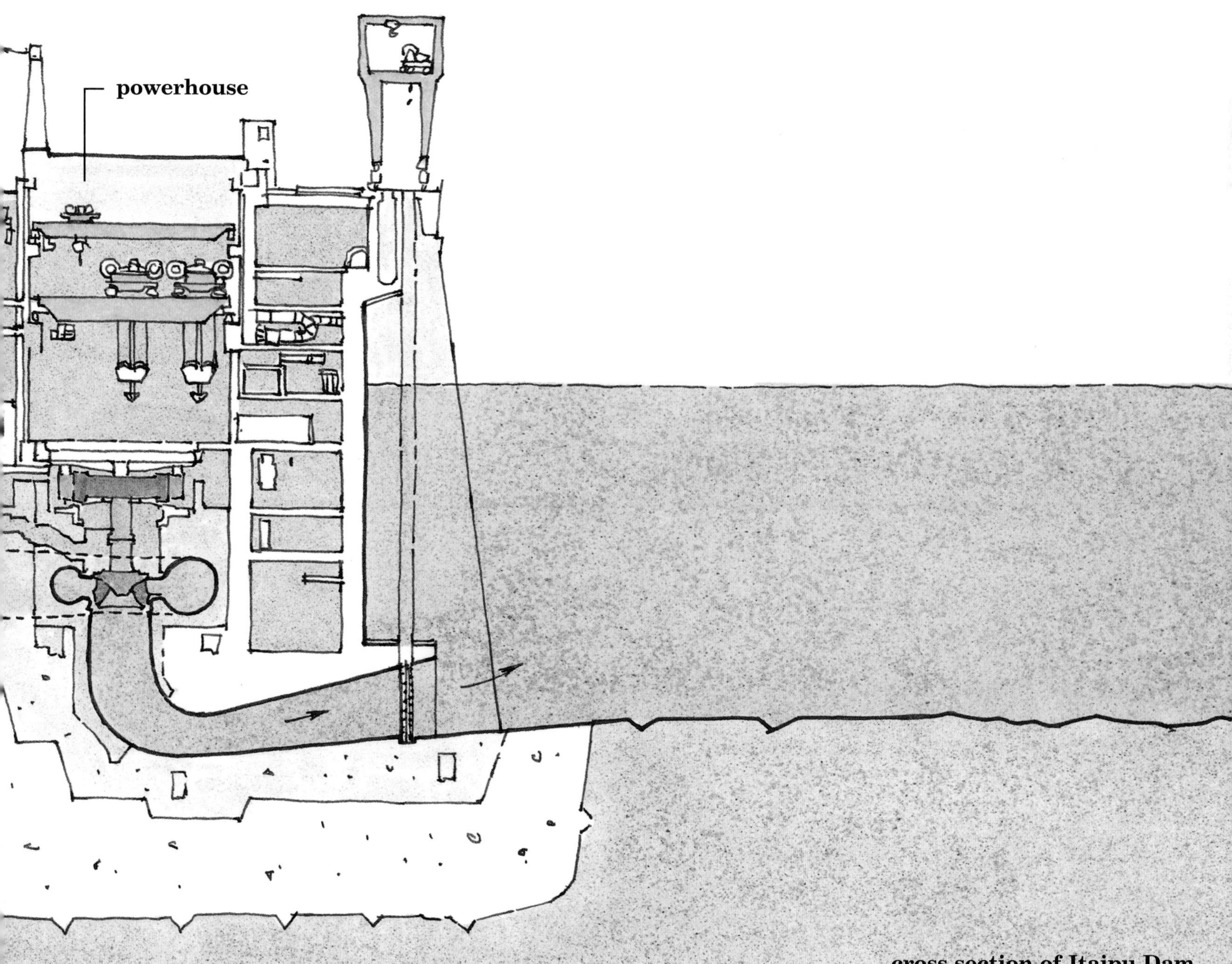

cross section of Itaipu Dam

The world's great domes have the ability to move us, both literally and figuratively. On the one hand, we find ourselves spinning around just to take them in. On the other, they elevate our spirits by drawing our gaze heavenward or by appearing to float weightlessly. But the builders of these remarkable structures would be the first to remind us that defying gravity isn't something to undertake lightly. Domes are, after all, roofs. No matter how big or impressive they may be, they are up there for a reason, and up there they must stay.

The earliest and purest domes were single masonry vaults, and their interior shape was more or less reflected in their exterior lines. Over the centuries, however, domes began to serve as beacons, and as such they were built higher and higher above the ground. In time, the proportions of the interior shape were no longer satisfying from below, so architects solved the problem by building a second dome within the first. Eventually, as many as three domes or domelike shapes were stacked one above the other. As the complexity of these structures continued to grow, so did their importance as symbols of religious, cultural, and government institutions.

During the twentieth century, as technology developed and materials grew stronger, enormous domes were built to cover sports arenas and meeting halls. By the end of the century, the word "dome" had become so synonymous with large gathering places that it was used to refer to a number of vast spaces covered with curved roofs of various kinds. "Domes" such as the Georgia Dome, the Millennium Dome, and the SkyDome are certainly considerable feats of engineering, but they are just too big to inspire. They may impress us, even overwhelm us, but transport us beyond ourselves, like the Pantheon or the dome of St. Peter's in Rome? I think not.

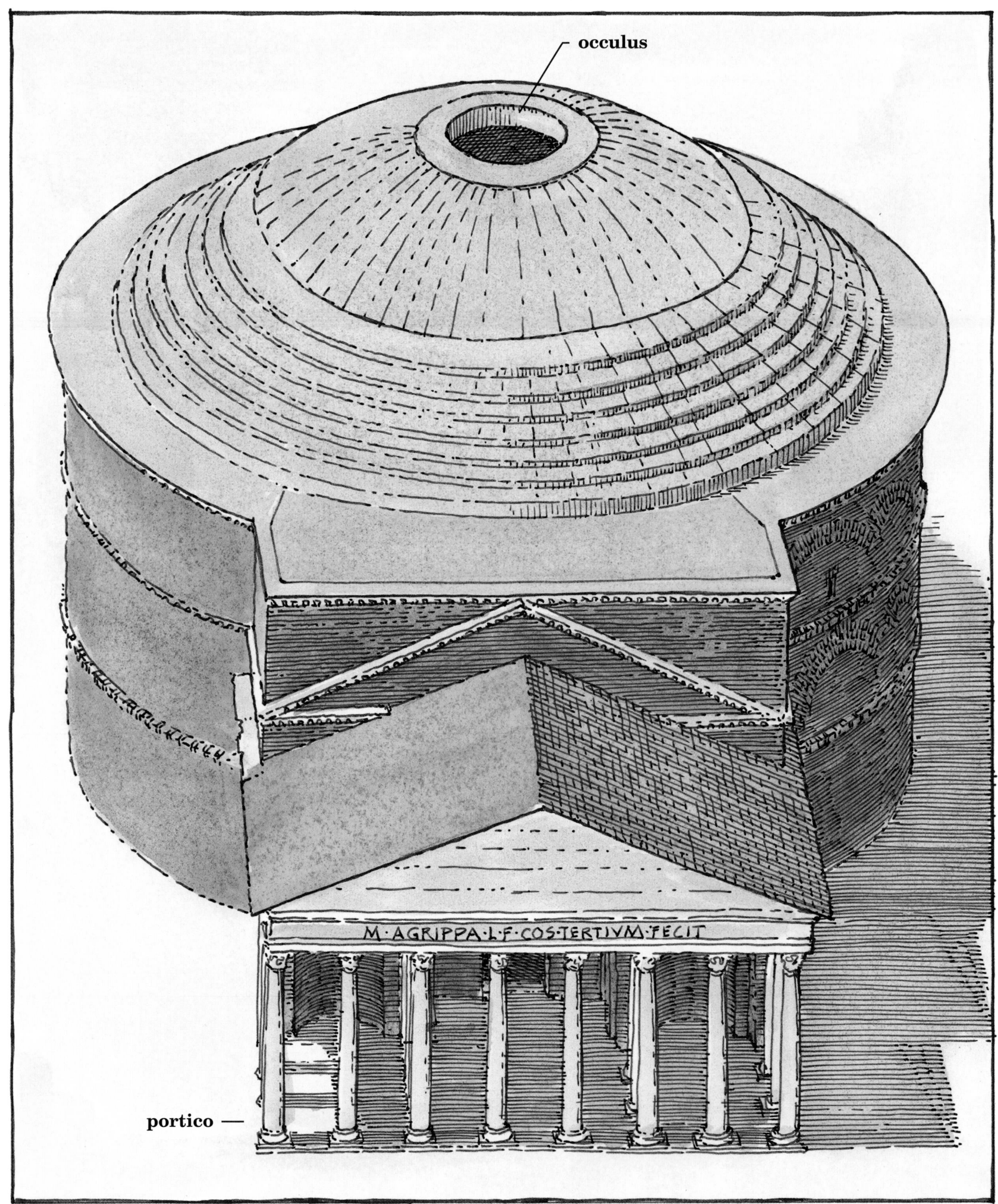
occulus
M·AGRIPPA·L·F·COS·TERTIVM·FECIT
portico

The Pantheon

Rome, Italy, 118–125: Upon his ascension to the throne, Hadrian, the thirteenth ruler of the Roman Empire, inaugurated something of a public relations campaign. As was traditional, he forgave certain debts and provided elaborate and generally gruesome entertainments at the Colosseum, but he also wanted to create something for which he would be remembered. As a gifted amateur architect, Hadrian understood how much power a building could have—especially a big building. Knowing also that even an emperor can use a few allies beyond his earthly realm, he worked with his architects to design a pantheon—a temple to all the gods—to replace Agrippa's old pantheon, which was now in a state of considerable disrepair.

The building they designed had two main parts. The first was the kind of entryway people would expect in front of a temple—a raised portico, complete with columns and a triangular pediment. The second, however, was to be something of a surprise—a vast circular room covered entirely by a single dome. This enclosed but unobstructed space beneath a manmade concrete sky would be linked directly to the heavens by a 27-foot-in-diameter eye, or occulus, right at the top. It was a brilliant design. Not only would a very large audience be able to see Hadrian conducting official business, but he would do it beneath the gaze and therefore with the implied support of the gods themselves.

Regardless of whether domes are hemispherical, egg-shaped, or saucer like, all of them obey certain fundamental principles. To understand how a dome works look at the one below which is covered with a grid. The vertical lines are called meridians. The horizontal lines are called parallels. At the top of the dome, as in an arch, the meridians lean in toward the center, forcing the parallels into compression. At the bottom, the meridians push outward, stretching the parallels and putting them into tension. At a particular point between the two sets of parallels is an area that is neither in compression nor in tension. This is represented by the dotted line. If a dome is to stand, the tension and compression forces must both be safely handled.

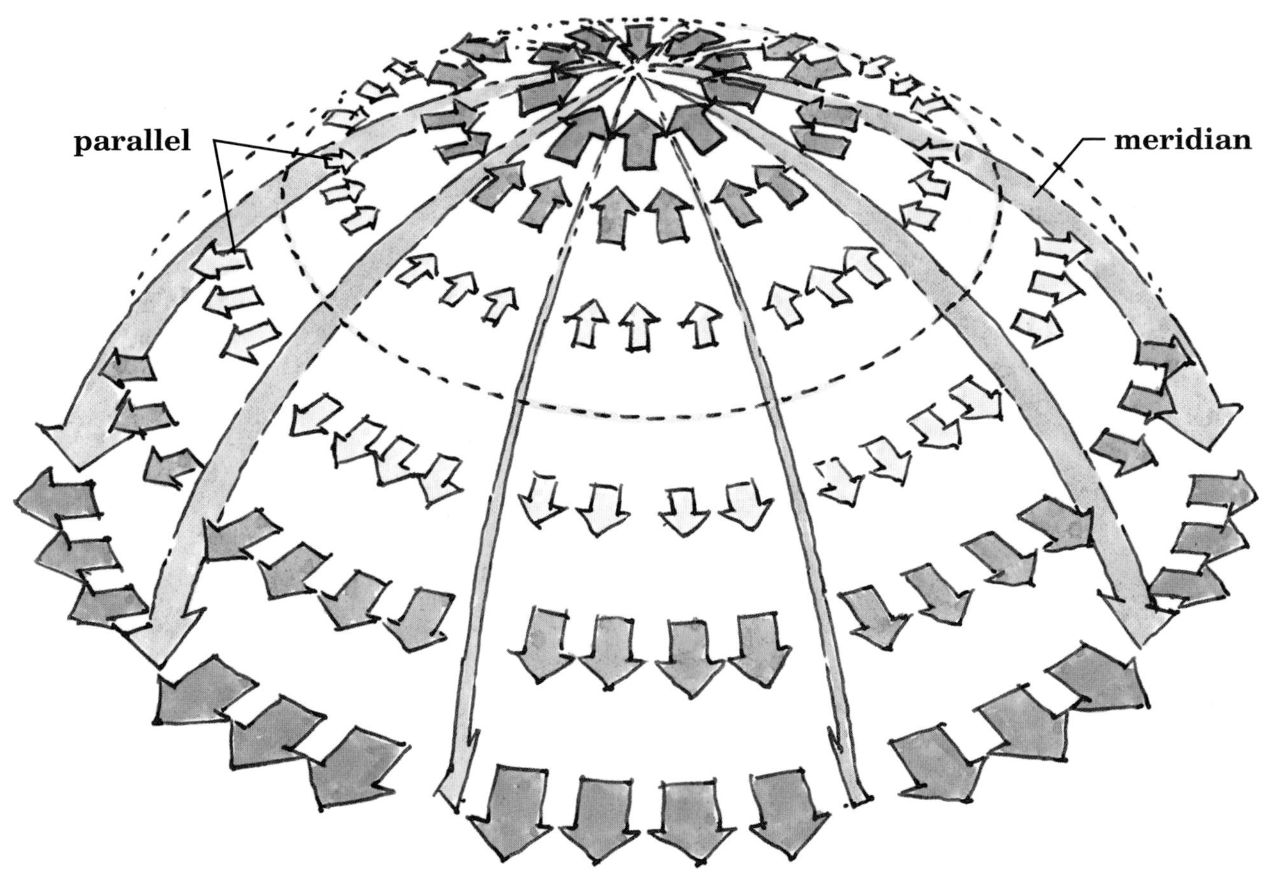

relieving
arches

Though the Pantheon was to be the largest concrete dome in the world, Roman builders were not inexperienced with either the shape or the material. Its form was a logical extension of the vault, which in turn had been a logical extension of the arch. The brick-faced concrete cylinder upon which the dome would rest was actually a ring of massive piers, linked by relatively thin walls and large buried arches. These arches were designed to carry the tremendous weight above them and channel it around windows, passages, and niches to the piers and foundations below.

Although the Pantheon was to be made almost entirely of concrete, wood played a very important role in its construction. Workers filled the space that would eventually be enclosed by the cylinder with a huge timber scaffold. This manmade forest provided platforms for the wall builders and supported the hemispherical form over which the concrete dome would be poured. Five horizontal rings of trapezoidal indentations called coffers were to be cast into the interior surface of the dome. These would not only add to its visual complexity, they would also reduce its weight. These shapes first had to be built as projections on the surface of the form.

Concrete is created by mixing aggregate, such as stone and sand, with cement and water. To further reduce the weight of their dome, the builders of the Pantheon used different types of aggregate in its construction. For instance, the material at the base of the dome is a heavy stone called basalt, while at the top it is a much lighter volcanic stone called pumice.

Around the base of the dome, several layers of concrete were added to counteract the tension forces. Called step rings, they provided the additional weight required to redirect the horizontal forces down into the walls below. The upper portion of the dome is approximately 5 feet thick, but with the addition of the seven step rings, the dome widens to more than 16 feet.

Perhaps the most remarkable feature of the dome is the occulus. Just where the compressive forces are the greatest, the architects chose not to place any material at all. Instead, the forces are resisted by a $4\frac{1}{2}$-foot-thick ring of bricks, called a compression ring. Like the cross section of a round tunnel, this ring withstands the compressive force from every angle, allowing the enclosed space to remain open. Instead of trains or cars, however, this opening admits light, and occasionally even a little rain.

The shape inside the dome is a perfect hemisphere with a diameter of 143 feet. This matches exactly the distance from the occulus to the center of the floor below. Add to this geometric perfection the daily movement of a circle of sunlight around the interior, as well as the nighttime view of the stars, and the Pantheon goes well beyond being just a temple to the gods. It is a representation of the heavens themselves, firmly fixed at the center of Hadrian's empire.

cross section of the Pantheon

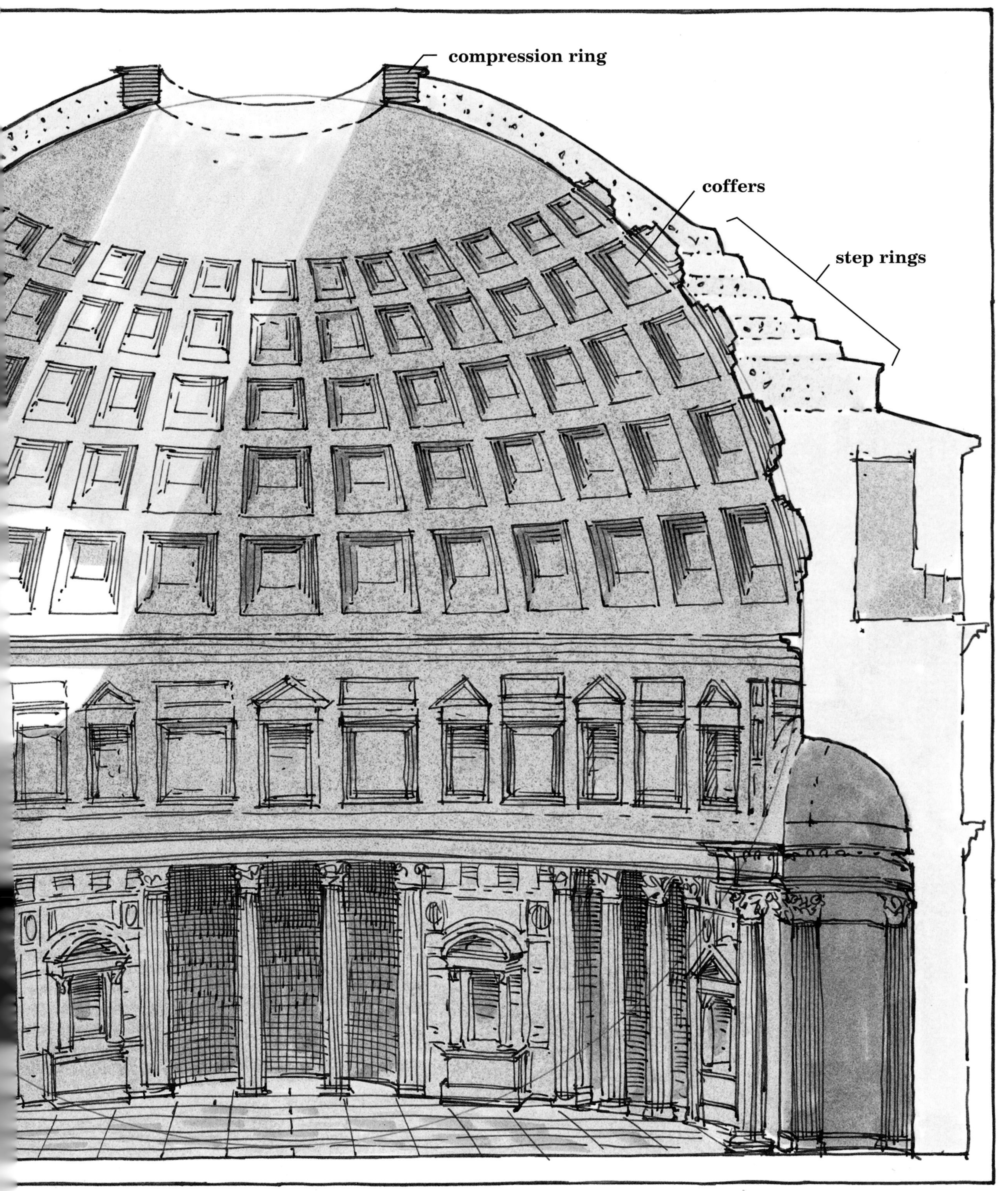
compression ring
coffers
step rings

Hagia Sophia

Constantinople (Istanbul, Turkey), 532—537: Once again the leader of the now Christian empire was in need of a little public relations help. Having put down riots that left 35,000 people dead, the emperor Justinian, following Hadrian's example, turned his attention to the creation of a great domed building—in this case a church, to be called Hagia Sophia, or Divine Wisdom.

The architects, Anthemius of Tralles and Isidorus of Miletus, began by dividing a 200-foot square into three parallel rectangles. This created a wide central space for processions and two narrower aisles for viewing. In the middle of the wide rectangle they marked off a square a little over 100 feet along each side. Above this square they located the dome.

Supporting a round dome above a square created challenges that Hadrian and his architects had been spared with their cylindrical wall. Anthemius and Isidorus first had four massive limestone piers built, one at each corner of the central square. From the tops of these piers they built four enormous brick arches, one over each side of the square. Above each pier, the space between the arches was then filled in with masonry, creating a slightly spherical triangular shape called a pendentive. When finished, the tops of the four pendentives formed a continuous circular base for the dome.

Like the rest of the building, the dome was built of flat bricks, 2 inches thick and approximately 25 inches square. They were laid with very thick mortar joints over a wooden centering.

To admit more light into the space, the architects set windows into the base of their dome. This meant that they could not use continuous step rings, like those of the Pantheon, to counteract the horizontal thrust. Instead, they buttressed the brickwork between the windows with segments of step rings and strengthened the dome with shallow ribs. Without the benefit of continuous step rings, the remaining tension forces from the dome, and from the four arches supporting it, had to be restrained in some other way.

Along the main axis of the church, the architects placed two half domes, one against each of the main arches. These in turn were buttressed with a sequence of smaller semi-domes and vaults. Working together, this system of masonry shapes carried all the principal forces down through the piers and walls to the foundations. To resist the forces pushing perpendicular to the main axis, the architects built four massive rectangular blocks right up against the main piers. They then filled the spaces below the two main arches with a second smaller arch and a combination of walls pierced with windows and colonnades.

a simplified look at Hagia Sophia

Just over twenty years after Hagia Sophia was completed, earthquakes brought down part of the dome and one of the semi-domes. When Justinian ordered the church rebuilt, his new architect recognized that one of the main problems had been the

cross section along main axis

tremendous tension forces created by the shallowness of the original dome. He reduced those forces by using a more hemispherical shape, and that is what we see today.

Sehzade Mosque

Istanbul, Turkey, 1544–1548: When Constantinople was invaded around 1450, Hagia Sophia suddenly went from being a Christian church to being an Islamic mosque. And a hundred years later, when the great Ottoman engineer and architect Sinan undertook the design of several new imperial mosques, he undoubtedly looked to Justinian's one-thousand-year-old creation for inspiration—not only for its size and forms but for its durability.

By this time, the general plan of a mosque was well established. It included an exterior courtyard, a high central prayer chamber, and one or more minarets. With the plan more or less a given, Sinan concentrated on enclosing the main interior space with efficiency and elegance. At Hagia Sophia, all the forces from the great dome and its supporting arches were held in check by two different systems, one along each axis. At Sehzade, the same system of smaller domes and semi-domes was used along both axes, creating a symmetrical structure. The external buttress piers were also smaller and more discreetly integrated into the building.

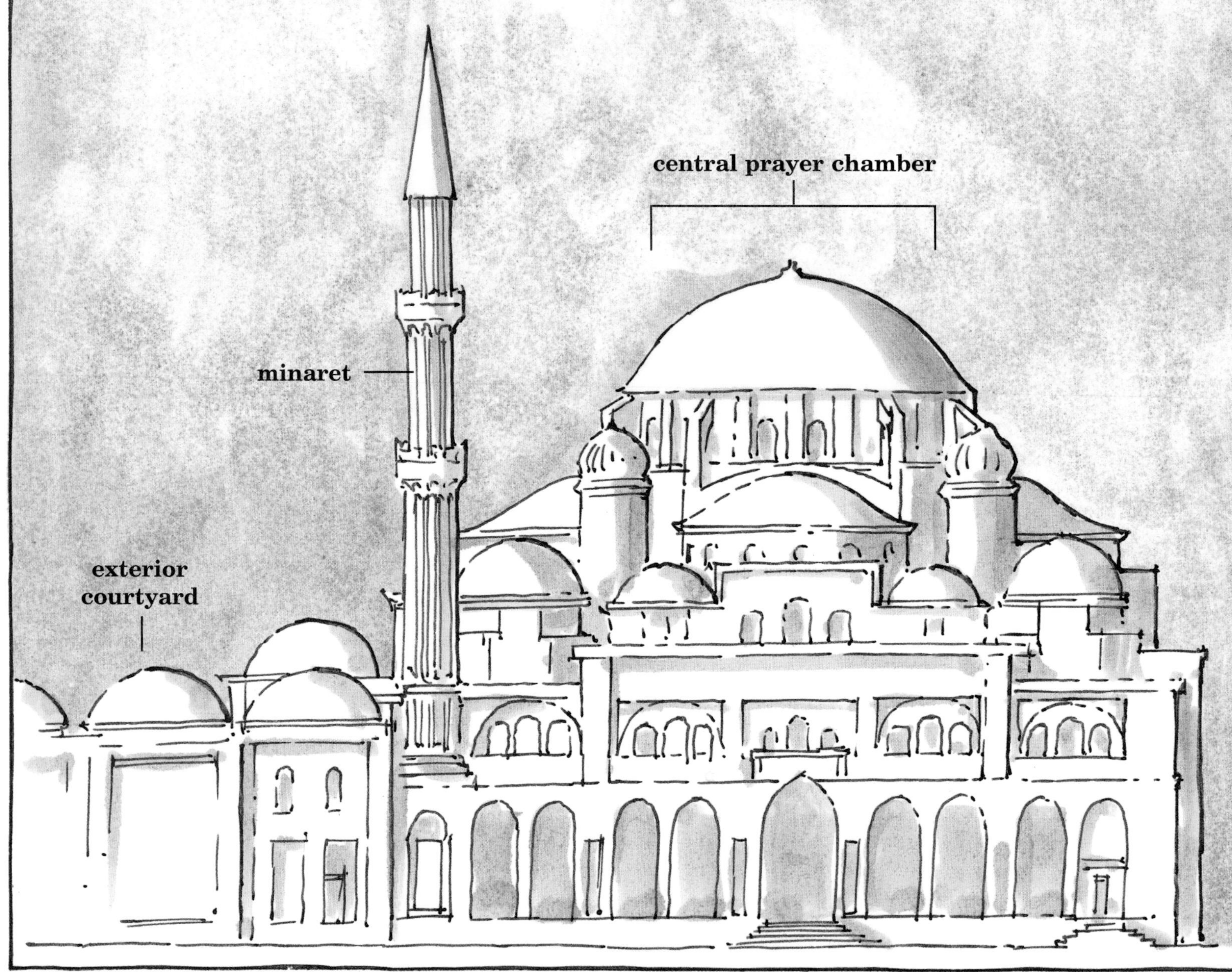

ST. PETER'S BASILICA

Vatican City, Italy, 1585-1590: Since 1506, just about every Italian architect and artist of note had been called into service to help in the building of the great basilica of St. Peter's. Having already contributed his Sistine Chapel ceiling, Michelangelo returned to Rome in 1546 to take over as chief architect. He was now seventy-two. The massive central piers of the basilica's crossing were already standing and the exterior wall was under construction. His main hope was to unify the entire structure beneath a monumental dome.

Unlike the dome of the Sehzade, which seems to grow naturally out of the structure beneath it, the dome of St. Peter's appears to be a very independent structure for which the building below is merely a starting point. It is divided into several distinct layers. The lowest one—the base—rests on the main pendentives. The next two layers, the first of which is ringed with double columns, make up the drum. Springing from the drum is the cupola, which in turn supports the lantern.

Perhaps in admiration of Hadrian's dome, Michelangelo designed his to be 6 feet less in diameter. But what he gave up in breadth, he more than made up for in height. The base alone began 10 feet above the height of the entire Pantheon, and the complete distance from floor to lantern top was approximately 450 feet.

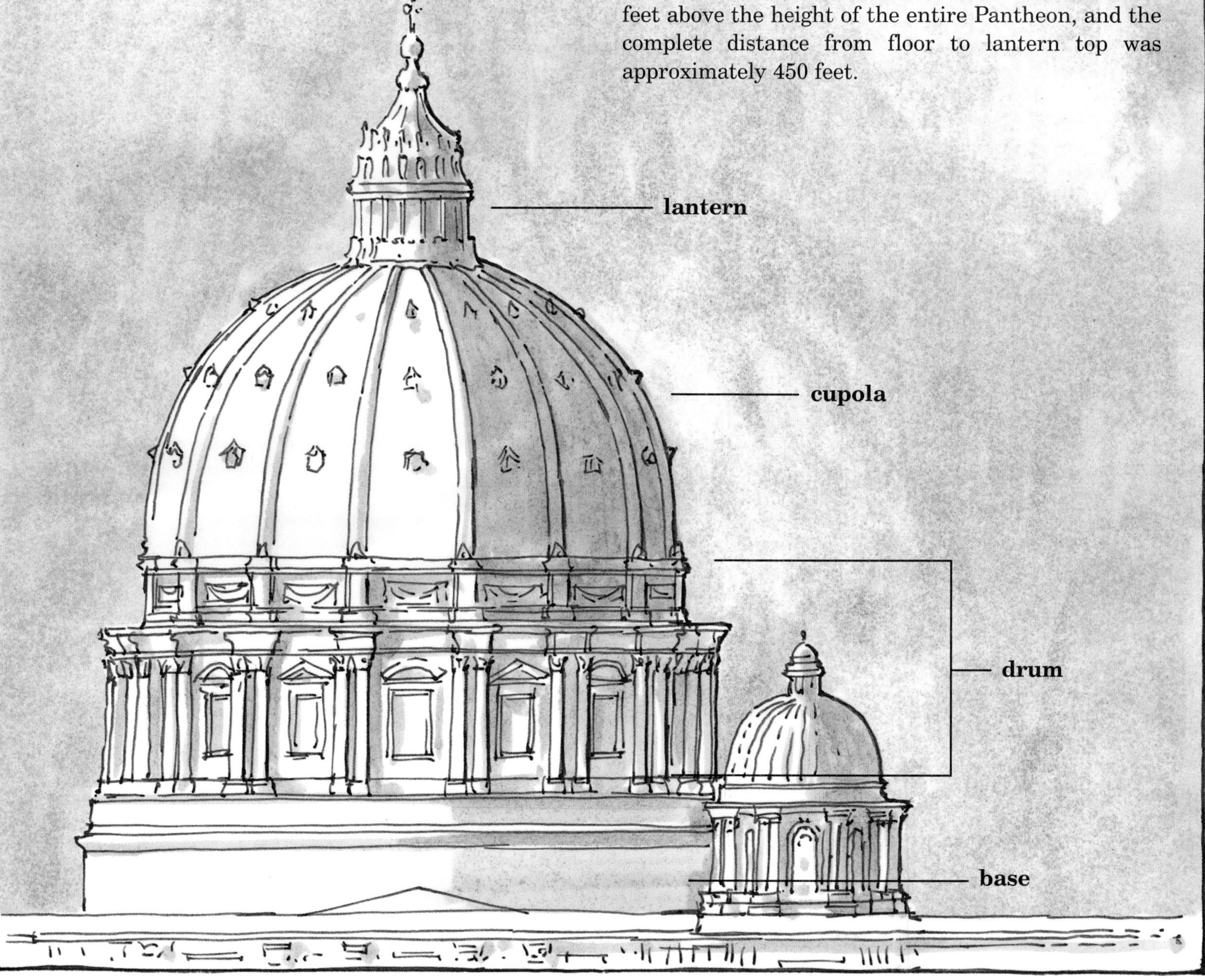

Also influencing Michelangelo was a remarkable dome built only a century and a half earlier by fellow Florentine, Filippo Brunelleschi. To cover the large crossing of that city's cathedral, Brunelleschi had constructed an octagonal dome with a thick inner shell and a thin protective outer shell. Both shells were made of brick and were tied together by a stone grid of vertical ribs and horizontal bands. This brilliant design not only reduced the weight of the structure, it made it stronger and easier to maintain. So famous was Brunelleschi's solution that the entire building is referred to simply as the Duomo.

Both shells of the Duomo follow the same elliptical contour. Only the outer dome of Michelangelo's cupola is elliptical. The inner dome is hemispherical—more like the Pantheon. This difference may be due to Giacomo della Porta, the architect who actually oversaw construction some twenty years after Michelangelo's death. Although the elliptical shape of Brunelleschi's dome created less outward thrust than the hemispherical shape of St. Peter's, both were ringed by a number of iron chains for additional stability.

One of the most extraordinary things about the Duomo is that it was built without scaffolding. Brunelleschi accomplished this by tying the masonry together in such a way that it would act as a compression ring even though the uppermost course of bricks was still unfinished. However, the more independent inner and outer domes of St. Peter's cupola were probably built using some kind of temporary centering. This would most likely have been supported from the drum rather than the floor. In any event, Michelangelo didn't bother himself with such details, relying instead on the ingenuity of the craftsmen who would construct his masterpiece.

cross section of Brunelleschi's dome in Florence

cross section of St. Peter's with outline of suggested centering

Les Invalides & St. Paul's

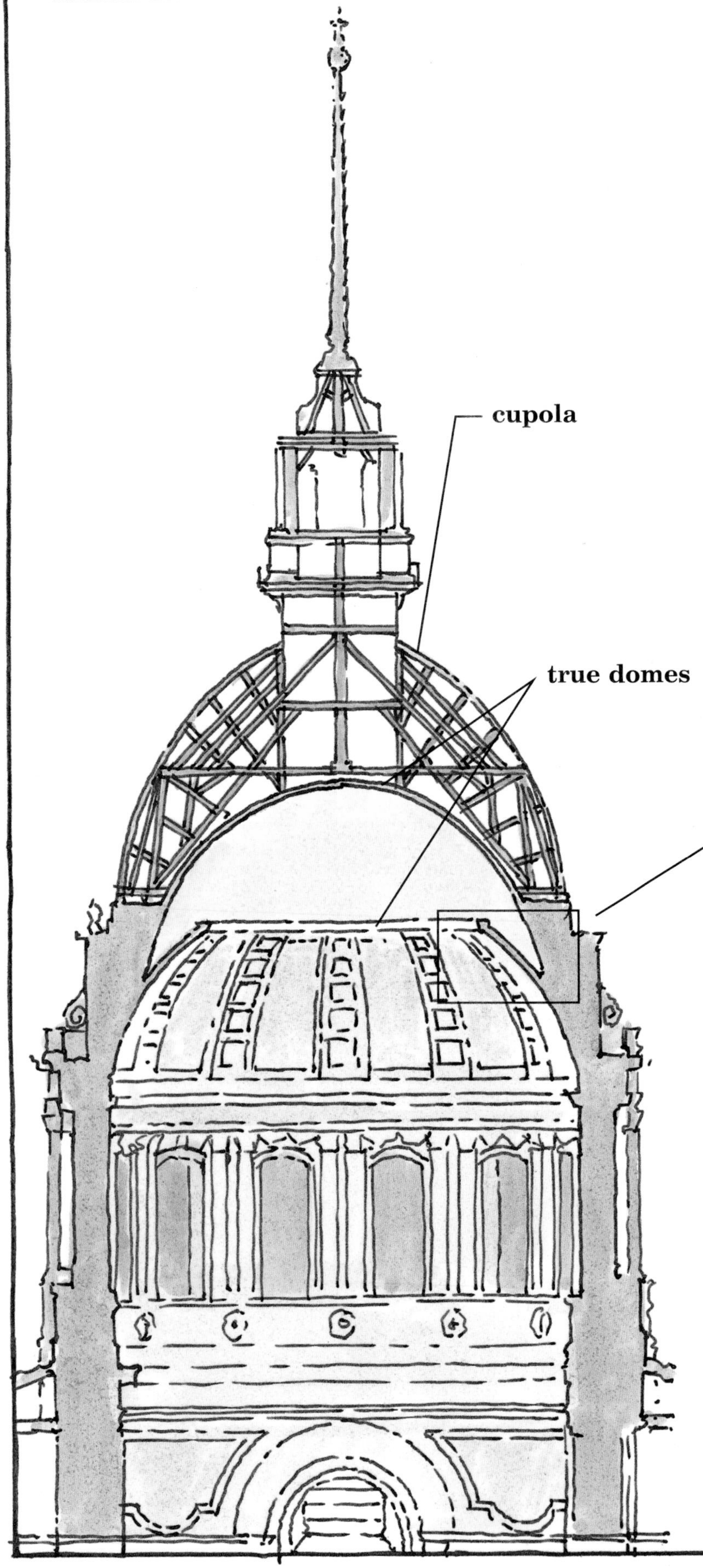

cupola

true domes

Paris, France, 1680–1691: While the dome of St. Peter's would remain the basic model for years to come, the continuing desire to build domes high led to a variety of inventive modifications on the inside. When J. H. Mansart built his dome over the church of Les Invalides, he decided on a three-part structure. The lowest one, a true dome with an occulus and a hint of coffering, is made of stone. Above it rises a second stone dome, the great weight of which is seemingly reduced, if not eliminated, by an assortment of painted clouds and deities. Mansart increased the amount of stone around the bases of both domes to counteract any outward thrust. Rising from and protecting the upper dome is the cupola—in this case a dome-shaped timber roof sheathed in lead.

London, England, 1675–1710: In Sir Christopher Wren's remarkable construction over the crossing of St. Paul's Cathedral, an inner dome of brick, once again complete with occulus, stands some 214 feet above the ground. Between it and the outer cupola is a towering brick cone. Wren obviously chose this very strong shape primarily to hold up the massive stone lantern, which is estimated to weigh more than 800 tons. The cone is ringed with four iron chains to resist any tension created by its own weight as well as that of the lantern pushing down on it. The combined weight of the cone and lantern, along with that of the upper portion of the drum, counteracts the horizontal forces around the sides of the real dome.

cupola
brick cone
brick dome

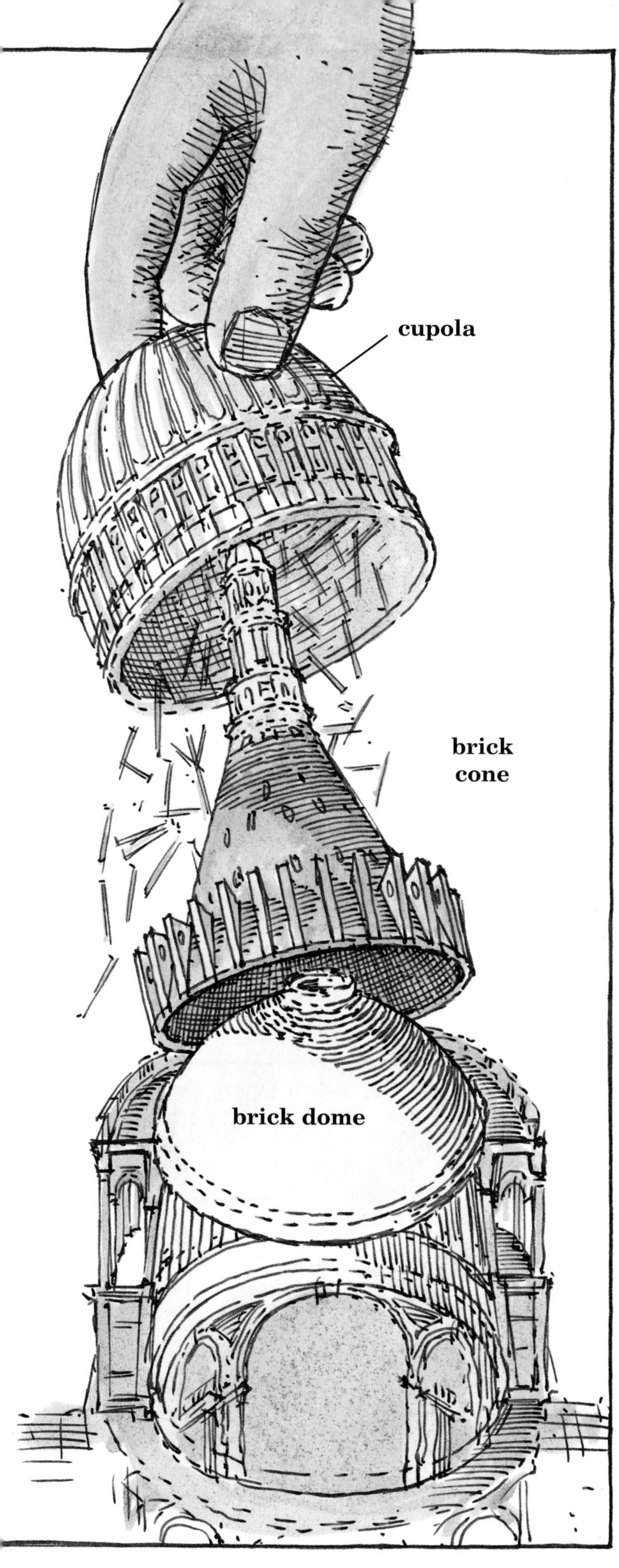

THE U.S. CAPITOL

Washington, D.C., 1856–1863: Near the turn of the nineteenth century, the symbolic, or perhaps propagandistic, possibilities of the dome were recognized by none other than George Washington himself. Although he'd never actually seen a dome in person, he believed that a new country's most important building—its capitol—would be taken a lot more seriously with a dome on top.

The first capitol dome, completed in 1824, combined an inner masonry shell modeled on the Pantheon with a dome-shaped roof of timber and copper cladding. At the urging of President James Monroe, this outer structure had been built much higher than it had been designed to be, creating an architectural compromise that never completely satisfied anyone. When a devastating fire in the Library of Congress almost reached this vulnerable and not terribly popular roof, the decision was made to give the central rotunda a completely new covering.

protective outer roof
original dome

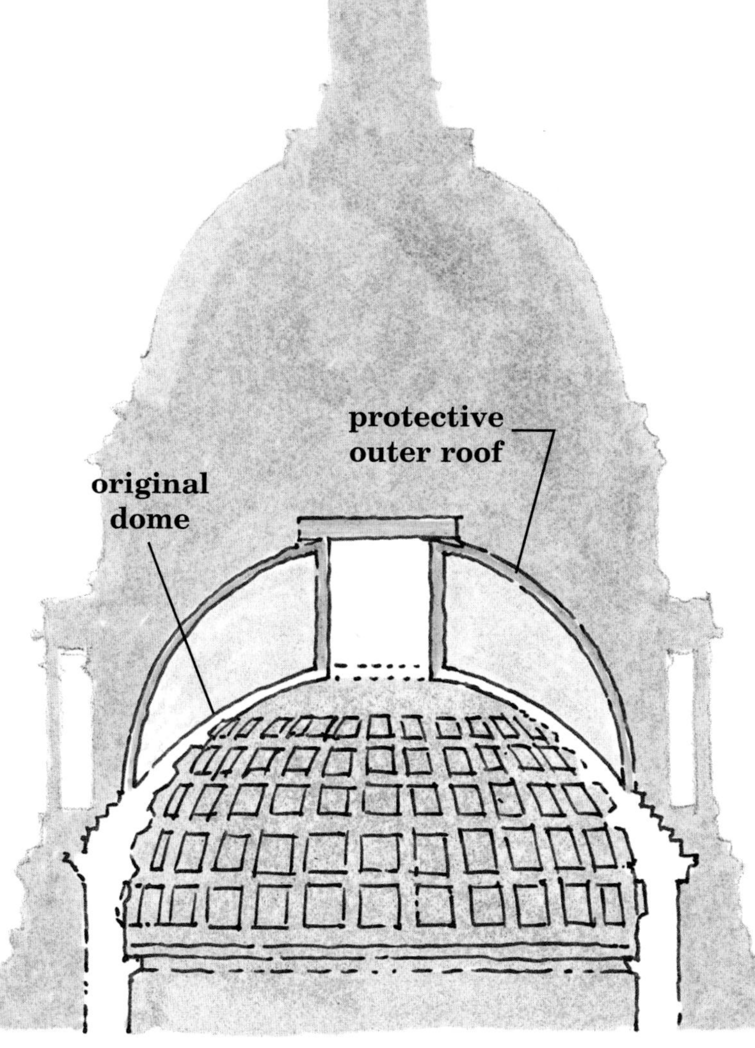

The first drawings of the new dome were created by an architect named Thomas U. Walter. While traveling in Europe, Walter had visited St. Peter's, Les Invalides, and St. Paul's, among others, and his design was certainly inspired by them. But it was also influenced by St. Isaac's Cathedral in St. Petersburg, Russia—a building Walter had only studied in drawings. All four structures employed the traditional base, two-part drum, cupola, and lantern, but St. Isaac's had the additional distinction of being made of cast iron. Cast iron could create the look of the great domes of the past, and it could do it far more economically than masonry. It was the ideal solution for an impatient young country wishing to import a little traditional respectability—and it was fireproof.

Under the watchful eyes of Walter and Captain Montgomery C. Meigs of the Army Corps of Engineers, work began in 1856 with the removal of the old dome and the installation of a temporary roof. Because of its increased diameter, the new dome would require a new larger base—the only part of the structure Walter intended to build of stone. Because of its dimensions and tremendous weight, however, this would have meant making major and costly changes to the existing structure, right down to the foundations.

Meigs had a better idea. He had the upper portion of the rotunda wall rebuilt and reinforced without altering its diameter. On top of the wall, extending almost 10 feet from the outer edge, he placed a ring of large iron brackets—two for each of the thirty-six columns that would surround the drum. The brackets were tied together by a thick iron ring and buried in the masonry. To create the appearance of a sturdy stone base, he then had a thin curtain of cast iron installed between the ends of the brackets and the roof below.

Since the entire structure was being bolted together piece by piece, no traditional centering was needed. Only a single timber tower was built from the floor of the rotunda to support a boom and the necessary tackle for lifting.

Moving around the wall, workers guided each of the 27-foot-long cast-iron columns into place and secured them to the base. About 6 feet behind each column and resting directly on the wall, they then erected four cross-shaped cast-iron columns. Not only would these form the base of the ribs, which in turn would support the dome, they would also anchor the wall that enclosed the drum.

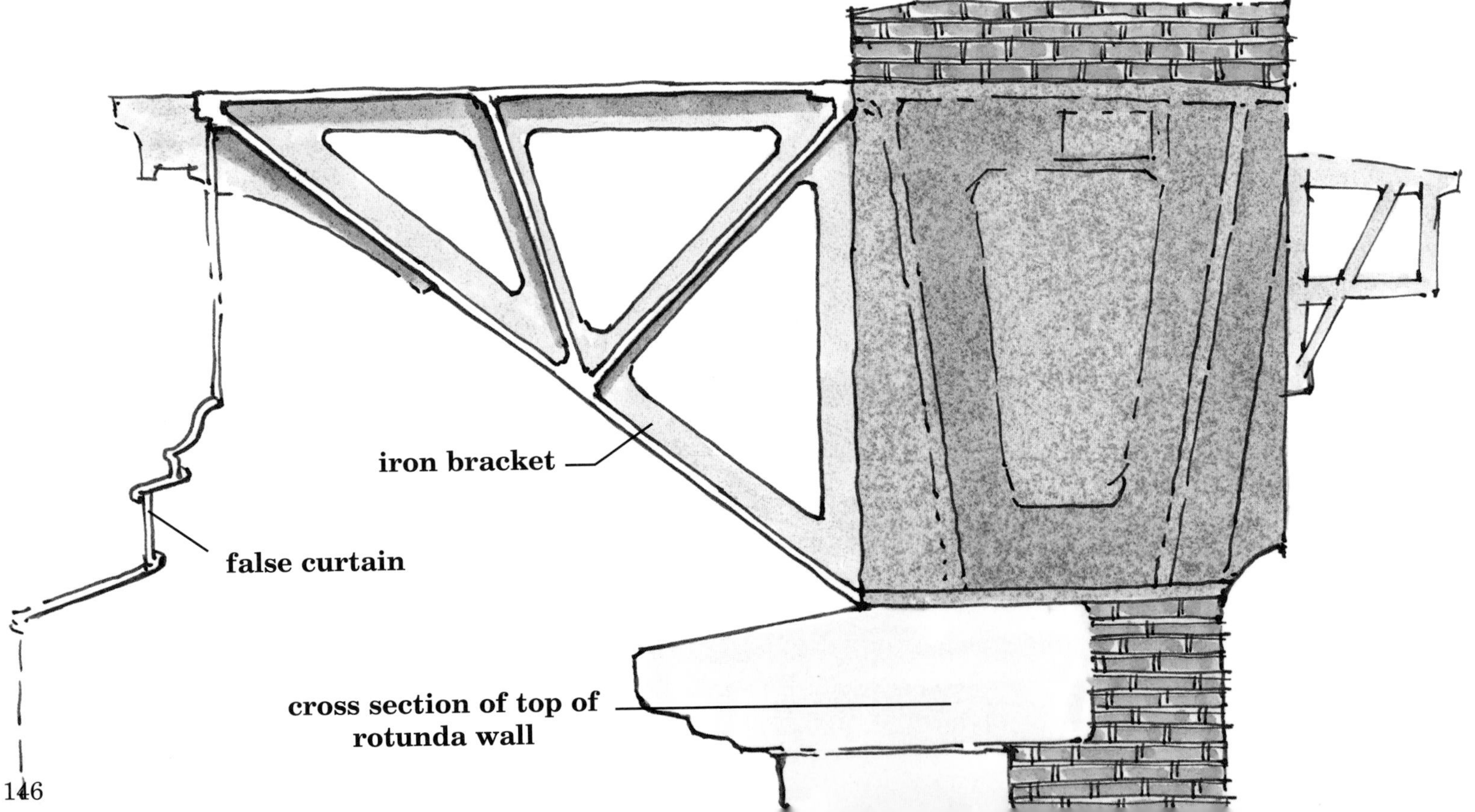

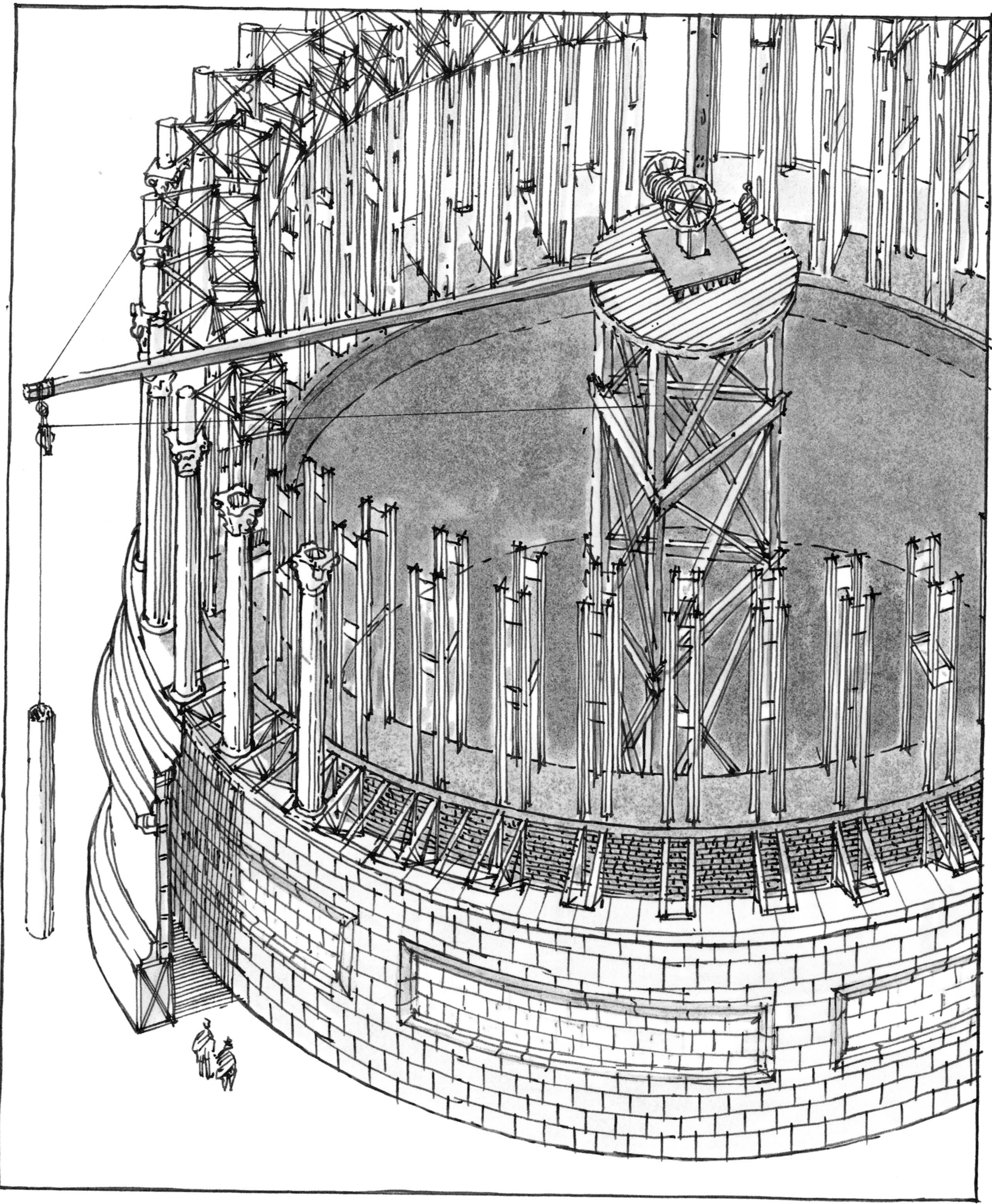

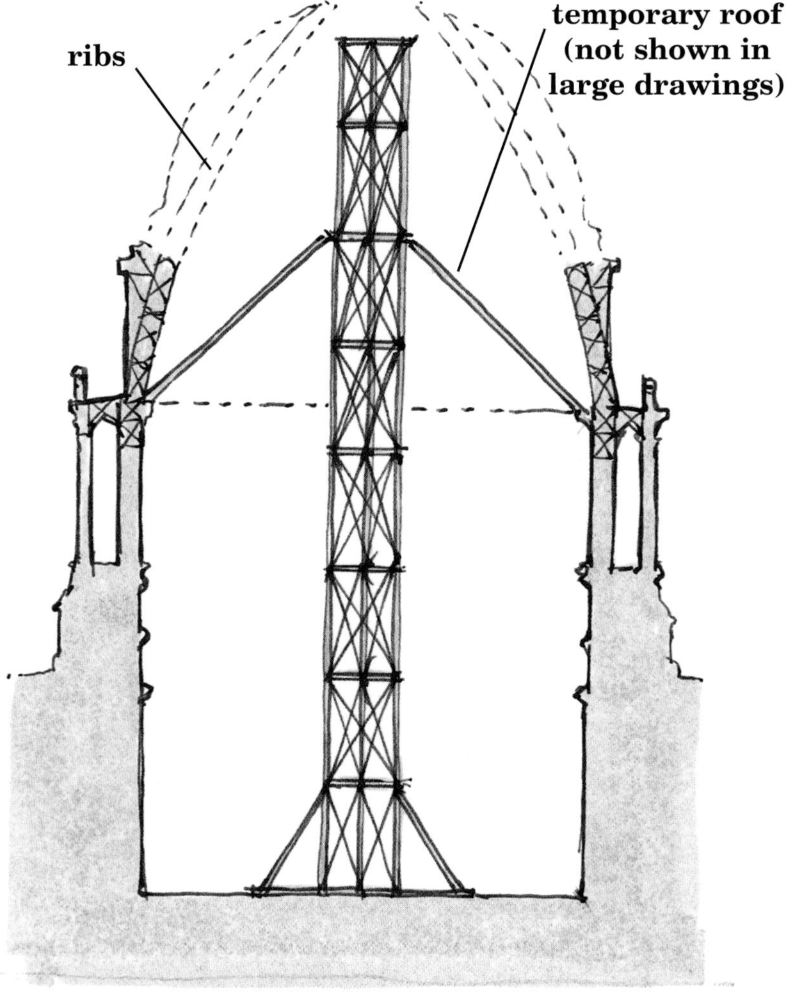

Once the lower level of the drum was finished, workers began extending the thirty-six curving ribs, adding the ornate pieces of the upper drum as they went. With the completion of the entire drum, the wooden tower had to be extended so that the highest pieces of the structure could be assembled.

In the middle of 1861, full-scale civil war broke out. Suddenly the resources allocated for building a dome were more urgently needed for equipping and feeding soldiers. All contracts were suspended, and no new materials were delivered. For the next year, the few workers who remained assembled only those pieces of cast iron already on hand.

Once again, though, the importance of a dome as a public relations symbol would prevail. In 1862, as the war raged on, it was decided that work on the Capitol should resume as a display of determination and of faith in the survival of a united land.

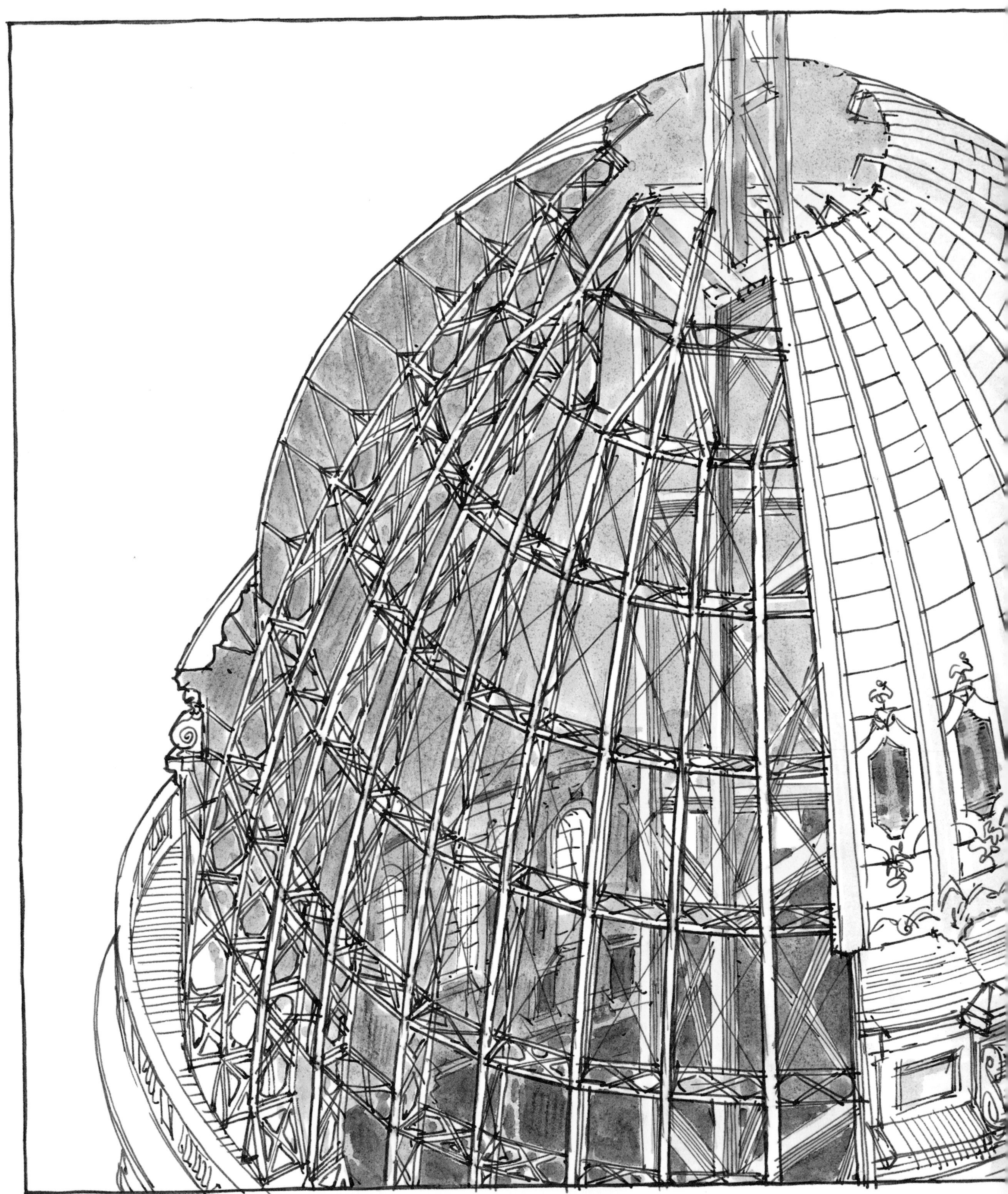

Soon new pieces of the structure were arriving, and they were quickly fastened into place. As the ribs rose, the builders tied them together with horizontal belts of cast iron and further secured them with cables, whose tension could be precisely adjusted. Projecting from the outer face of each rib were the supports to which the pieces of the cupola were attached.

At around 200 feet above the rotunda floor, the tops of the thirty-six ribs were connected into groups of three. Just twelve ribs would continue on to support the lantern. In early December 1863, the great bronze Statue of Freedom was secured to the top of the lantern and the exterior of the dome was finished.

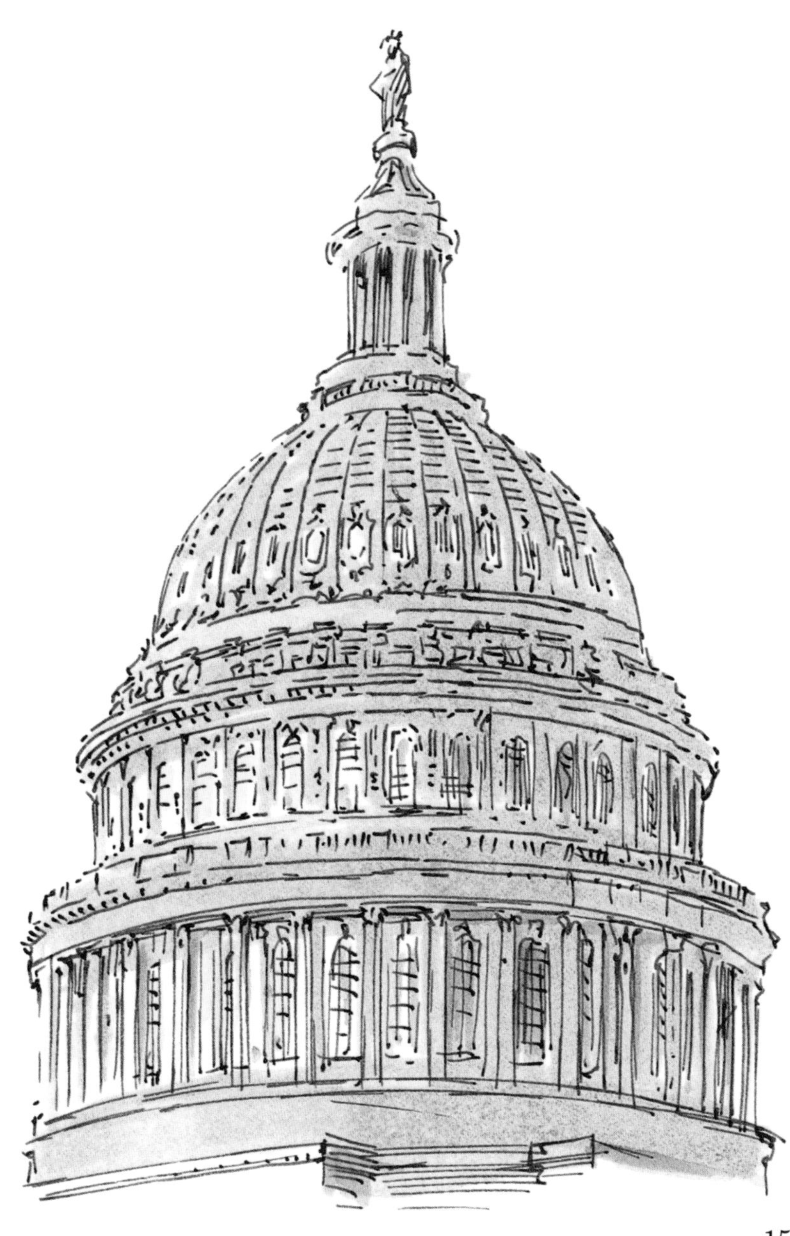

Work could now safely begin on the interior. An ornate inner dome, complete with coffers and occulus, was hung piece by piece from the ribs. A dome-shaped canopy was then suspended immediately above it, upon which a monumental painting would be created to provide an appropriately dramatic vista through the occulus. The artist, Constantino Brumidi, was still at work on his masterpiece in the spring of 1865, when the body of Abraham Lincoln was laid in state in the rotunda below.

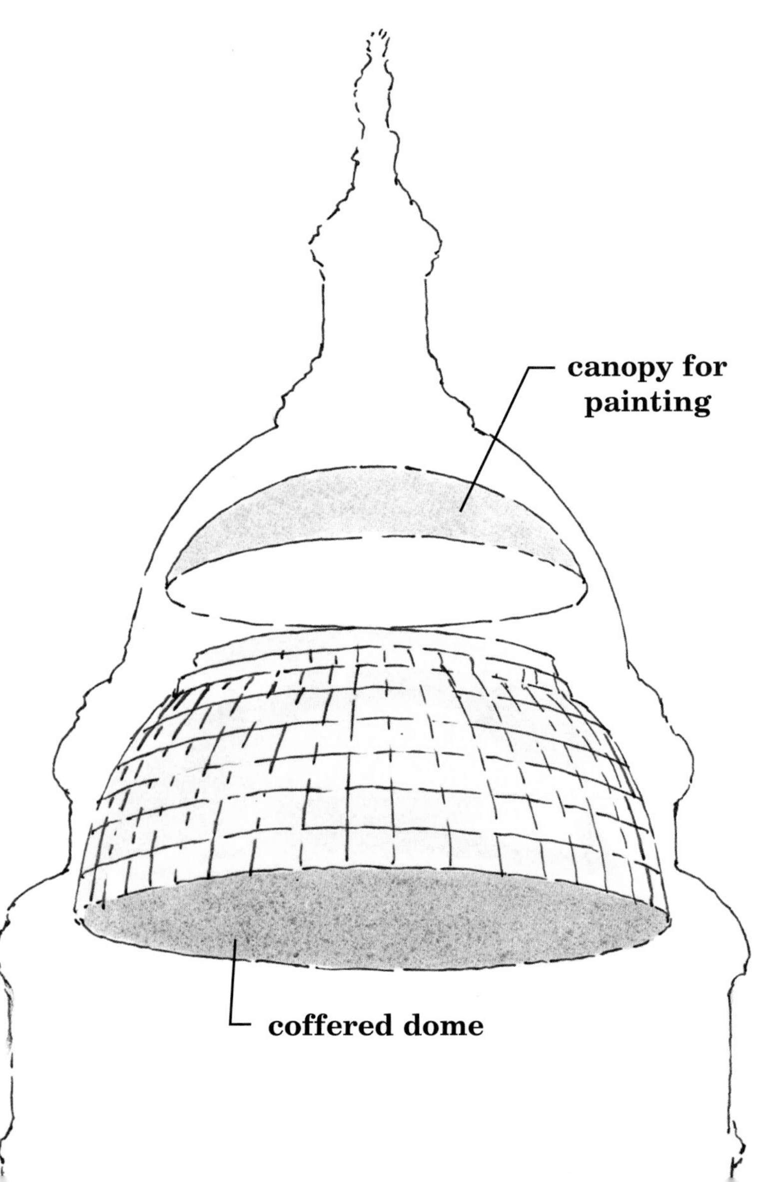

Astrodome

Houston, Texas, 1962–1965: Houston needed a stadium large enough to house a baseball field and seating for 50,000 fans that could be sealed off from heat, humidity, and insects and then air-conditioned. Given the more-or-less circular arrangement of seating around a baseball field, and the need to eliminate any columns that would interfere with both playing and watching the game, a dome was a very logical choice. And since domes had a solid two-thousand-year track record when it came to raising the profiles of both places and individuals, why wouldn't one with an unencumbered span of 642 feet do the same for Houston? This apparently was the thinking of one Judge Roy Hofheinz—showman, baseball fan, and Texan.

The dome he eventually got, called a lamella roof, was built of prefabricated steel trusses fastened together to form arches, which were then linked by a lattice of interlocking diagonals. Unlike any of the domes we've seen so far, the Astrodome was built from the center outward, using thirty-seven temporary towers. To overcome the tremendous outward

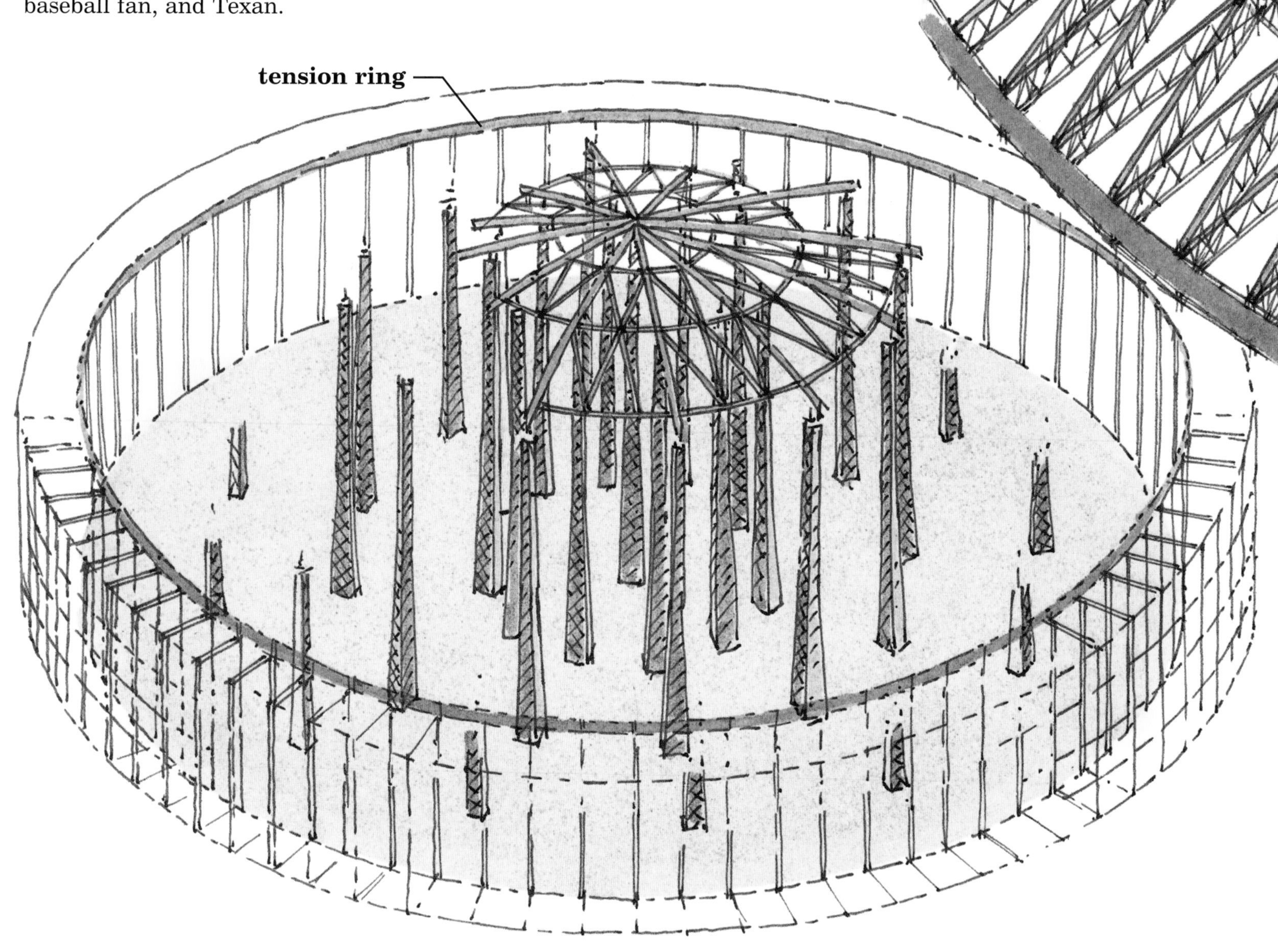

thrust created in this relatively shallow structure, the sides of the dome were contained within a strong steel truss tension ring. Seventy-two columns below the tension ring carry the weight of the dome to the foundations. The actual connections between the lamella roof and the tension ring were hinged to allow the dome to expand and contract.

When the entire steel structure was finished workers carefully lowered the hydraulic supports on the tops of all the towers at the same time, and only a sixteenth of an inch at a time, so that the dome would settle the few inches to its final height.

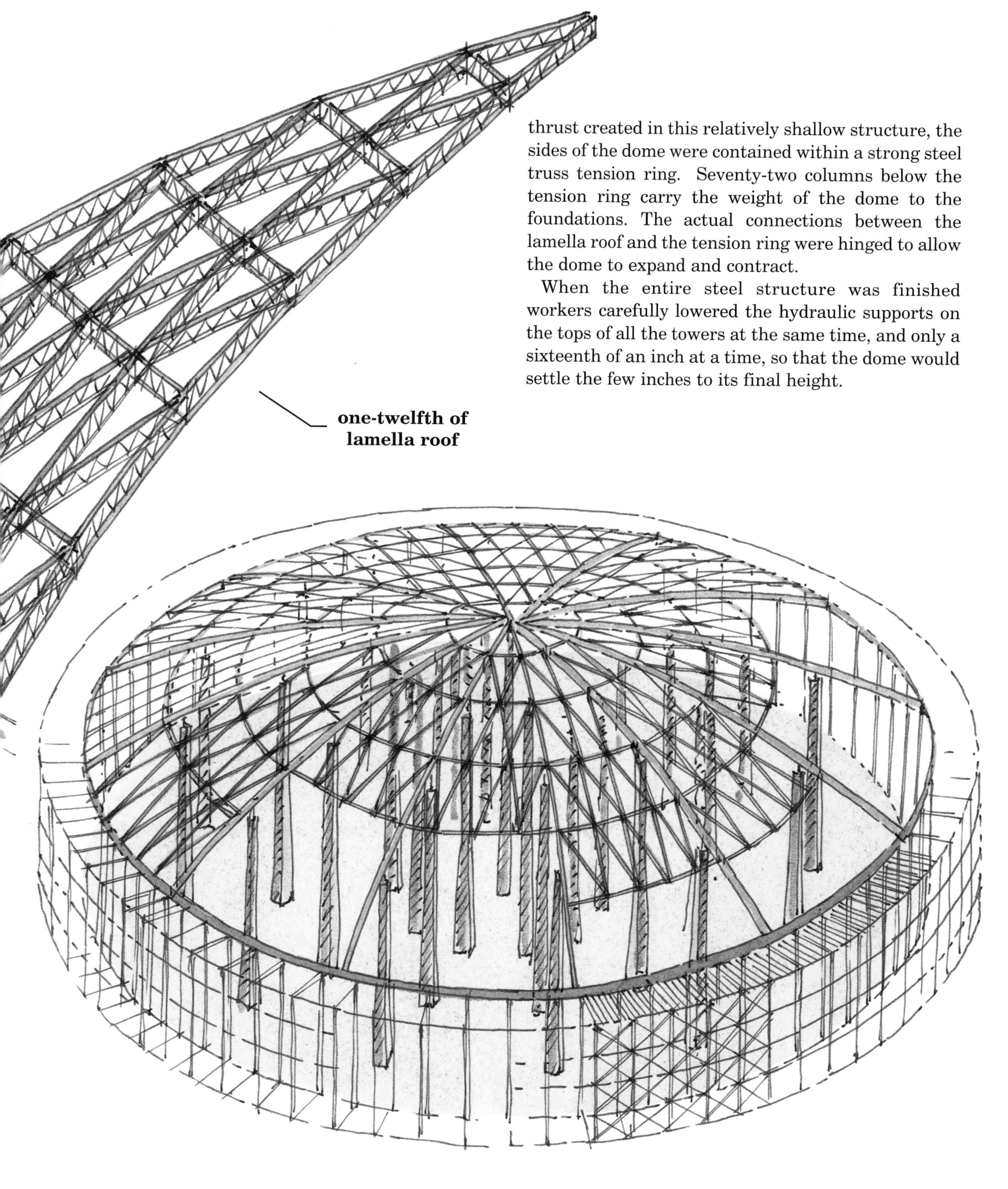

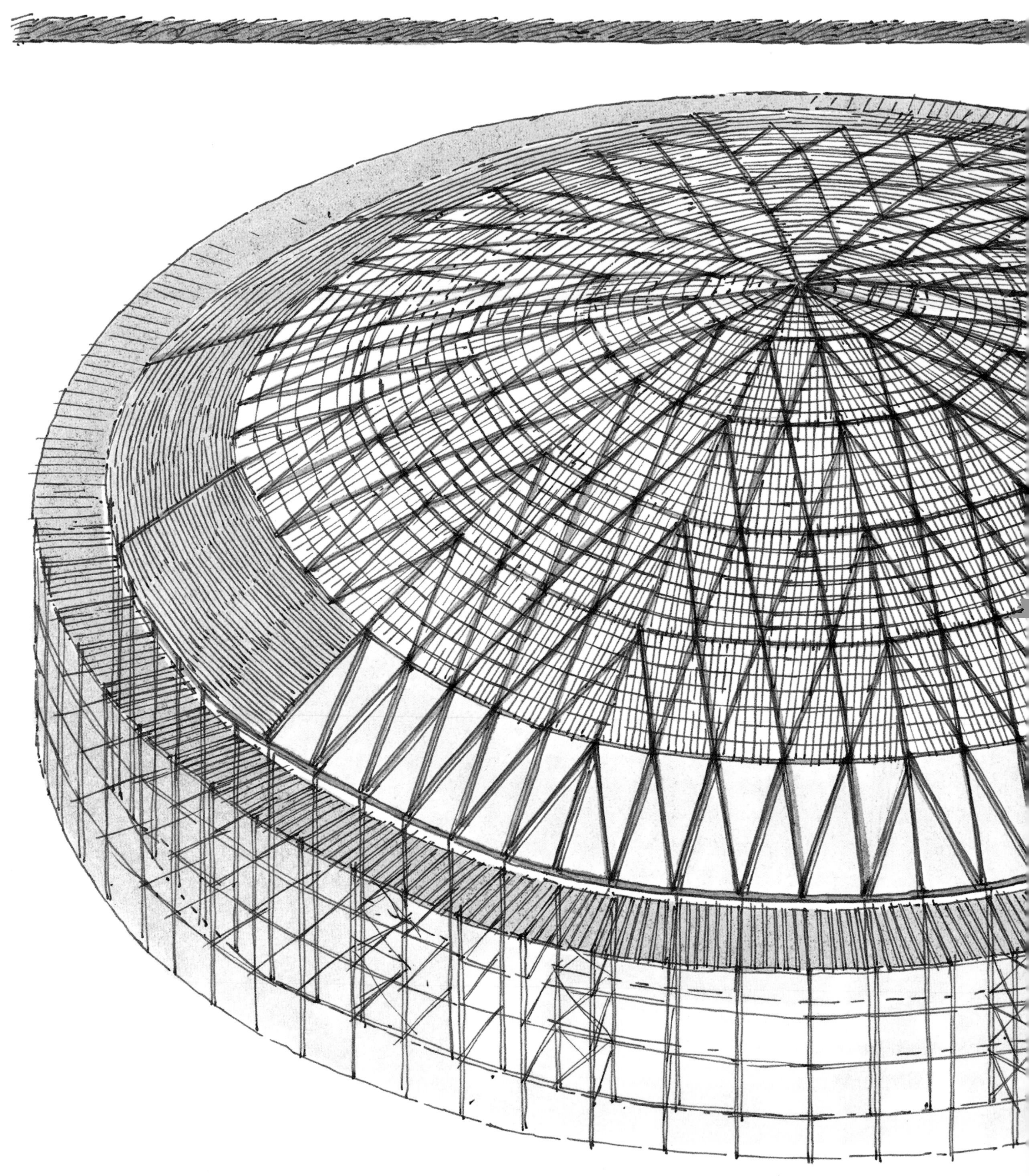

The surface of the finished dome was then covered with acrylic skylights and as at any self-respecting ballpark, the ground was planted with grass. It was not until this "eighth wonder of the world" was actually operating that a few problems arose. The skylights not only admitted natural light, they intensified it, making it almost impossible to see fly balls. When they were painted over, the grass, which had been specially developed for the Astrodome but still depended on sunlight, promptly died. This led to the invention of a plastic grass substitute called AstroTurf, which was glued in thin sheets to the unforgiving concrete slab below.

The Astrodome continued to offer baseball games right through the 1999 season. Now, however, the old building has been abandoned by the Astros and their fans for a brand-new stadium with a retractable roof right in the heart of the city. In theory, at least, Enron Field, as it is called, should provide the best of both worlds.

So what do you do with an often empty though still impressive domed stadium surrounded by a huge parking lot with easy access from the highway? I would use it to house the world's first international dome exposition. What could possibly be more fun than comparing domes side by side, and all in air-conditioned splendor? Of course, the success of such an undertaking would depend entirely on the generosity of the lenders, as it would be astronomically expensive to put on—but hey, this is Texas. Right, Judge?

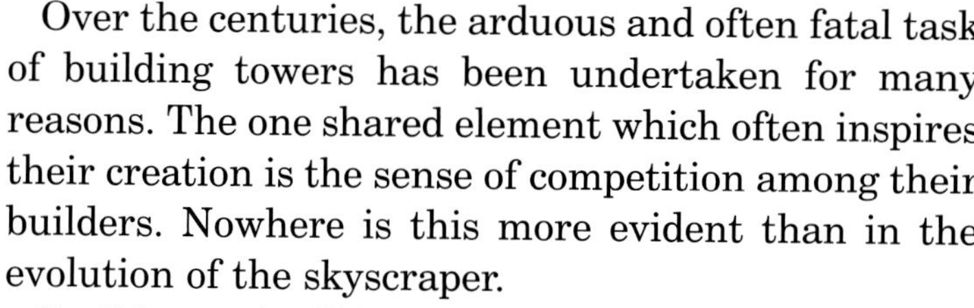

SKYSCRAPERS

Over the centuries, the arduous and often fatal task of building towers has been undertaken for many reasons. The one shared element which often inspires their creation is the sense of competition among their builders. Nowhere is this more evident than in the evolution of the skyscraper.

It all began in Chicago at the end of the nineteenth century. In the years following the devastating fire of 1871, the city's prosperity steadily grew along with its population, creating, among other things, a booming real estate market. Some of the most sought-after properties were located in the heart of the city—an area of just a few blocks bound on the north and west by the Chicago River and on the east by Lake Michigan. By the 1880s, the amount of remaining downtown space could not satisfy the demand. For the developer or businessman, there was no longer any alternative but to pile floor upon floor, as high and as quickly as possible.

In 1893, when a number of buildings approached and then exceeded the 200-foot mark, city fathers grew nervous. Fearing that these tall, out-of-scale boxes would turn the sunny streets into dark, inhospitable canyons, they imposed a ten-story limit on all new construction. Although this proved a significant hindrance to the appearance of real skyscrapers in the very city that had given birth to this quintessentially American architecture (a fact for which Chicago is still overcompensating), the high-rise office building was alive and well and ready to travel. It quickly went east. In less than twenty-five years, the tallest buildings in the world rose above the streets of New York City. It would be sixty years before Chicago could make that claim.

Reliance Building

Chicago, Illinois, 1892–1895: William Hale's new building was intended to house a number of different businesses. The basement and ground floor would be used as a department store. Smaller spaces on the second floor would be offered to jewelers, tailors, and hat makers. The upper floors were to provide the most up-to-date offices for the growing number of doctors and dentists and their patients.

The area the building would cover—56 by 85 feet—was fixed on two sides by State and Washington Streets and on the other two by an existing L-shaped building. Because the building was started before the new height limits were imposed, it was designed to be fifteen stories tall. Anything taller would have concentrated too much weight on the layer of clay that began just a few feet below ground level.

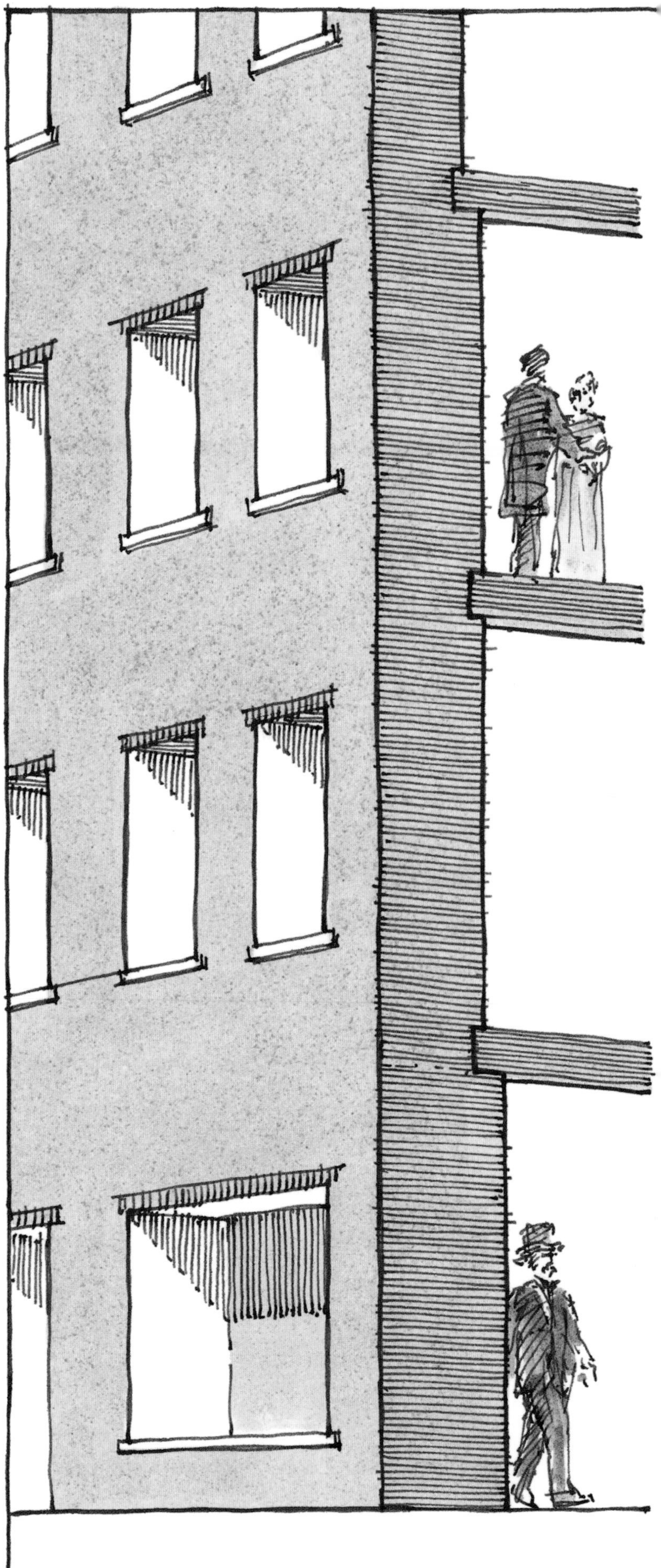

load-bearing wall

Up to this time, almost all tall buildings were enclosed by masonry load-bearing walls. To support a building's great weight, these walls had to be thick, particularly at the base. This imposed serious limitations on the number and sizes of windows. But an alternative was emerging in Chicago that would eliminate the need for exterior weight-bearing walls altogether: a three-dimensional grid of beams and columns capable of supporting all the loads to which a building might be subjected. These included the vertical forces created by the weight of the floors and their occupants, as well as horizontal forces caused either by the wind or, in some regions, by earthquakes.

Hale's Reliance Building, designed by the architects John Root and Charles Atwood, was to follow this concept. Since all the structural requirements would be handled by a steel skeleton, the exterior covering could be quite thin. Its only function now was to let in light and keep the weather out.

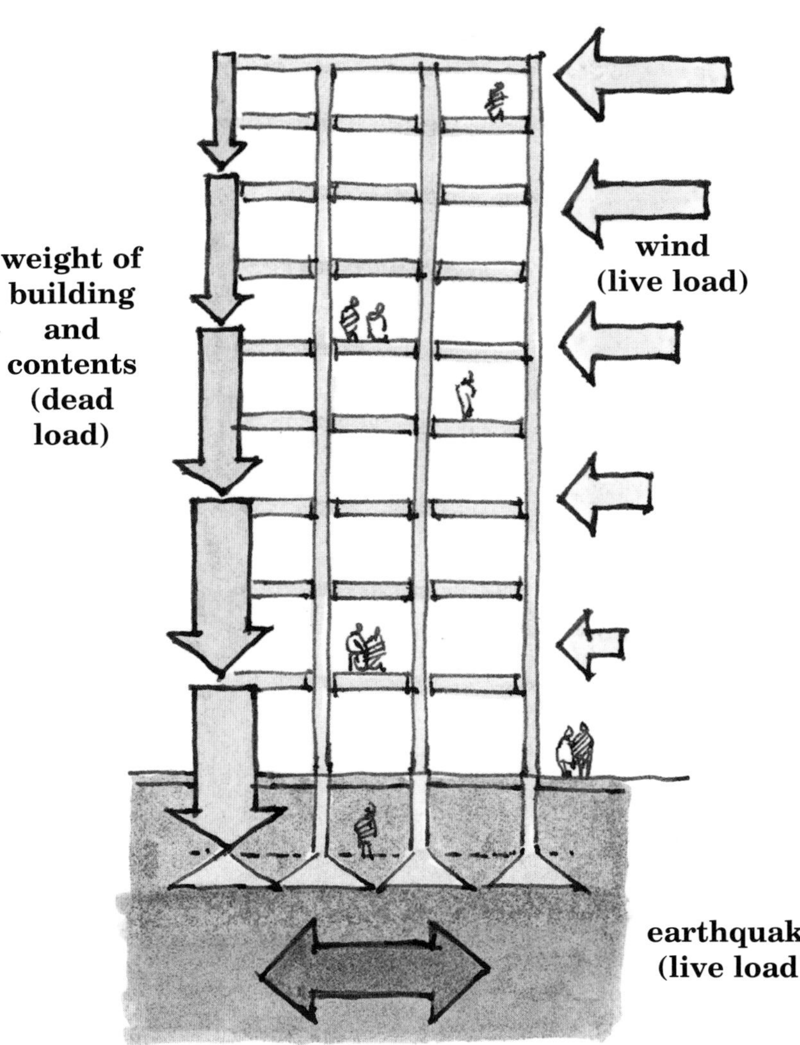

steel skeleton and curtain wall

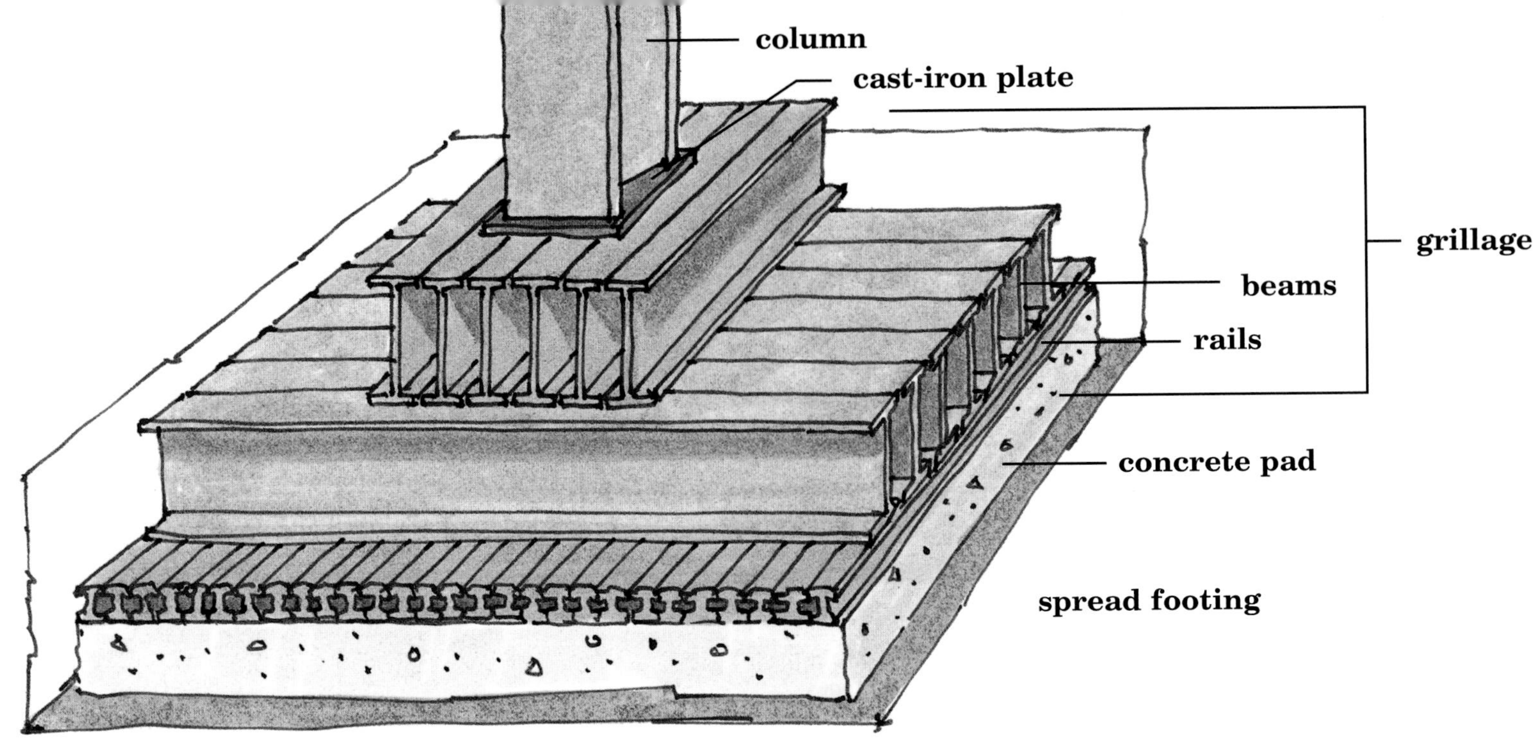

By the time the various loads on a building reach the bottom of each supporting column, they have become a strong vertical force concentrated in a very small area. Foundations have to distribute this force over a wider area or, if that is not enough, to carry it all the way down to firm soil or bedrock. By choosing the appropriate foundations, engineers hope to minimize the distance a building will settle and to ensure that it does so uniformly.

Before the foundations for the Reliance Building could be built, the site had to be excavated to a depth of 14 feet to expose the firm clay upon which it would rest. However, the process was made complicated by the fact that there was already a building on the site—complete with tenants. But Hale was nothing if not persistent. Rather than wait for the occupants' leases to expire, he decided to support the occupied floors on temporary beams and columns so that his workers could safely remove the ground from beneath them.

Since the columns of the building could not rest directly on the clay, each had to have its own especially constructed support. Called spread footings, these pyramid-shaped structures were built up in layers, starting with a thick concrete pad poured right on the clay. Two or more layers of steel rails or beams, set perpendicular to each other to form what is called a grillage, were then placed on top of the pad and buried in more concrete. A thick cast-iron plate on top of the grillage carried the actual base of the column.

In 1893, when the last of the tenants were finally gone, the old masonry building was demolished and construction of the steel frame began. As the two-story sections of column arrived at the site, workers hoisted them into place and riveted them together. To further stiffen the skeleton against the horizontal forces of the wind, they bolted deep beams called girders into place between the exterior columns at each floor level. The entire skeleton was assembled in only four weeks.

The architects designed the outer skin (eventually to be called a curtain wall) as a series of horizontal bands which alternated between high windows and narrow molded pieces of terra cotta. These glazed clay blocks not only gave the building's façade some decoration, they also protected the skeleton from fire. Although steel will not burn, it will weaken if exposed for too long to very high temperatures. Such improvements in fireproofing, along with the provision of adequate escape routes and a reliable water source on each floor, represented another important innovation in skyscraper development.

One more thing helped nurture this new architectural form—the development of safe, efficient elevators. No one understood better than Hale that stairs lose their charm for most people after about five stories. In the early 1880s, he and his brothers had bought out the company founded by Elisha Otis, the inventor of the elevator. The Hale Elevator Company claimed to offer the most advanced elevators in Chicago, and the architects were only too happy to install four of them in the Reliance Building.

construction of the Reliance Building

Woolworth Building

A healthy business climate and lots of reliable bedrock just below the surface set the stage for New York City's incredible foray into the world of skyscrapers. When Frank W. Woolworth asked the architect Cass Gilbert to design a new skyscraper, he requested something gothic and at least 50 feet higher than the nearest competition—the 700-foot-tall Metropolitan Life Insurance Tower.

What he got was an extraordinary building. Its overall shape was to a great extent the result of the amount of floor space that had to be fitted onto the site. But Gilbert greatly emphasized its verticality by setting the bands of ornate terra cotta—once again the material of choice—on end and slightly recessing the columns of windows between them.

Although built to provide first-rate office space, with the fastest elevators and latest safety features, the Woolworth Building was first and foremost about height. Both its existence and its striking appearance owed a great deal to Frank W. Woolworth's determination to nickel and dime his way into the record book—which he did. His building was the world's tallest from 1913 to 1930. Beneath the skin of this truly "modern" skyscraper, a heavily braced steel frame rises some sixty stories on the backs of caissons sunk deep in the waterlogged soil below.

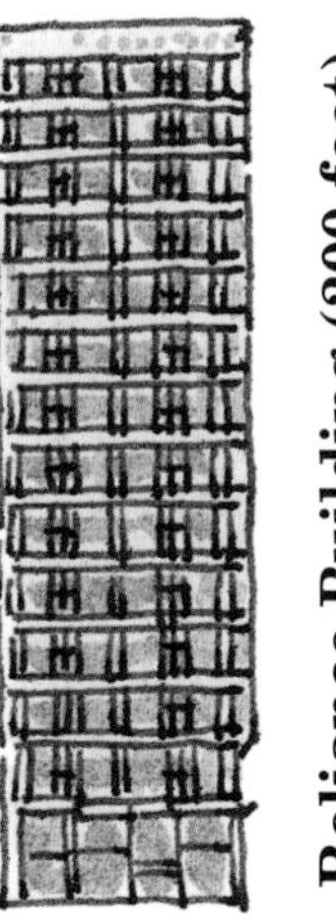

Reliance Building (200 feet)

Metropolitan Life Insurance Tower (700 feet)

Woolworth Building (792 feet)

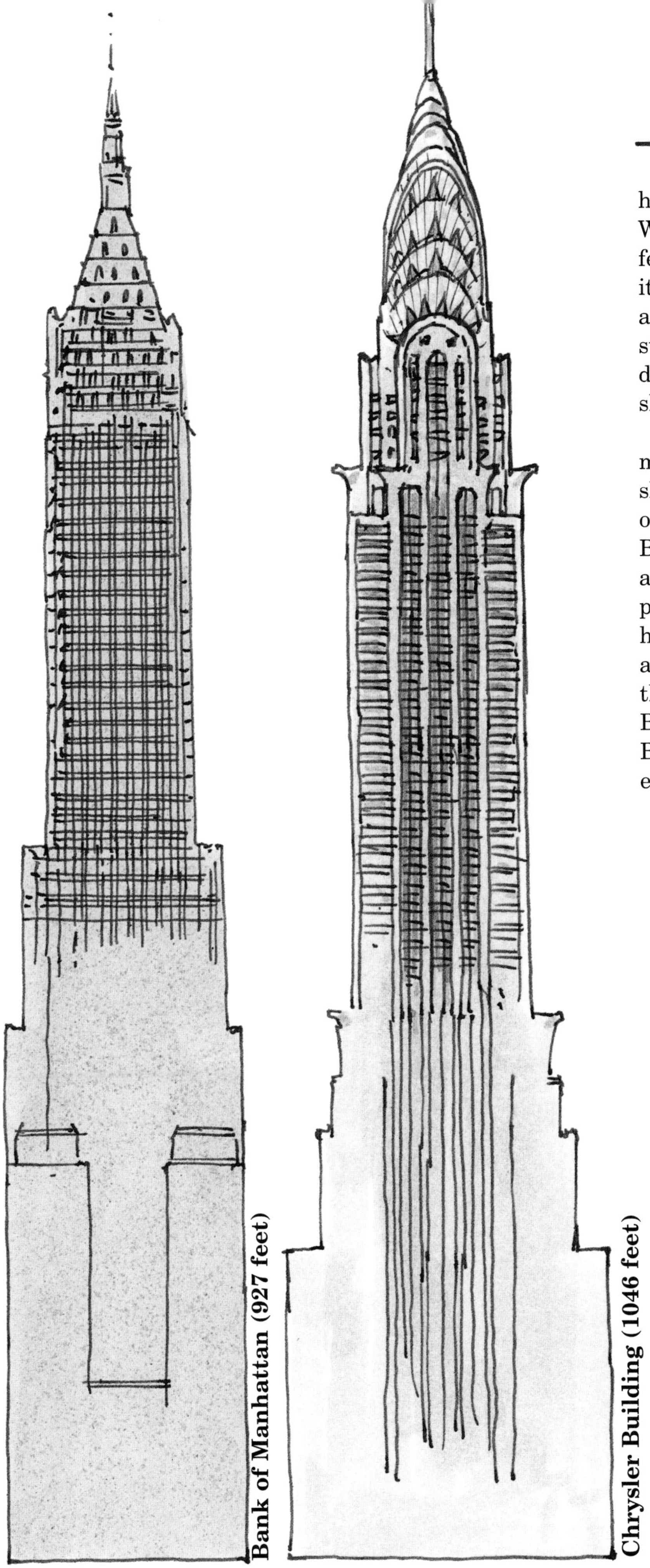

CHRYSLER BUILDING

When the title of "tallest" eventually changed hands, it left the neighborhood but not the island. William Van Alen's Chrysler Building—almost 300 feet higher than the Woolworth Building—was, like its predecessor, a towering tribute to both ego and advertising. And it too rises on a heavy steel frame strengthened against the lateral forces of the wind by diagonal bracing sandwiched between the elevator shafts.

A modest skin of white and gray glazed brick covers most of the building. The only hints that something slightly unusual may be afoot are the oversized hood ornaments that occasionally slow our upward gaze. But waiting for us at the top are crescents of radiating sunbursts sheathed in chrome-nickel-steel and punctuated by triangular windows. Once our eyes have adjusted to this gleaming madness, they arrive at the spire whose surprising last-minute emergence through the top of the roof guaranteed the Chrysler Building's height superiority over its closest rival, the Bank of Manhattan. But even this trickery was not enough to fend off the next challenge.

Bank of Manhattan (927 feet)

Chrysler Building (1046 feet)

Empire State Building

New York City, 1929–1931: Having determined how much office space the Empire State Building should provide, an approximate budget for the enterprise, and the fact that it should be the tallest building in the world, the project backers turned the job over to the architectural firm of Shreve, Lamb, and Harmon. As chief designer, it was William Lamb's job to oversee the process that would eventually give the building its final form.

Many factors had to be taken into consideration, including a few, such as city zoning regulations and site limitations, over which the architects had no control. One such regulation, intended to maintain at least a minimum amount of light and air at street level, demanded that tall buildings be stepped back at certain predetermined heights based on the width of the adjacent streets. Another stated that the portion of a building rising above the thirtieth floor could be of any height as long as the square footage of any individual floor didn't exceed 25 percent of the area of the site.

Bound by these requirements, Lamb had to determine how to give his clients the floor space and building height they required and at the same time satisfy his own wish that no office worker would be any farther than 28 feet from a window. With each significant increase in floor space, he had to provide more elevators, so that passengers wouldn't be left waiting. The more elevators he provided, the more floor space they consumed. The more floor space they consumed, the more floors he had to add. The form eventually created by the banks of elevators grew in response to the building's height and regulated massing. By the time the calculations were done, everyone's practical needs were realized in a building of eighty-five stories.

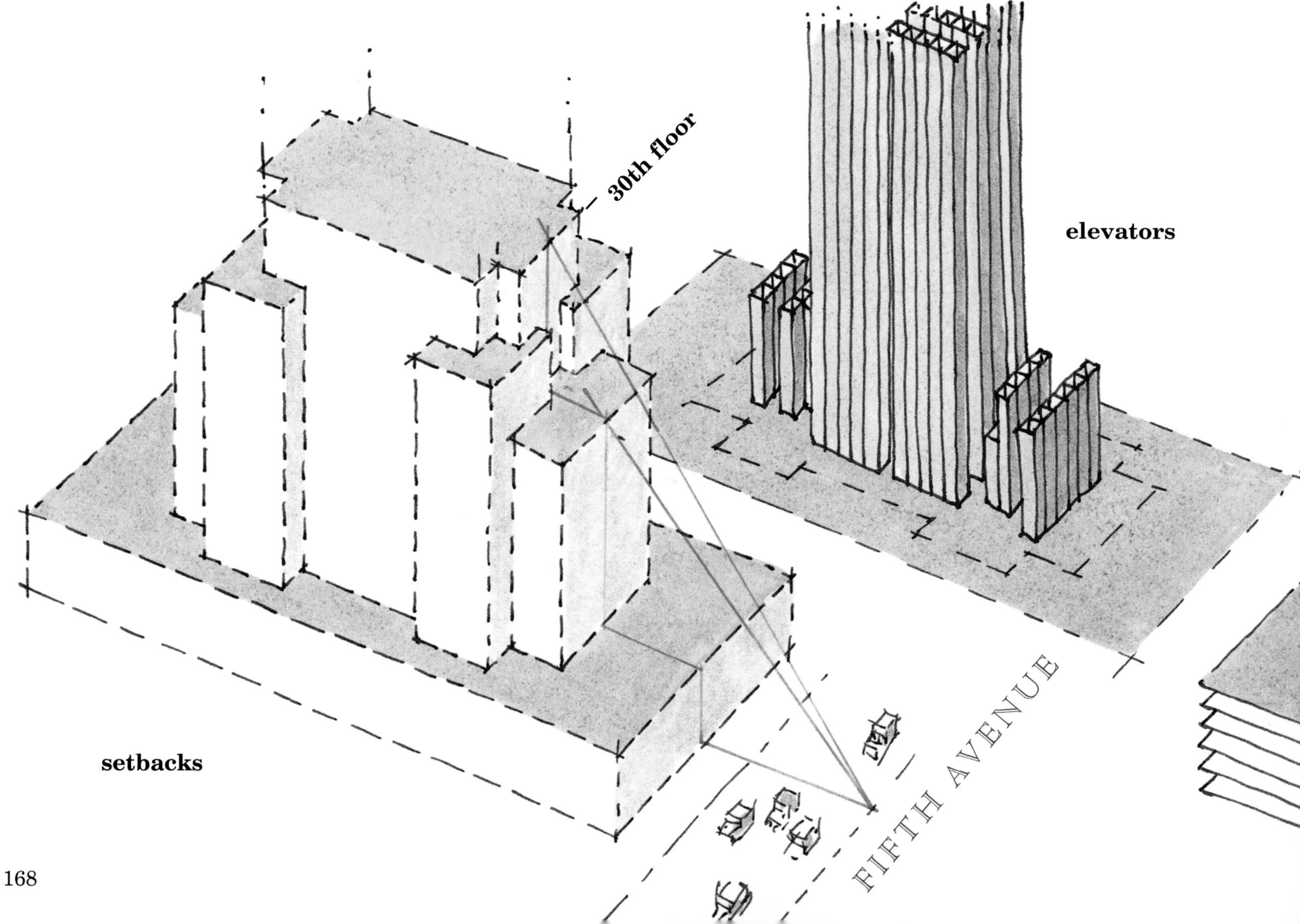

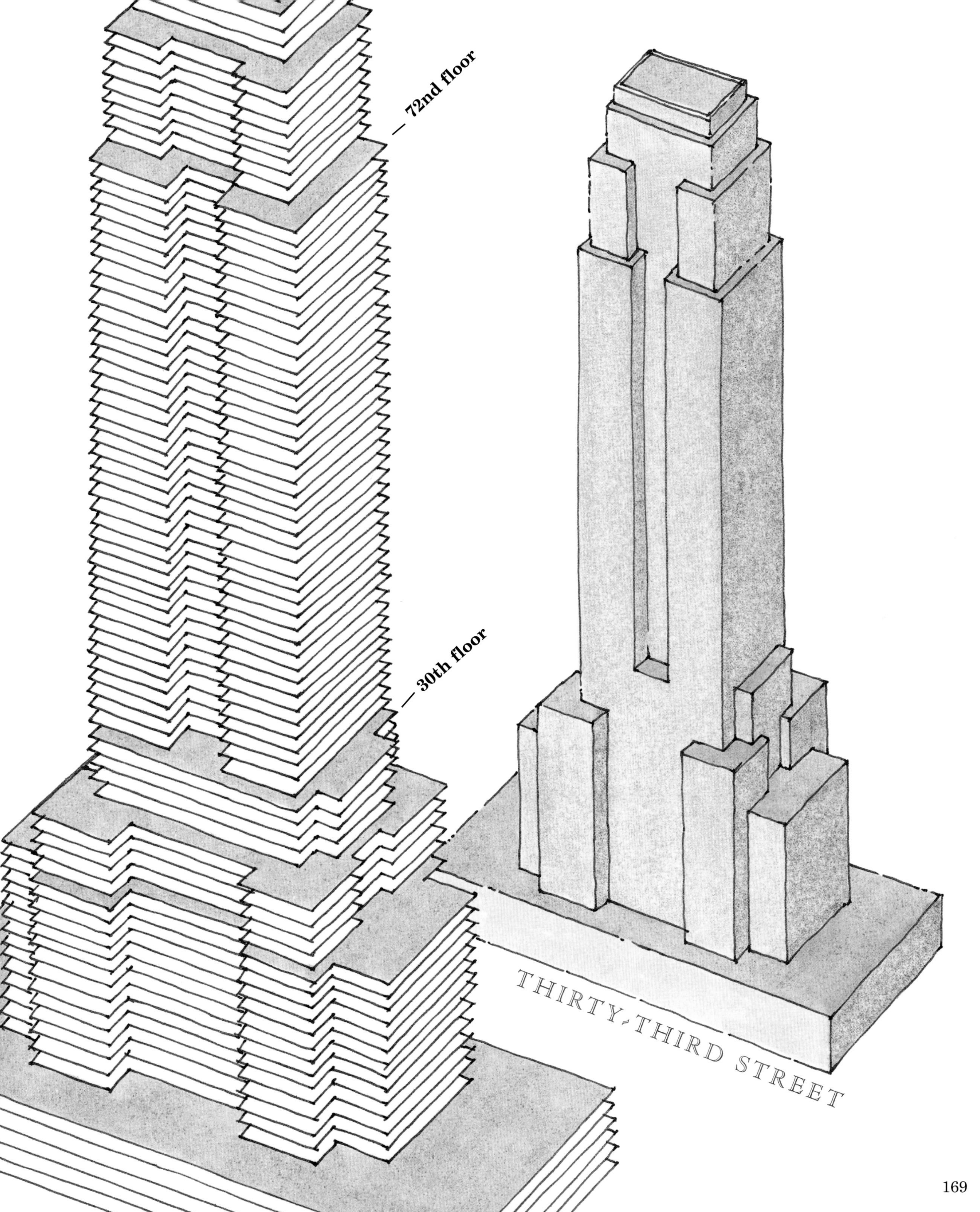
72nd floor
30th floor
THIRTY-THIRD STREET

WHY AN *I*?

When a beam or column bends, one side goes into compression while the opposite side goes into tension. The area along the centerline between the two sides experiences neither. This means that in a solid rectangular beam there is some material right in the middle of the beam's depth that isn't doing much. In an iron or steel beam, it is possible to move much of that underutilized material to where it will be more effective in resisting these forces. The result is a beam in the shape of an I. The two parallel parts, called the flanges, do most of the work. The piece that holds them together, called the web, can be thinner because it doesn't have to carry as much force. Although the girders of the Reliance Building were not single rolled pieces like those of the Empire State Building—they were built up of angles and thick steel plates riveted together—their overall shape remains the same.

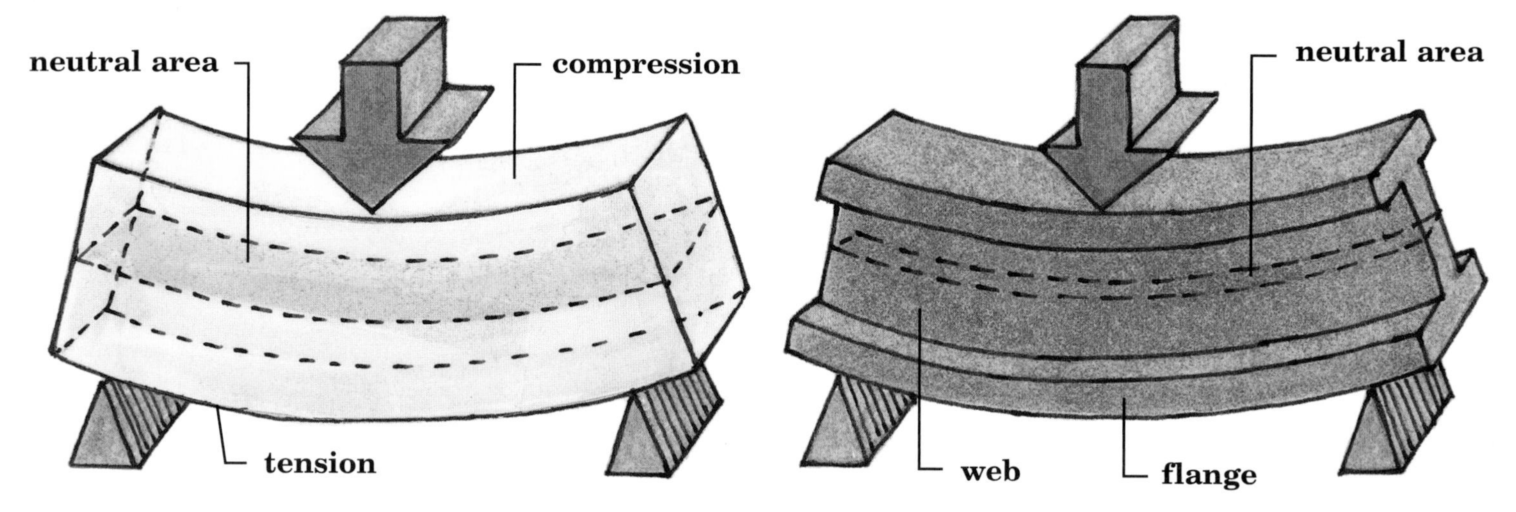

As soon as the architects had determined the number of floors and their exact square footage, the engineers located all the beams and columns and calculated how strong they would need to be. While beams can be more or less the same size regardless of which floor they are on, the strength and therefore the sizes of the columns depend very much on their placement in the skeleton.

Once the site for the Empire State Building had been cleared, it was excavated down to bedrock (only about thirty feet below street level), and spread footings were prepared.

Meanwhile the various pieces of the skeleton were being fabricated. The heaviest columns, those at the very bottom of the building, were built up from I-beams and steel plates. They were delivered in two-story sections with rivet holes already drilled and brackets for the girders already in place. As soon as the first columns had been set on their bases, girders were inserted between them to stiffen the building and to support the smaller floor beams. When workers had made sure that the columns were perfectly vertical, they riveted the various connections permanently.

After the first few tiers were in place, temporary lifting devices called derricks were set up. These would hoist the various pieces of steel into position. Every few floors, workers had to dismantle and raise the derricks to keep up with the building.

As the steelworkers continued to assemble the frame above them, other workers were busy making the concrete floors. They erected temporary wooden forms around the girders and beams and then draped a heavy wire mesh over the steel to help reinforce the four inches of concrete that would serve as the base of each floor.

No sooner had the concrete set than another group of workers began installing the limestone blocks, aluminum panels, chrome-nickel-steel trim, and windows that made up the curtain wall. To help maintain the very tight building schedule, all of these pieces were designed to be installed independently of the others.

construction of the Empire State Building

In less than seven months, workers had reached the level of the observation deck on the eighty-sixth floor. Although the structure now rose four feet above the tip of the Chrysler Building's spire, they continued the framing so they could build a 200-foot-tall tower, ostensibly for docking dirigibles. When such aerobatics turned out to be much too risky—only two attempts were made—the idea was abandoned. Yet even though the mooring mast failed on the transportation front, it perfectly concludes the building's journey to the sky. It also gave the Empire State Building a solid 200-foot edge over its art deco neighbor and a height superiority that would last for forty years.

Lamb and his engineers knew that the real problem with height isn't the rivalry between buildings so much as the increasingly fierce battle all tall structures must wage with the wind. Even a skyscraper as heavy as the Empire State Building will sway a couple of inches off center in strong winds.

While a building's sway rarely presents a structural threat, it can test the stamina of its inhabitants, especially those living or working near the top. Over the last fifty years, only a handful of buildings have grown taller than the Empire State, but many have grown narrower, and all are lighter. Walls of glass now cover steel skeletons instead of the heavy masonry cladding that helped stabilize buildings like the Empire State. Some of these newer structures can sway more than two feet in each direction, which is why engineers have had to develop additional ways of stiffening their buildings.

From the beginning of skyscraper construction, engineers used connections that attempted to counteract rotation and flexibility at the ends of beams and columns. In what are called rigid connections, both the flanges and the webs are attached. This makes the joined beams and columns act more like a single piece. On the Empire State Building, these rigid connections were achieved with rivets. Today rigid connections are far stronger, because they use a combination of high-strength steel bolts and welding. However, because they are complicated and time-consuming to make, they are also expensive.

Beyond a certain height, even rigid connections won't be strong enough on their own to adequately reduce a building's sway. This is why the engineers of buildings like Woolworth, Chrysler, and the Empire State strengthened the central cores by installing diagonally braced steel trusses between the elevator shafts. In more recent buildings, reinforced concrete walls running the full height of the structure have been used to create even stronger cores. Whether built of steel or concrete, a building's core usually houses elevator shafts, stairwells, toilets, and other mechanical systems.

By solving the problem of sway in tall structures from the inside out, engineers can often make the surrounding skeleton lighter and significantly reduce the number of expensive connections. However, in the tallest buildings, requirements for stiffness have forced exterior walls to reclaim their load-bearing responsibilities.

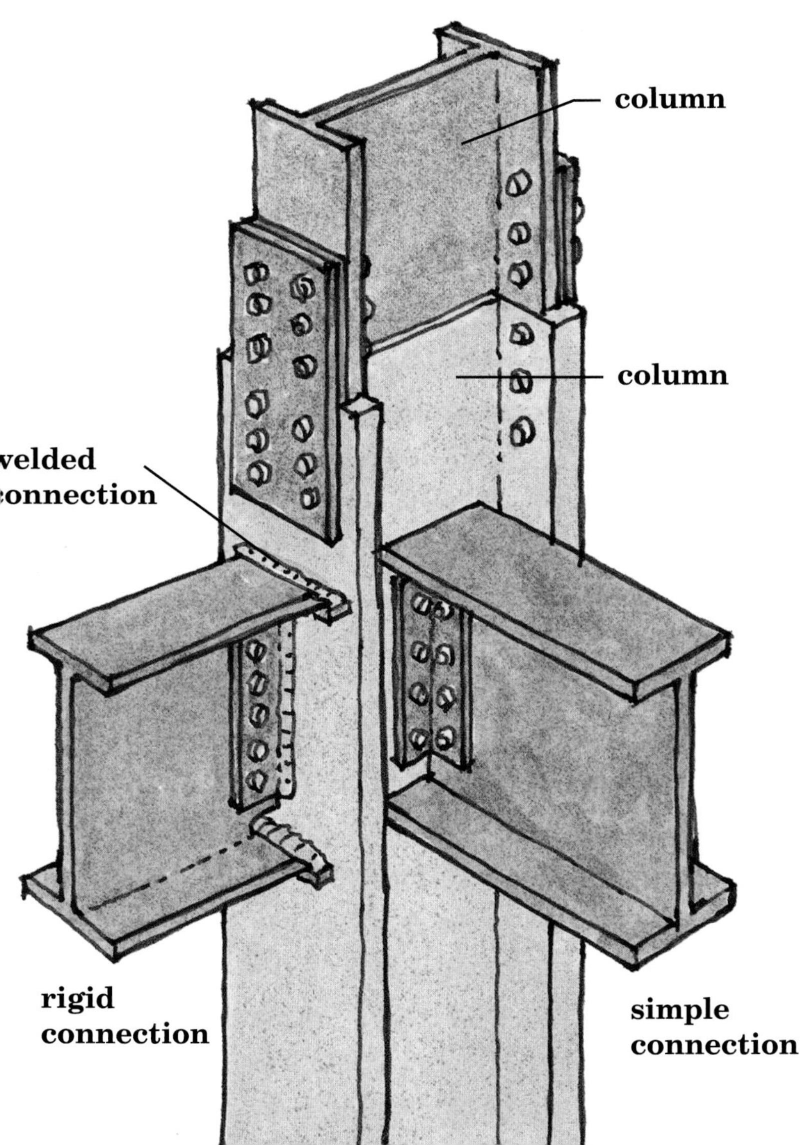

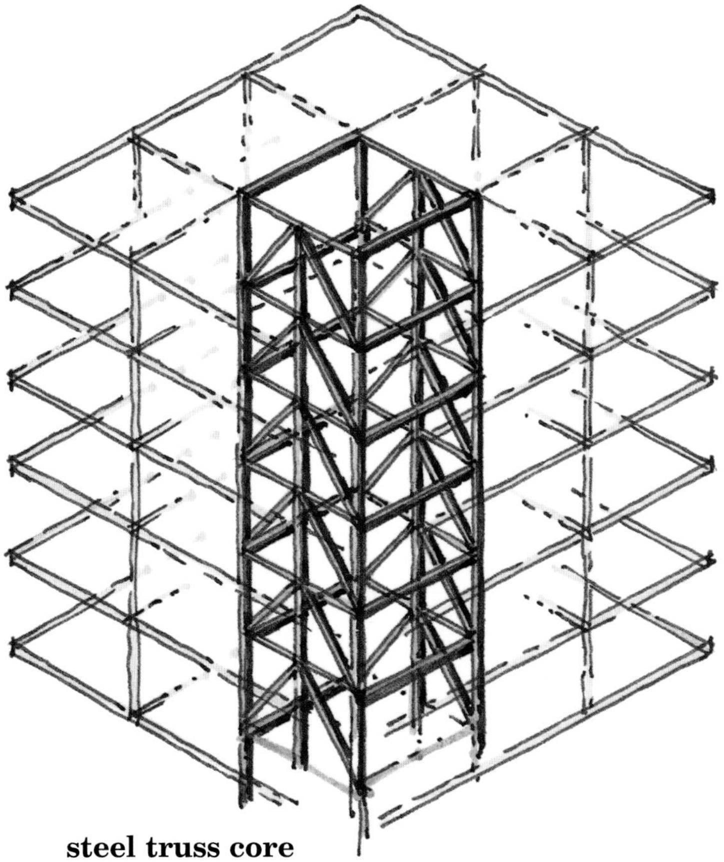

steel truss core

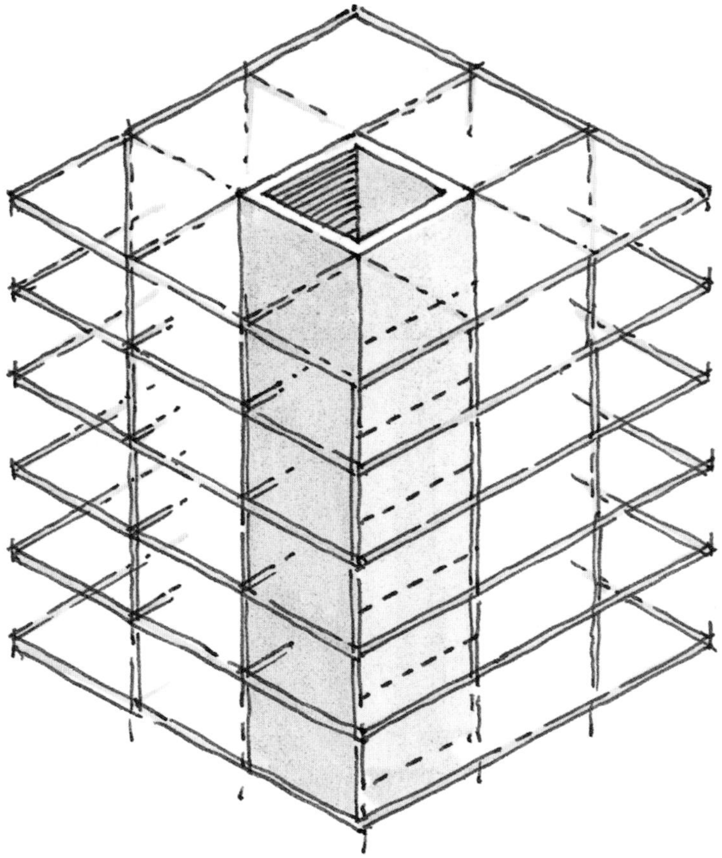

reinforced concrete core

John Hancock Center

Chicago, Illinois, 1969: There are two obvious things about engineer Fazlur Khan's John Hancock Center that remind us of the ongoing battle between all tall structures and the wind. The first is its shape. The second is the enormous exterior cross-bracing.

The shape is both familiar and logical. At Garabit, that other master engineer Gustave Eiffel made the towers under his railway track wider at the bottom and narrower at the top to increase their stability. Of course, he had the additional advantage of being able to let the wind pass through the structure. Although Chicago, too, has something of a reputation when it comes to wind, this approach would not have been received too well by the residents of this 1100-foot-high building.

The cross-bracing around the Hancock Center is also very logical, though perhaps less familiar at this scale. Like any good engineer, Khan was always looking for ways to reduce the amount of material his buildings would need. By tying continuous columns and occasional floor beams together with enormous diagonal wind braces, he significantly increased the building's rigidity. And by transferring more of these loads to the outside, he was able to reduce the number of columns required inside.

World Trade Center

New York City, 1972: Architect Minoru Yamasaki and engineers John Skilling and Leslie R. Robertson took on vertical weight and horizontal forces in a different way. In their 1360-foot World Trade Center Towers, the load-bearing exterior columns have become the wall. They are spaced only three feet apart and are tied together at every floor by a deep horizontal beam. The result is a strong lattice that completely encloses both towers with a very stiff square tube. The core is also a very strong tube. Floors connect the inner and outer tubes and bridge the distance between them, creating large office spaces completely free of columns.

The exterior wall was built in sections, either 24 or 36 feet high (two or three stories) and three columns wide. As in the Reliance Building, they were connected at staggered heights so all the joints wouldn't be on the same level, which could slightly weaken the wall. Each column was eventually sheathed on the outside with an aluminum skin, into which a stainless steel track was recessed to guide the window-washing platform.

The floors also arrived in prefabricated sections, some as large as 60 by 13 feet. They were covered with a light steel decking over which the concrete floor would eventually be poured. All the pieces of the structure were lifted into place by one of four climbing cranes housed in elevator shafts in the central core. Each time the building reached the level of the cranes, they were raised to a new height by powerful hydraulic jacks.

North Tower

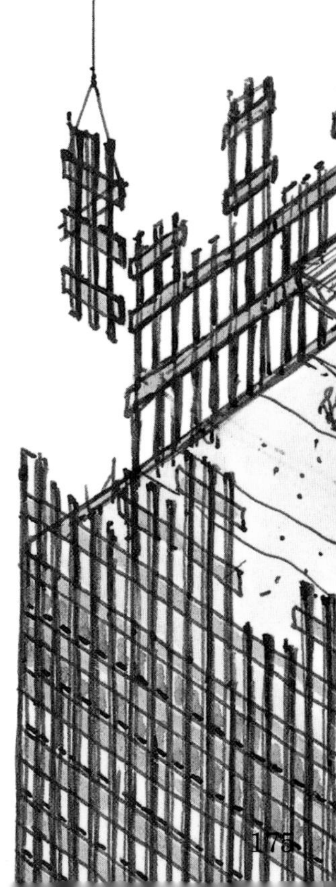

South Tower

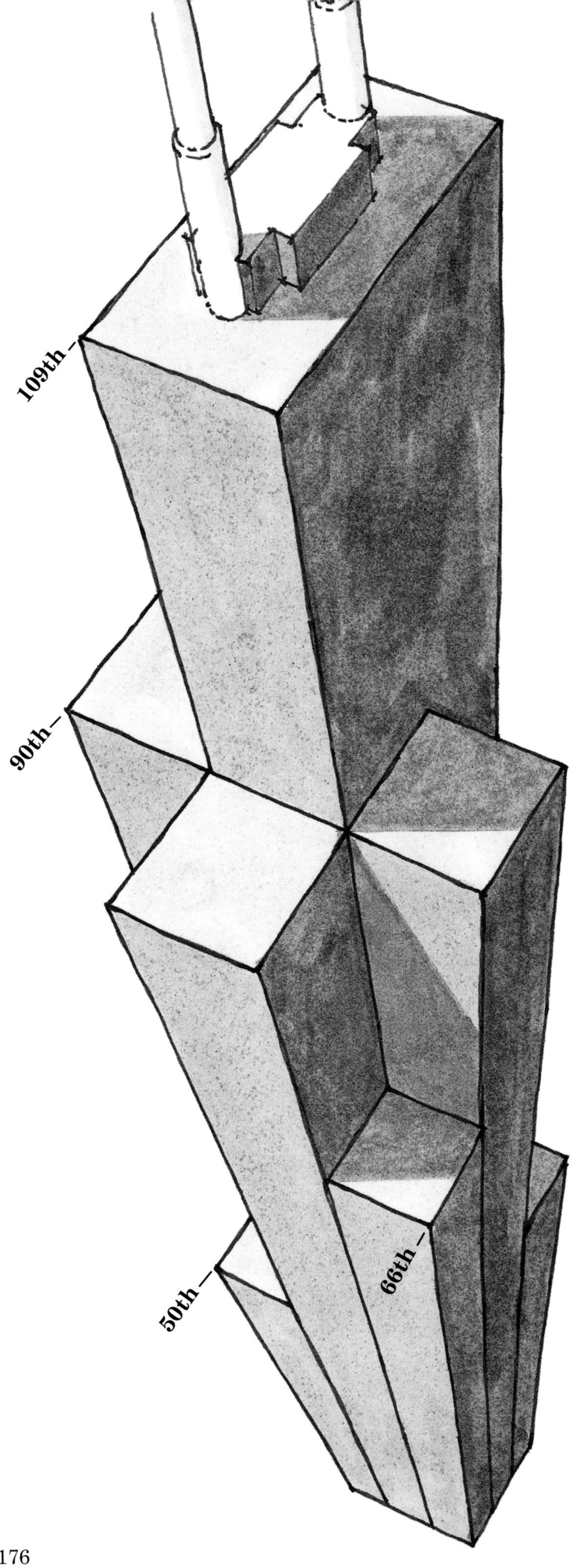

Sears Tower

Chicago, Illinois, 1974: If one tube is good, then nine must be better. The Sears Tower, also engineered by Fazlur Khan of Skidmore, Owings, and Merrill, finally brought the title of world's tallest building (1454 feet) almost literally into the back yard of the Reliance Building. (The tower lost it in 1997 by a mere 22 feet, but in the record business a foot is foot.) The idea here was to use several smaller tubes and bundle them together, creating a single huge footprint 325 feet square. As the building rises, all but one of the outer tubes drop off at certain heights, creating a stepped effect that is both structurally sound and psychologically reassuring. Only two of the tubes, clinging to each other for dear life, rise the full height.

Instead of spacing a lot of smaller columns close together, as at the World Trade Center, Khan enclosed each tube with huge columns set 15 feet apart and connected by 42-inch-deep girders. Deep trusses span each tube at every story, once again creating unobstructed floor space. The entire building is clad in a combination of bronze-tinted windows and black aluminum panels, which suggest the locations of the columns but completely obscure their scale.

For a building of this size, spread footings on clay were not going to do the job. Each of the main columns rests instead on a 7-foot-in-diameter concrete pier three levels below the street. The piers travel 60 feet down to bedrock, where they are firmly embedded.

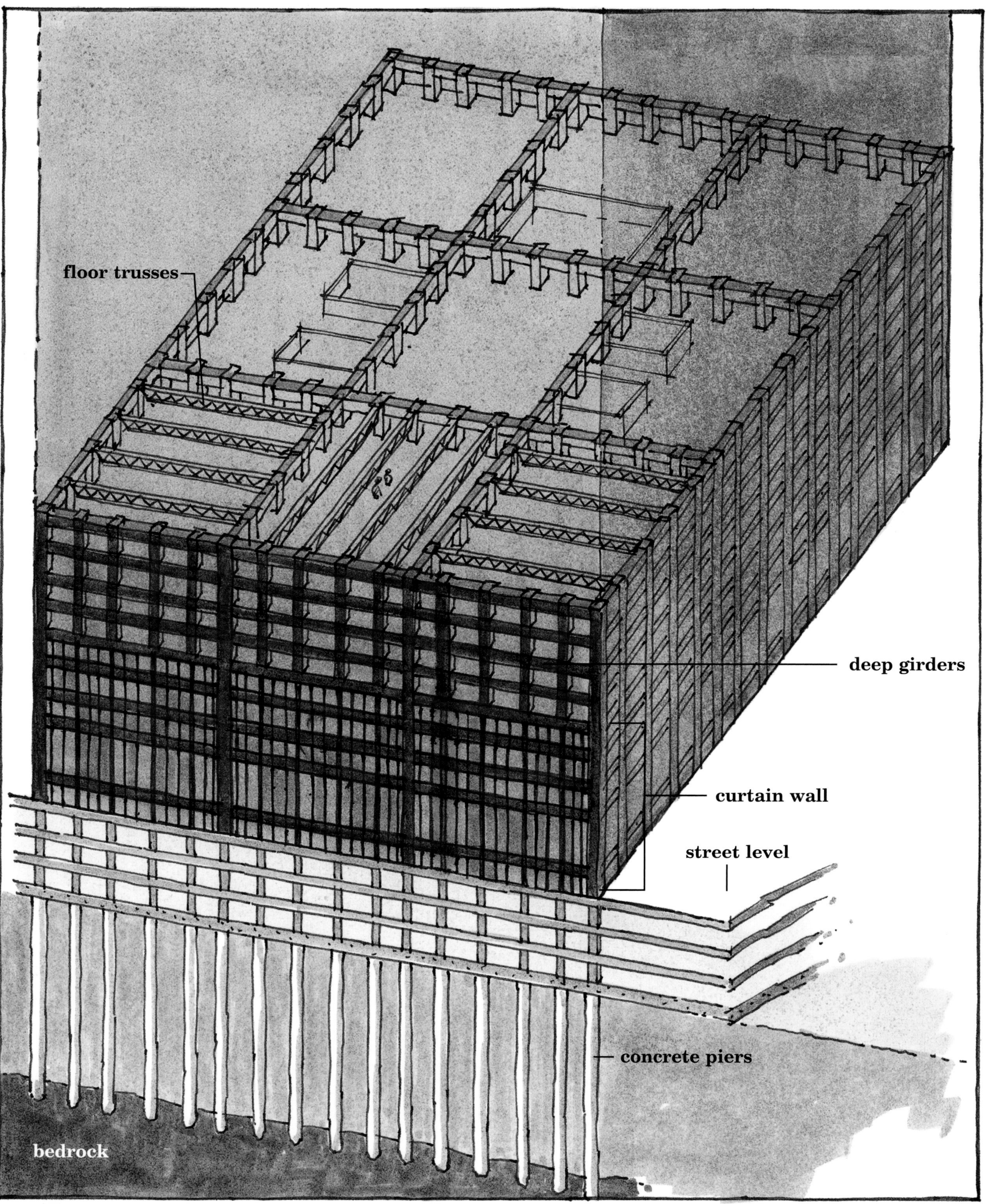
floor trusses
deep girders
curtain wall
street level
concrete piers
bedrock

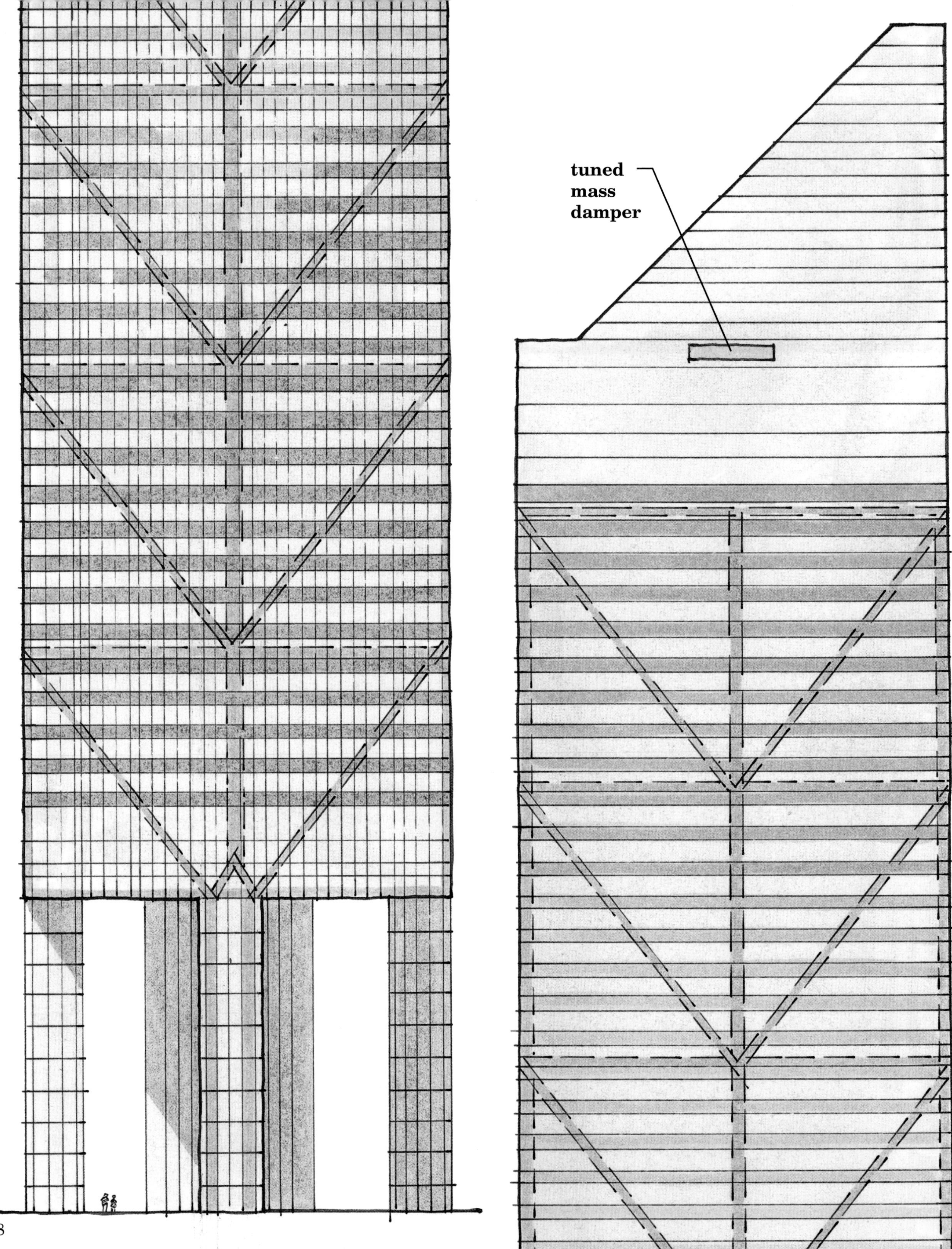
tuned
mass
damper

Citigroup Center

New York City, 1977: There are a number of interesting things about the former Citicorp Building (now Citigroup Center) designed by architect Hugh Stubbins and structural engineer William Le Messurier. For one thing, there is the way in which the top of the building has been lopped off at a forty-five degree angle, giving it an immediately identifiable shape. Then there are the four large columns at the base which have been moved from the corners, where you might expect to find them, to the middle of each side. This was done to open up space at street level and create room for a new church which replaces the one demolished to make room for this building. Although it is hidden behind the aluminum and glass skin, inverted triangular bracing carries the loads on the exterior walls to those columns. And finally there is the way in which this building addresses the problem of sway.

The key is something called a tuned mass damper, the centerpiece of which is a block of concrete 30 feet square, about 6 feet high, and, most important, weighing 400 tons. (For obvious reasons, it was poured in place before the top of the building was enclosed.) This block is supported by a three-foot-high concrete base, which sits on twelve 24-inch-in-diameter disks. The whole contraption rests on a smooth concrete bed in the middle of the sixty-third floor.

When a computer system detects an increase in the wind, oil is pumped out through the disks elevating the block ever so slightly. As the building moves, the damper is activated by a series of pistons and starts to follow, but because of the oil, it has difficulty catching up. After several seconds the building reaches the end of its swing and begins moving back in the opposite direction. The damper will continue to travel in the first direction for a short time until various springs and arms stop its movement and send it back after the building. Try as it will, it can never actually catch up with its host until both have stopped moving. But by maintaining this slightly out-of-sync choreography, the tuned mass damper reduces the building's sway by almost half.

Numerous types of dampers are in use, not only in buildings but at the tops of the tallest suspension bridge towers. One designed for a very tall (yet so far unbuilt) skyscraper in Paris would use a 600-ton pendulum, a portion of which would hang in a large tub of silicon. As the building sways, the pendulum will try to keep up, only to have its movement severely restricted by the extremely dense silicon. Through this deceptively simple device, the energy of the wind is actually being transferred to the silicon, sparing the building some of that force and reducing the sway in the process.

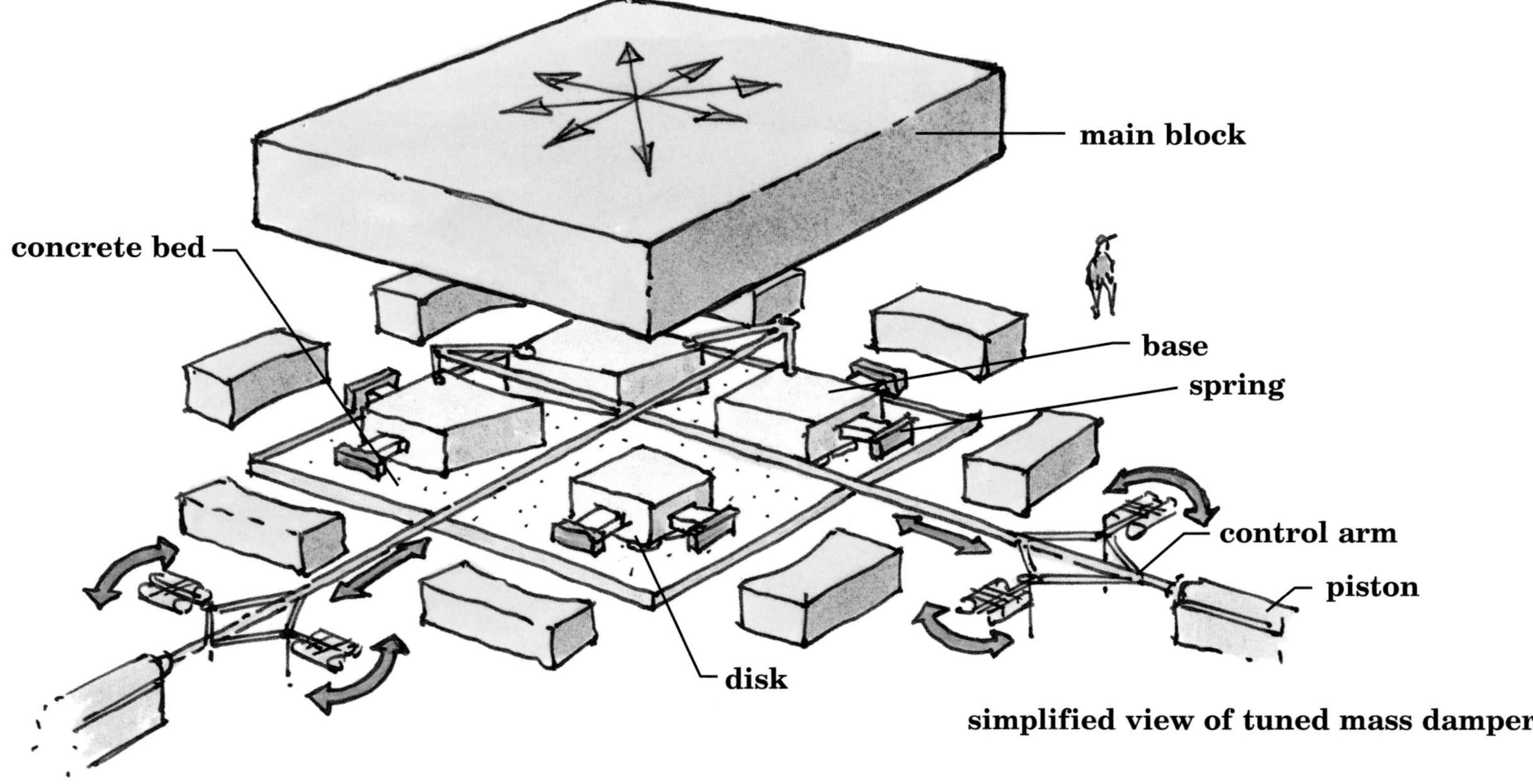

simplified view of tuned mass damper

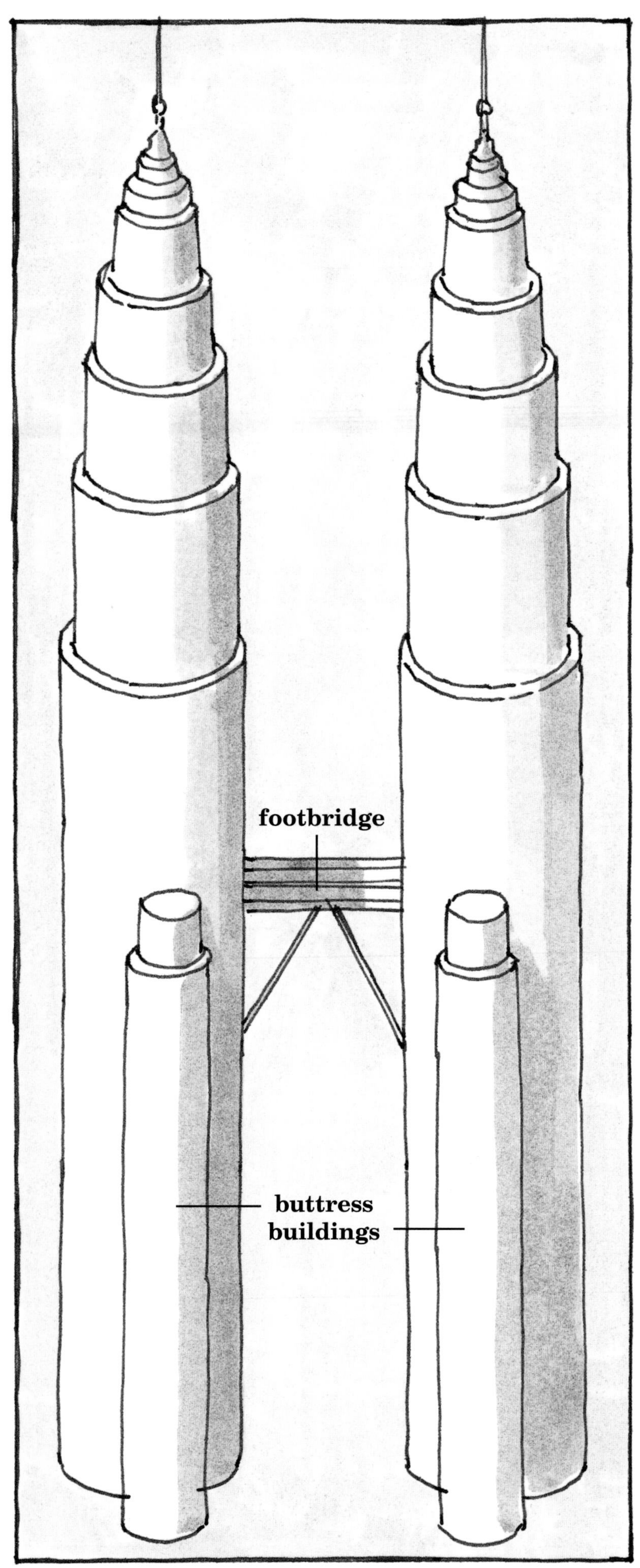

Petronas Towers

Kuala Lumpur, Malaysia, 1993–1997: In 1991, a number of world-famous architectural firms were invited to submit designs for a pair of skyscrapers to house the offices of the state-run Petronas Oil Company. The two towers, which were to be of different heights, would serve as the centerpiece of a new urban redevelopment project. In Cesar Pelli and engineer Charles Thornton's winning design, the towers, which rise like giant minarets, are both 1476 feet high. In fact, their symmetry is emphasized by their side-by-side placement. A two-level footbridge at the forty-first floor not only eases the traffic flow between the towers and provides an important escape route if one is needed, it also gives the entire structure the appearance of an enormous symbolic gateway.

The shapes of the floors themselves evolved from an eight-pointed star—a familiar form in Islamic design. However, when the core space was subtracted, particularly at the higher levels, there wasn't enough usable floor space left. This problem was eventually solved by cantilevering a curved projection between each of the points of the star.

Because of their height and relative slenderness, the towers had to be very stiff. Two attached cylindrical structures called buttress buildings provide some stability while ensuring that the square-footage requirements are met. Stiffness of both skyscrapers was primarily achieved by the use of high-strength concrete. In all concrete buildings, the connections between beams and columns are automatically rigid. Each tower is basically a tube within a tube. The outer tube is a spacious grid of thick circular columns (8 feet in diameter at the base) tied together at each floor by a continuous ring beam. The lateral forces working against the building are carried between the outer tube and the thick walls of the inner core by the steel-framed concrete floors and by deep concrete beams about halfway up called outriggers.

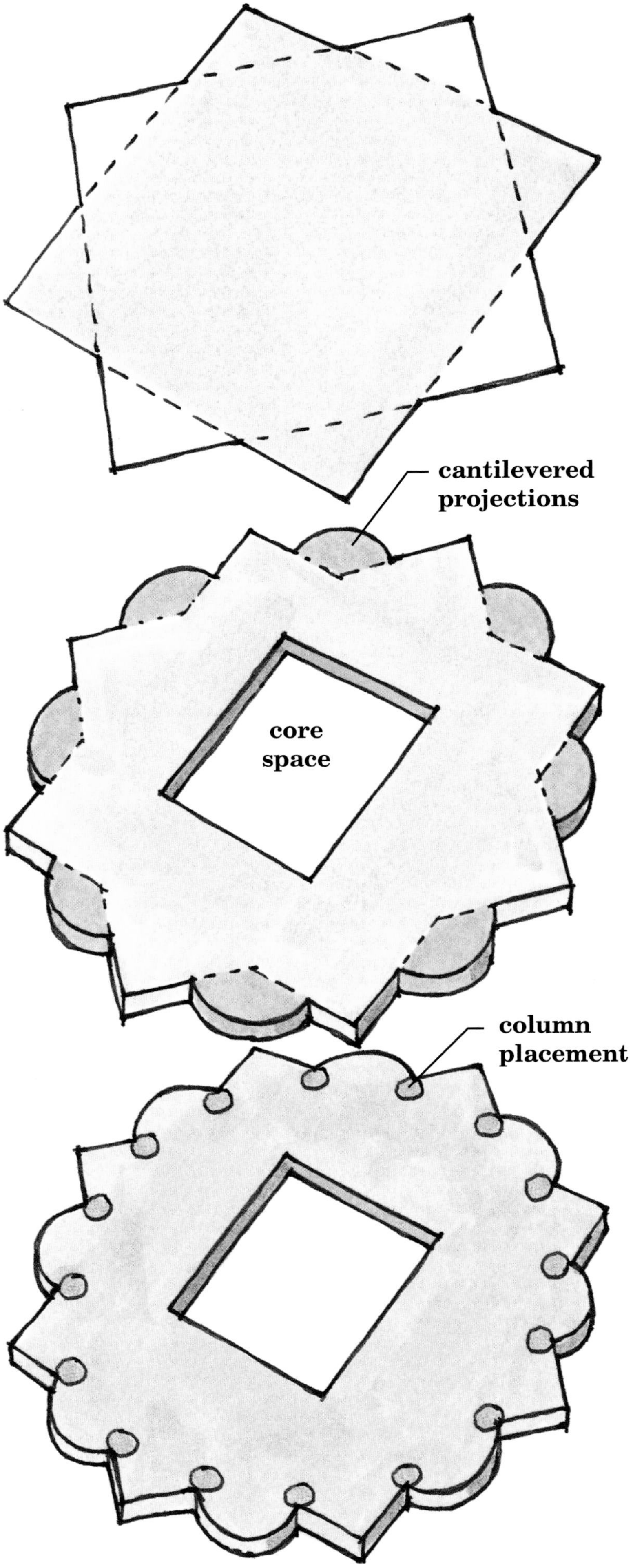

cantilevered projections

core space

column placement

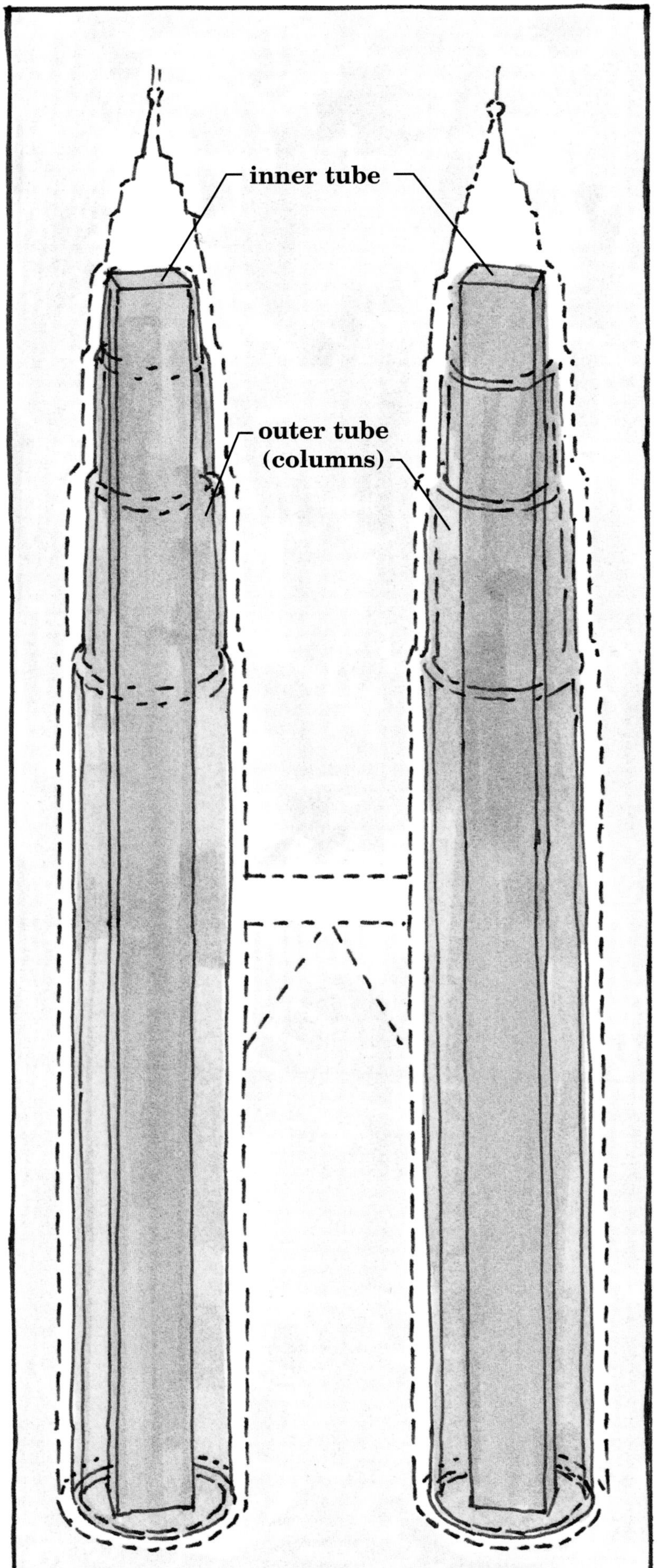

inner tube

outer tube (columns)

The Petronas towers may be an impressive sight, but it is unfortunate that we can't see what goes on below them. The foundations of these two buildings are at least as dramatic as the structures they support.

Knowing from the beginning that the soil in this area was weak, the engineers initially planned to support the columns of both towers on pairs of concrete piers that would carry their weight all the way down to bedrock. Further investigation revealed, however, that while the piers at one end of the foundation would have to go down only 50 feet, those at the other end would have to descend almost 600 feet. Since piers shorten over time (as do both concrete and steel columns), there was some uncertainty that the resulting settling would be uniform. A leaning Italian belltower is one thing, but no one was willing to take the chance with such an expensive and prestigious national symbol. Fortunately, the site—a former racetrack—was large enough so that the towers could be moved to a more favorable location.

Eventually, the engineers decided that each structure should rest on a thick reinforced concrete mat that in turn would be supported by approximately a hundred rectangular friction piles. These piles varied in size, but the largest were approximately 4 by 8 feet in area and 400 feet deep. The pressure that builds up around the piles as the weight of the building squeezes the soil between the bottom of the mat and the surface of the bedrock keeps the foundation from sinking. The friction is so great, in fact, that while the bottoms of the piles follow the profile of the bedrock, they don't need to touch it. Workers injected grout to form bumps on the sides of the piles, which further increased the amount of friction.

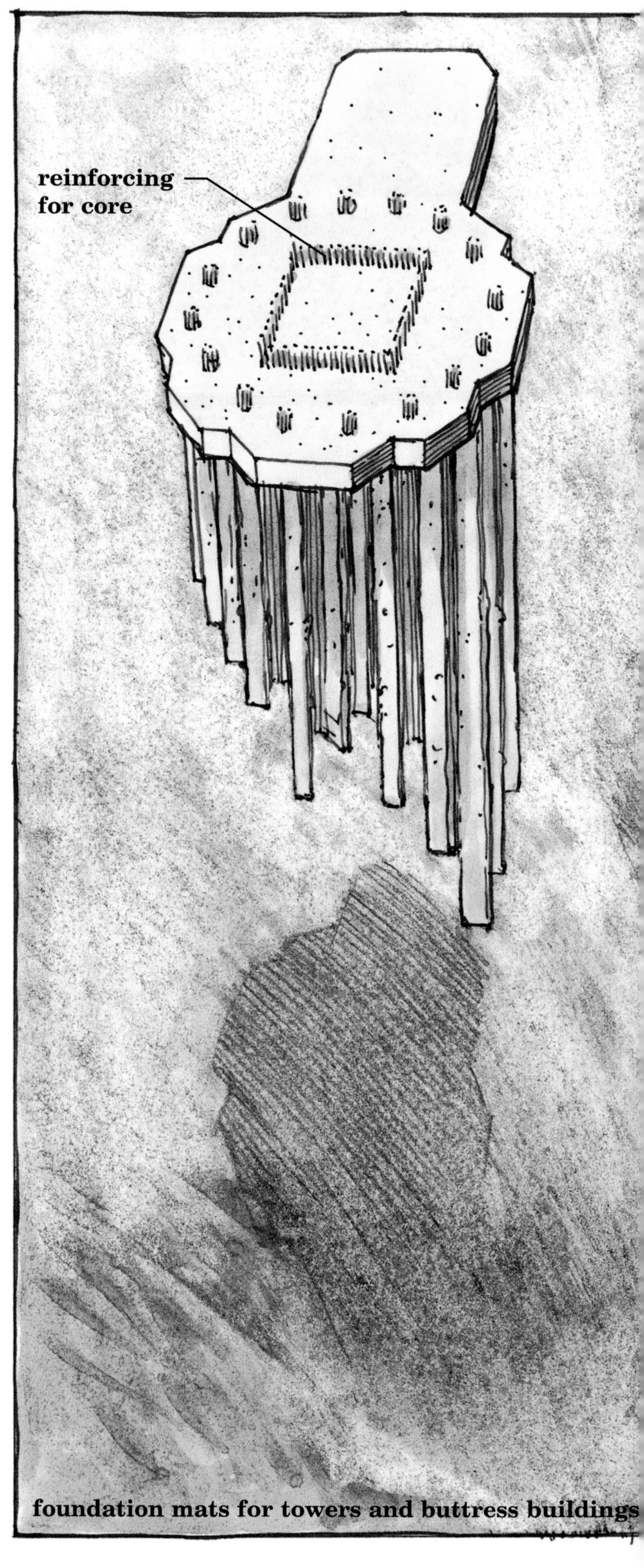

foundation mats for towers and buttress buildings

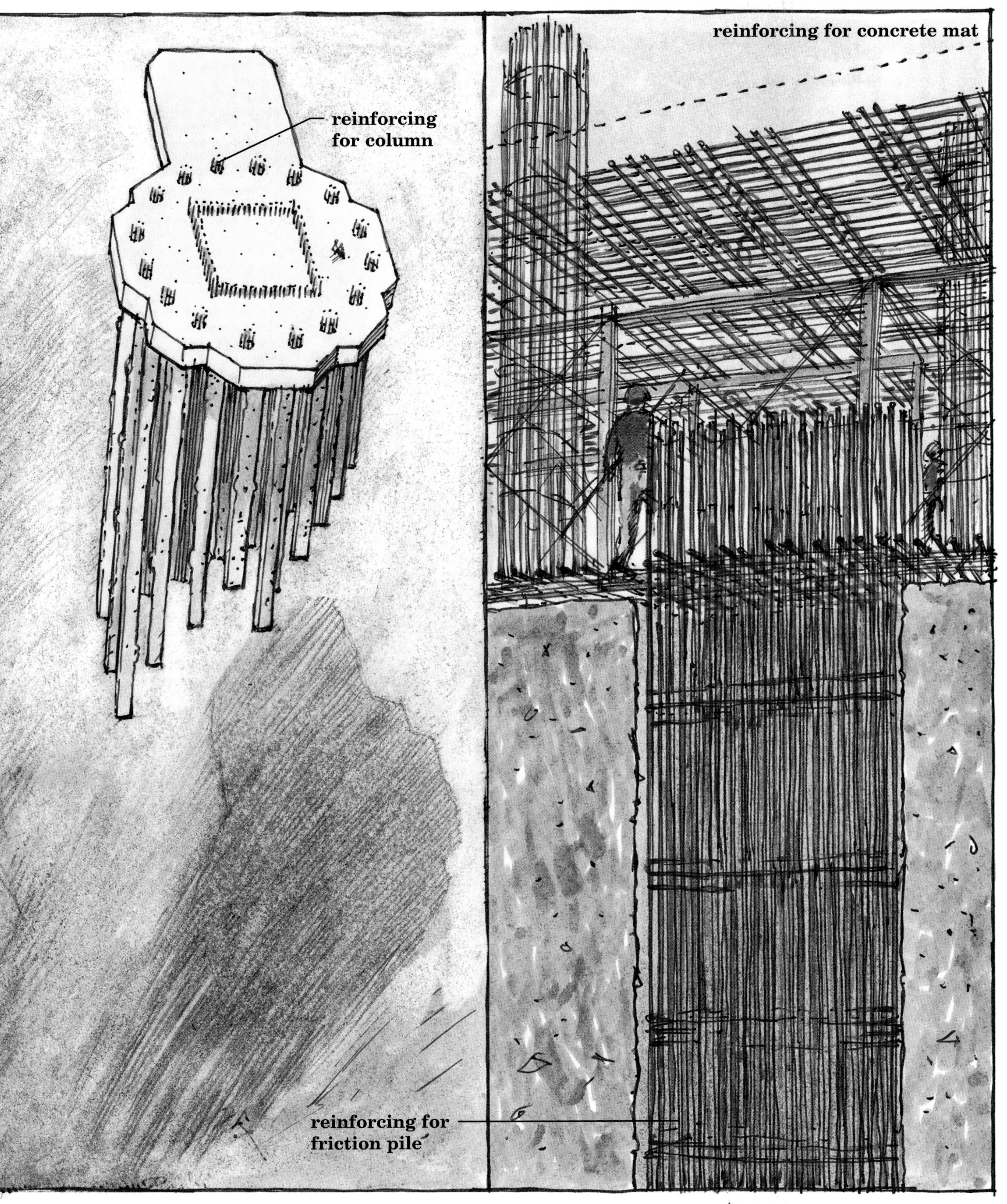
reinforcing for column
reinforcing for concrete mat
reinforcing for friction pile

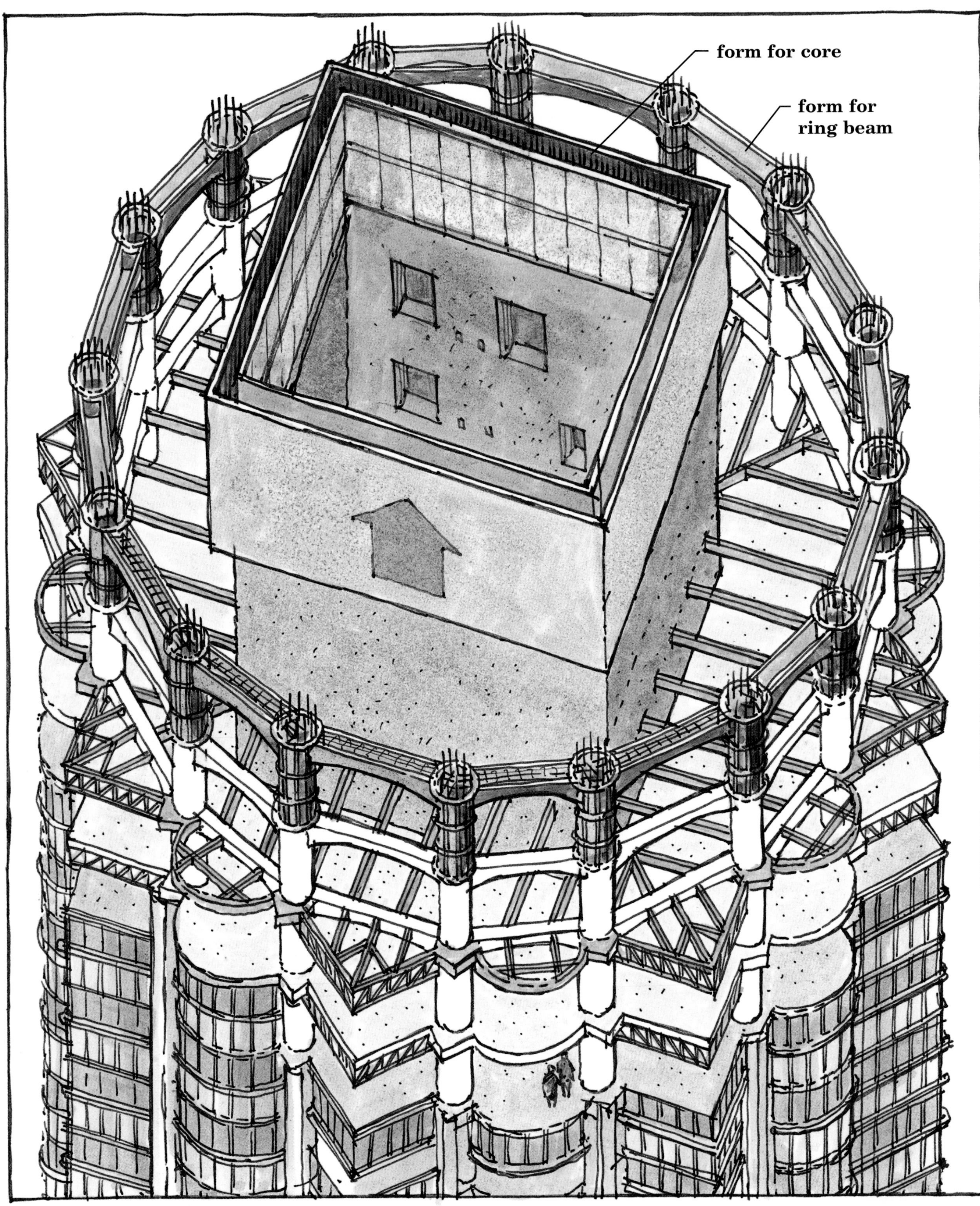
form for core
form for
ring beam

Concrete was chosen as the primary material for the Petronas towers because of the tremendous strength and rigidity it offers, and also because it is a familiar building material in Malaysia. The core walls were built first, using an enormous form that could be jacked up a level after each pour. The columns were formed next, and then the ring beams that tie them together. Last, steel beams and cantilevered supports were installed and the floors slabs were then poured over them. To keep up with demand and ensure that the concrete would all be of the same high quality, a number of concrete mixing plants were built on site. As the buildings continued to rise, workers near the bottom were already hiding the rough concrete surfaces behind a smooth skin of stainless steel and tinted glass.

The masts at the top of each tower were jacked into place from inside, much as the mast of the Chrysler Building had been. One wonders if the architect isn't already anticipating the arrival of the world's next tallest building. How difficult would it be, after all, to sneak a few more sections up the elevator shafts? In the meantime, for practice, the two towers can just compete with each other.

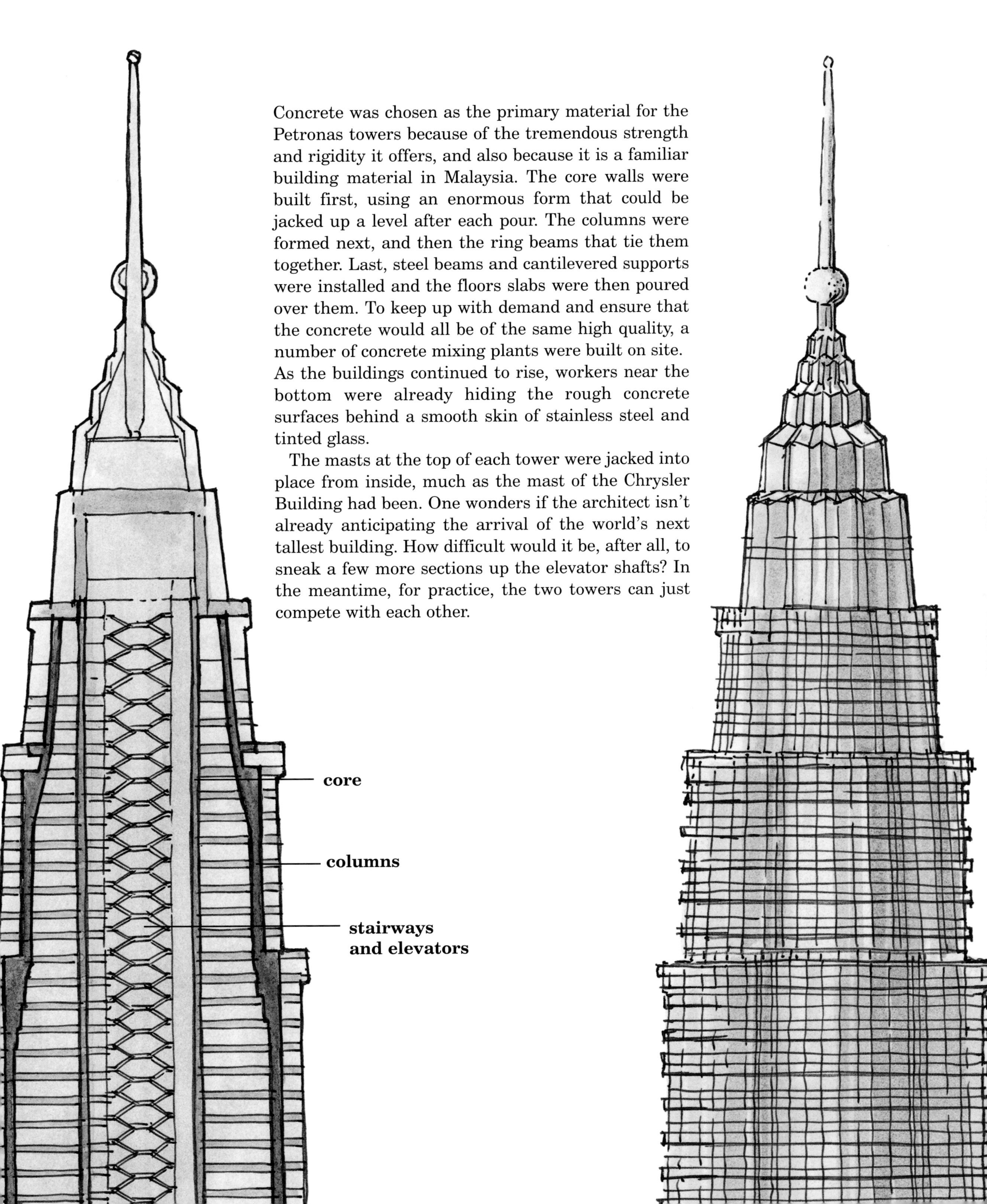

COMMERZBANK FRANKFURT

Frankfurt am Main, Germany, 1991–1997: Right from the beginning, the building that would occupy this site was intended to be open in the middle and to provide some kind of interaction with nature. The designers were required to give the bank's employees access to natural light, fresh air, and a view, no matter where their desks happened to be. The building was also supposed to be inviting from the outside, rather than imposing and aloof like most corporate headquarters. The actual footprint or shape of the building on the ground could have been just about anything. But in the end, a slightly rounded equilateral triangle seemed to offer the best possibilities. It would provide natural shafts at each of the three corners for elevators, stairwells, and mechanical systems, creating an interior space or atrium free of obstruction.

Knowing the amount of square footage required, it was a fairly straightforward task for architect Sir Norman Foster and his design team (which included the engineers Arup, Krebs and Kiefer) to then estimate the number of floors. On their own, however, these numbers were not likely to produce a very distinguished skyscraper. And if nature, in the form of a garden, remained at the bottom of the resulting atrium, no one above the fourth floor would really notice it.

In order to bring the garden to the workers, the architects clumped the floors into blocks and then separated the blocks vertically with spaces large enough for trees. Initially, there were two problems with this approach. First, only the lowest and highest floors of each block would have any visual connection

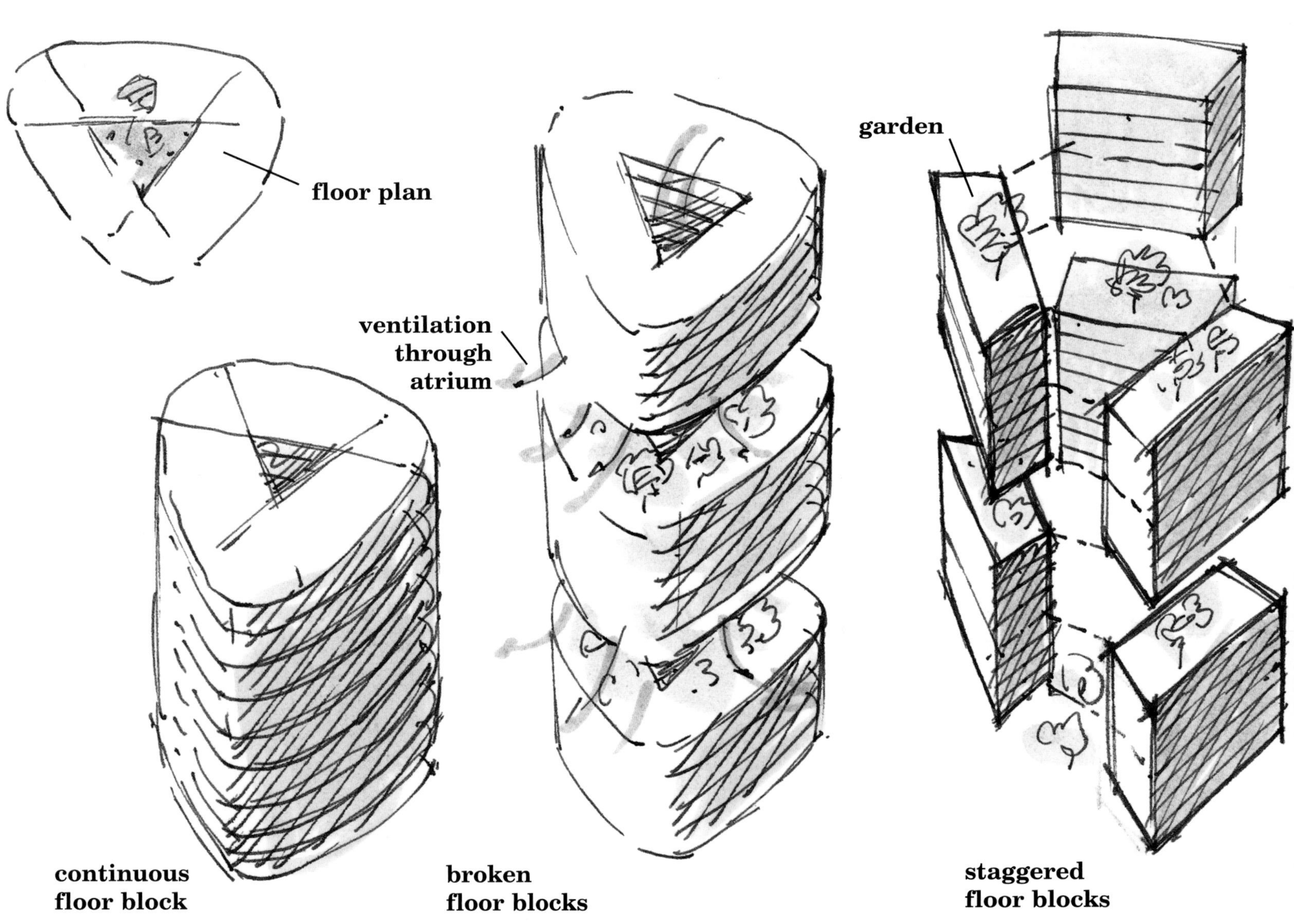

with these gardens. Second, placing these blocks at the same height on all three sides of the building would create an inherently weaker structure (the same problem we saw avoided by the staggering of the exterior columns at the World Trade Center). Both problems were eventually solved by arranging the blocks in a kind of spiral pattern. Now everyone in the building, no matter what floor they were on, would be able to look across the atrium, through a garden, and out over the city.

Having determined how the offices and open spaces should be arranged, the engineers then had to figure out how to hold them up. The relative smallness of the building's footprint—roughly 156 feet along each side—compared to its height, 840 feet, was going to make stiffness a critical issue. They decided to move as much of the supporting structure as possible out from the center of the building to its perimeter to increase stability. They did this by placing all of the building's columns in the three corners along with the elevators, stairwells, and utilities. In essence they created three individual cores.

Each core contained two vertical steel trusses called megacolumns and three smaller columns of triangular cross-section. Once the columns were tied together at every floor level, these cores would become very strong. The space between each pair of cores would then be spanned by the floors. The outer edges of all the floors were to be supported by eight-story-high rectilinear grids called Vierendeel trusses. The ends of these trusses were to be fixed to the megacolumns.

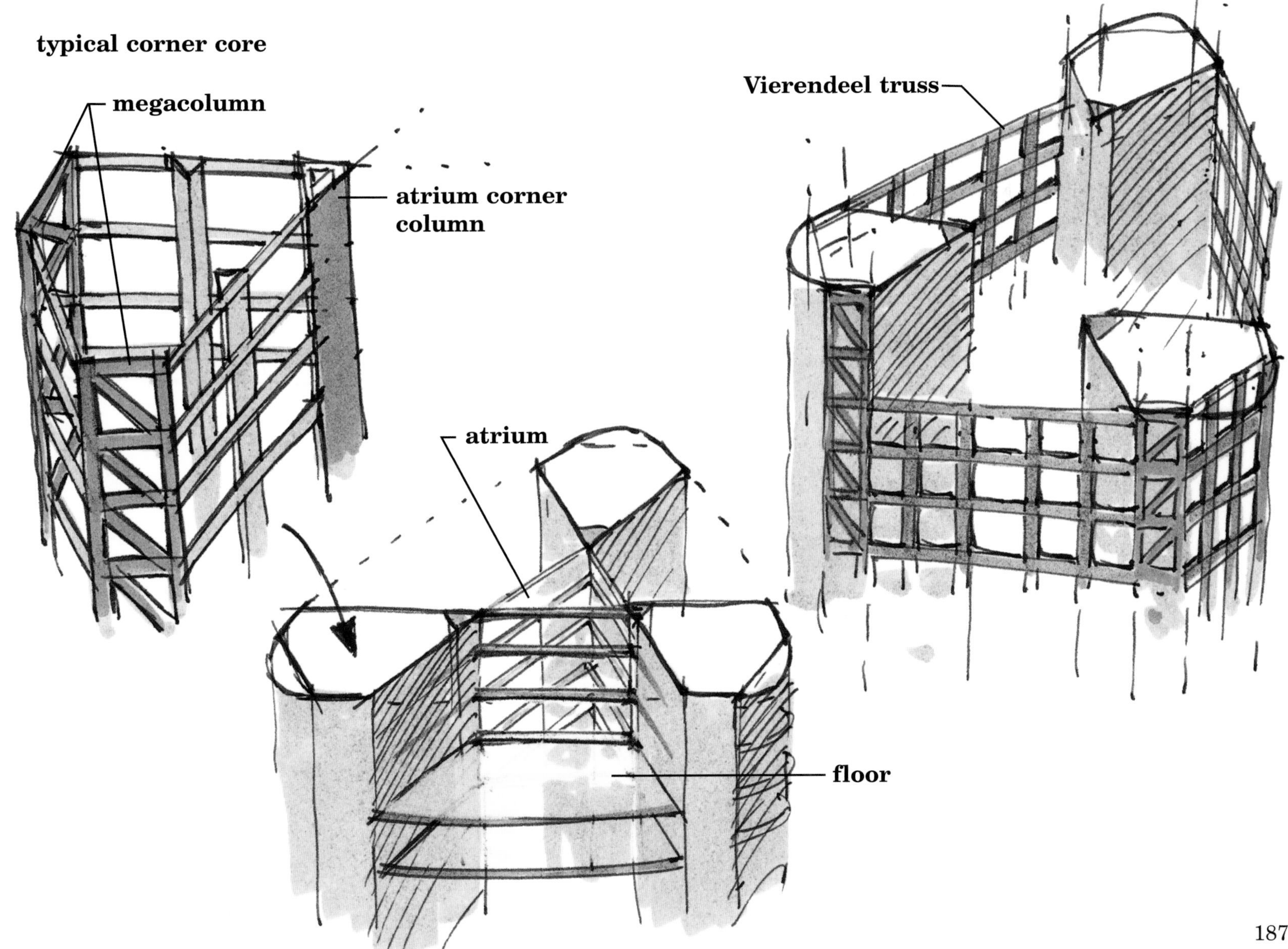

Located at each apex of the triangle, the foundations for the building consist of deep concrete boxes supported on clusters of piles. After about eleven months, they were ready to receive the steel framing.

Climbing cranes were erected at two of the building's corners and a third was set up alongside one of the main walls. The first part of the framing to be built was that of the atrium, which would always remain slightly ahead of the rest of the building. Next came the megacolumns. While new pieces of steel were being added to them, the bases of these columns were already disappearing in a thick wall of concrete. Unlike the columns of most buildings, the vertical steel members of the megacolumns remained the same size from bottom to top. It was the amount of steel reinforcing buried in the concrete around them that diminished as they rose. Ten months after work began on the steel framing, workers completed the fifty-first and final story of the main tower.

The Sears Tower hides the scale and to some extent even the existence of its structural frame behind a fairly uniform surface, making the building look even larger than it already is. The cladding around Commerzbank, on the other hand, was intended to acknowledge and even draw attention to the structural system. The color difference between the metal panels and the windows is subtle enough to unify the surface and at the same time distinct enough to remind us of what is actually doing the work. While Commerzbank remains an imposing building, this particular concession to those of us on the outside does give it a slightly friendlier face.

Unlike most skyscrapers, in which each floor is sealed off from the next and all of them are sealed off from the outside, Commerzbank relies on its atrium to create a dramatic spatial link between the various levels, one that delivers natural light into the heart of the building and promotes natural ventilation, since the windows in each of the garden terraces can be opened.

construction of Commerzbank

Although they are certainly technological triumphs, of all the big things we build, skyscrapers are my least favorite additions to the landscape. Those Chicago officials back in 1893 were right. When these massive structures rise side by side, they really do turn our city streets into dark, windy, inhospitable canyons. Even taken individually, these buildings seem intent on overwhelming, belittling, or at the very least ignoring us. The problem is, it is not so easy for us to ignore them.

Understandably, the primary influence on most of the skyscrapers discussed in this chapter has been the need to get as much floor space as possible out of their respective sites and still stay within the budget. This is not to say that these concerns were not high on Foster's agenda when he began thinking about Commerzbank. But since his building gives me a little hope, it seems like a positive and yet realistic way of wrapping things up.

When additional concerns were introduced into the basic design process, it became necessary for the architects and engineers to avoid a purely mechanical approach. In the end, the client and its design team worked together to create a different kind of skyscraper. Instead of raising yet another late-twentieth-century medieval tower, their collaboration suggests that it is possible to create a tall building that stimulates and nourishes those who work inside and welcomes rather than alienates those who live on the outside.

It would appear that building big successfully, especially when it comes to architecture, is more likely to occur when imagination is not reserved solely for the solution but is employed from the beginning in the framing of the problem.

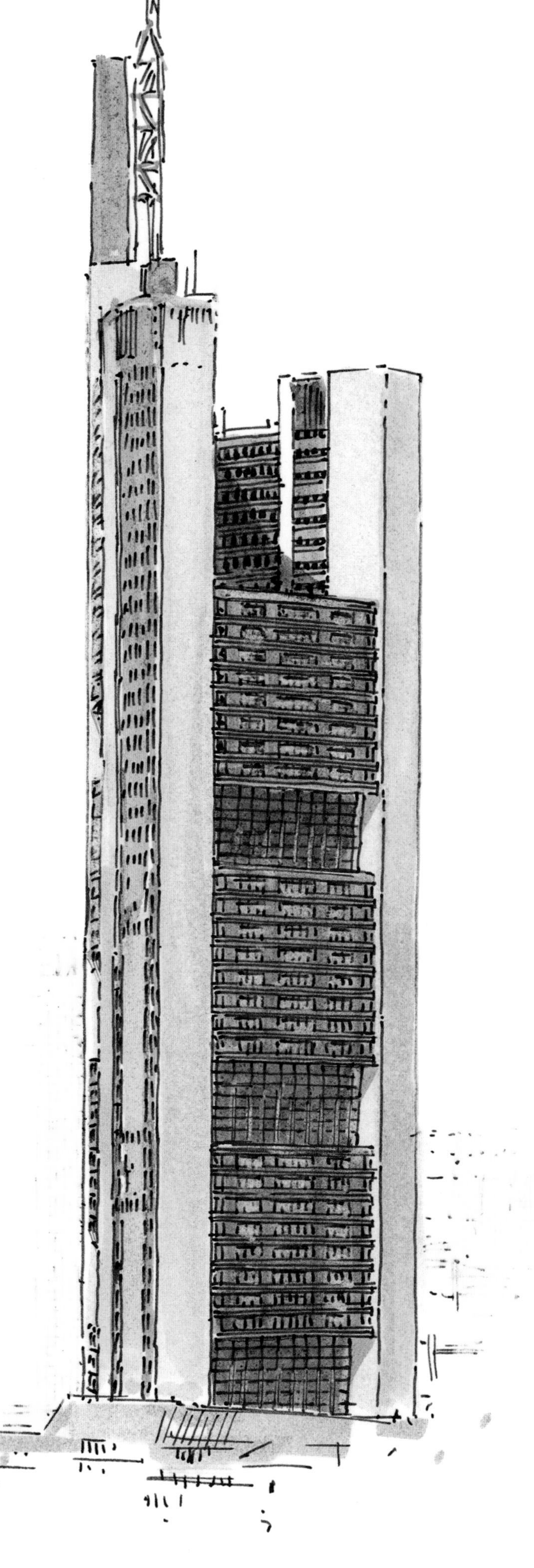

GLOSSARY

Arch—A curved structure that converts vertical force into angled forces that travel down through its sides to a foundation.

Bedrock—The solid crust of the earth, which often lies several hundred feet below the surface.

Bending—A combination of forces that causes one part of a material to be in compression and another part in tension.

Caisson—A watertight chamber in which people can work under water.

Cantilever—A structure that projects beyond its point of support.

Cast iron—Iron that has been melted, then poured into a form of the desired shape and cooled.

Centering—A temporary form over which an arch or vault is built.

Climbing crane—A crane that can be raised or lowered to keep up with the construction or demolition of a building.

Cofferdam—A watertight enclosure or barrier constructed in a river. Water is pumped out of the enclosure or from behind the barrier so workers can reach the riverbed.

Compression—A pressing force that squeezes material together.

Concrete—A building material made by mixing stone or sand with cement and water. Concrete is very strong in compression but very weak in tension.

Curtain wall—A non-weight-bearing wall used to enclose a structural skeleton.

Dead load—The weight of the permanent, nonmovable parts of a structure.

Derrick—A lifting device made up primarily of a boom and a mast. The base of the mast is fixed to the structure; and its top is secured by either steel cables or steel-frame legs.

Force—A push or pull on an object.

Form work—The temporary mold into which liquid concrete is poured to create a specific shape.

Girder—A large beam, often built up from smaller pieces. Girders usually support smaller beams.

Grout—A mixture of cement, aggregates, and water that can be pumped or poured into cavities to increase strength, or that can be used to create a watertight barrier, as in a grout curtain.

Keystone—The central, wedge-shaped locking stone at the top of an arch.

Live load—The weight of a structure's temporary, movable parts or contents, as well as the forces created by wind, rain, and earthquakes.

Load-bearing wall—A wall designed to support all or part of a building's weight.

Pendentive—A slightly spherical triangular shape used to form a continuous circular base for a dome above a flat-sided space.

Pier—A vertical support such as a column.

Post and beam—A simple structure using horizontal beams and vertical posts or columns.

Reinforced concrete—Concrete with steel bars embedded in it to improve resistance to tension.

Shaft—A vertical passage dug to the level of a proposed tunnel through which workers, materials, and equipment can be moved.

Slurry—A watery mixture of insoluble material used in trenches to prevent collapse by equalizing the pressure between the trench and the surrounding soil.

Spoil—The material removed in the process of excavating.

Steel—An alloy of iron and carbon that is hard and strong and can be pounded or rolled into desired shape.

Structural skeleton—A three-dimensional grid of beams and columns designed to carry all the loads in a building.

TBM (tunnel boring machine)—A highly automated piece of machinery that excavates a tunnel face, removes spoil, and places the lining.

Tension—A stretching force that pulls on a material.

Tension ring—A circle of material placed around the outside of a dome's base to prevent outward movement.

Transit—A surveying instrument that measures vertical and horizontal angles.

Truss—A rigid frame built up from short straight pieces that are joined to form a series of triangles or other stable shapes.

Tunnel face—The portion of a tunnel that is continually being dug away.

Tunneling shield—A movable structure, usually cylindrical, built to protect people working in unstable ground as they excavate and line a passage.

Wrought iron—An iron alloy that is less brittle than cast-iron.